C000175048

Th
b

UNKNOWN
WARRIORS

UNKNOWN
WARRIORS

THE LETTERS OF
KATE LUARD,
RRC AND BAR,
NURSING SISTER
IN FRANCE
1914–1918

PREFACE BY FIELD MARSHAL VISCOUNT ALLENBY

EDITED BY JOHN AND CAROLINE STEVENS
INTRODUCTION TO NEW EDITION
BY CHRISTINE E. HALLETT AND TIM LUARD

The
History
Press

This new edition is dedicated to the Unknown Warriors of the
First World War and all who cared for them.

Illustrations: Front cover: Stretcher bearers struggle through deep mud to
carry a wounded man to safety on 1 August 1917 during the Third Battle
of Ypres. Photograph by Lt J.W. Brooke (© Imperial War Museum); Kate as
a young woman (Author). *Back cover:* Envelope addressed to Kate at No.4
Field Ambulance and letter from Kate dated Wed 11 April 1917, during
the Battle of Arras (both Essex Record Office). *Frontispiece:* 'Removing the
Wounded, 60 Yards from the Enemy', pencil, watercolour and conte crayon
by Harold Sandys Williamson (1892–1978). (© Imperial War Museum)

First published 1930 by Chatto and Windus: London
Publication in this form 2014 by The History Press

The Mill, Brimscombe Port
Stroud, Gloucestershire, GL5 2QG
www.thehistorypress.co.uk

© Kate Luard 1930; ed. John and Caroline Stevens 2014;
Introduction © Christine E. Hallett, Tim Luard, 2014.

British Library Cataloguing in Publication Data.
A catalogue record for this book is available from the British Library.

ISBN 978 0 7509 5922 3

Typesetting and origination by The History Press
Printed in Great Britain

CONTENTS

ACKNOWLEDGEMENTS

We would like to thank all the wonderful people who have contributed to this new edition of *Unknown Warriors*, for their expertise and support throughout.

Denise Bilton for her speed, skill and patience in typesetting the text as the original 1930 edition and for coping with the numerous amendments as more and more information came to light.

Christine Hallett (Professor of Nursing History at the University of Manchester) and Tim Luard (great-nephew of Kate Luard) for co-writing the introduction: Christine with her extensive knowledge of First World War nursing and Tim who meticulously researched the Luard archives in the Essex Record Office transcribing many of the letters and documents. Thanks are also due to Christine for her help with the glossary.

The Luard family is indebted to Dr Midori Yamaguchi, Associate Professor at Daito Bunka University, Tokyo & Saitama, who inspired us all with her excellent account of the Bramston & Luard families of Essex in her PHD Thesis.

Much gratitude to Tim and his wife Alison with their expertise and experience of proofreading in checking the 1930 text and glossary; and to Tim for all his painstaking research and his valuable contribution to the postscript.

We are indebted to Sue Light, creator of the Scarletfinders website, who unfailingly helped with details of military nursing history and for checking the glossary, also for freely providing her collection of First World War photographs.

Our grateful thanks to Geoff Russell Grant, editor of the Parish News for Birch, Layer Breton and Layer Marney, for supplying Parish archive material relating to KEL and the Luard family of Birch.

Tim Luard and the family are grateful to the archivist and staff at the Essex Record Office, Chelmsford for their help in researching the Luard family papers deposited in the county archives.

Christine Hallett would like to acknowledge the invaluable assistance of Gertjan Remmerie and Jan Louagie-Nouf at the Archives of Talbot House, Poperinghe, Belgium.

Special thanks are due to my husband John for many hours spent researching and compiling the glossary, indexes and list of personnel and for his invaluable help throughout.

Many thanks to our daughter Louise for all her assistance and support, and for her skills in promoting the book through social media.

Last but not least, a debt of gratitude to my mother, who despite living in Africa all her married life, kept a constant record of family newspaper cuttings, photographs and letters and passed on to us all such respect and admiration for the Luards of Birch.

The help of the following people in providing illustrations for the book was much appreciated: Rob McIntosh, Curator Archives & Library, Army Medical Services Museum, Aldershot; Sally Richards at the Imperial War Museum, London; Miriam Ward at the Wellcome Trust, London.

Thanks are due to The History Press for recognising the value of the work and making it available to a wider public, and for their continued support.

Caroline Stevens
Great-niece of Kate Luard

Introduction to the New Edition,

Kate Luard (1872–1962) – Professional Nurse and Witness to War

Unknown Warriors is a long-lost jewel of First World War reportage. Its words resonate as powerfully today as when first written beneath a French sky split by thunderous shellfire and read days later over the breakfast table in a rural Essex vicarage. Since its publication in 1930, it has offered those who have managed to find it on obscure library and archive shelves an extraordinary vantage point from which to view the realities of the Great War: a privileged glimpse into the hidden world of the military field hospital, where patients struggled with pain and trauma and nurses fought to save lives and preserve emotional integrity.

The book's author, Katherine Evelyn Luard, was one of a select number of fully-trained professional nurses who worked in casualty clearing stations and on hospital trains during the war, coming as close to the battlefront as it was possible for an early-twentieth-century woman to be. This new edition of her book – produced by her own family and offering a fitting tribute to her remarkable work – is a timely reminder of the horrors of war and the courage and endurance of those who survive it. One hundred years after the events it describes, *Unknown Warriors* provides rare insights into both the experiences of soldiers and the work of nurses.

Having trained as a professional nurse in the 1890s, Kate served the British army in both the Second Boer War and the First World War. By the time she arrived in one of the earliest military hospitals to be established on the Western Front in 1914, she was already a war veteran. Apart from a few weeks absent on leave, she was to remain on the Western Front continuously until 1918.

Although clearly steeped in the values and attitudes of her own time, and fully believing in the right of the Allied cause, she seems to have written with the intention of placing before her readership the full horror faced by war's wounded. She succeeded brilliantly, and in doing so, managed to convey conflicting messages to her readers, challenging them to view war in new and perhaps disconcerting ways. Such contradictions are familiar to twenty-first-century audiences who honour those who fight in their wars, even as they deplore the havoc wrought and the suffering caused.

Above all, the author's intention appears to be to bear witness to the suffering of the ordinary soldier. Her 'Reggie, Walter, Joseph, Harry and Billy, and the armless, legless ones, who won't tell their mothers' are real men – often so young that they really seem to be no more than boys. Yet she does not want them to be viewed as victims; rather, she wants us to recognise the nobility with which they endured suffering and met death. Whatever their actions on the battlefield might have been, it is their patient suffering that makes them true heroes. She conveys vividly this sense of heroic endurance.

Kate Luard was not writing for the general public but for her family. She was reporting, in the simplest and most direct way possible, what she saw and heard and felt each day, so that those she knew most intimately could share her experiences. The arrival of her latest despatch, jotted down in pencil last thing at night or whenever there was a moment to catch her breath, was an exciting highlight of her family's otherwise mostly humdrum wartime existence. Several of Kate's numerous brothers and sisters, though all well into adulthood, were still living with their father, an elderly clergyman, at his large rectory in the village of Birch, near Colchester. Much of what she wrote had been censored before it arrived, with certain names and numbers and even whole sentences heavily scored out in purplish ink. But what remained was eagerly devoured and – apart from those letters marked 'Inner Circle' which were for the eyes of only her most trusted sisters – was passed on around the village and to other family members further afield. 'You are a lucky devil waltzing to the Front like that... Give our love to the fighting line', Kate's youngest sister Daisy wrote to her soon after the start of the war, adding: 'N and I spend hours reading and sending or copying your cards and letters'.

The family's shared belief in a man's duty to fight for his country and their obvious envy of Kate's privileged position at the cutting edge of the war persisted over the next few years, even as the horror of what she was witnessing became ever clearer and more unremitting. Evidence of their enthusiastic support is found not only in their almost daily letters to her but also in the many presents they sent, both for her and 'her boys'. These letters in their turn paint a vivid picture of village life in wartime Britain – of the daily struggle to carry on as normal with everything from haymaking to choir practice when almost every man and boy had gone off to fight.

It was Kate's family who eventually persuaded her to have her letters published for a wider audience. They were printed almost exactly as they were originally written. The present volume remains faithful to the 1930 edition, incorporating the original preface and footnotes, but adds an introduction, a glossary, a postscript and indexes.

Katherine Evelyn Luard was born in 1872, the tenth of thirteen children of the Reverend Bixby Garnham Luard and his wife Clara, who would die in 1907, seven years before the First World War began. The world into which she was born was one in which even middle-class girls had very few career choices. Women were only just beginning to free themselves from a domesticity which had, for centuries, circumscribed their lives.

Kate and women like her, with unflinching determination and a passionate zest for life, broke the boundaries of their time by entering worlds that even a creative mind like Charlotte Bronte's could not have imagined. They did more than merely step outside their late-Victorian drawing rooms. They took enormous leaps of faith into the worlds inhabited by their brothers; in doing so, they changed those worlds.

The Luard family, of old Huguenot stock, was a close one, imbued with a sense of service to society. The boys were sent to public school and had careers as soldiers or naval officers, doctors or clergymen. (Two of Kate's brothers, Frank and Trant, were colonels in the Royal Marines, serving respectively in Gallipoli and Palestine, where her letters were sent on to them.) Two of the six Luard girls, Georgina and Rose, went on to graduate from Lady Margaret Hall, Oxford.

Kate herself attended Croydon High School from 1887-90, where the headmistress, Dorinda Neligan, an active member of the suffrage movement who had served with the Red Cross during the Franco-Prussian War, may have influenced Kate in her choice of career. Kate worked as a governess and as a teacher for about a year in order to raise sufficient funds to pay her way through her probationary periods, first at the East London Hospital for Children and Dispensary for Women; and then at the prestigious nurse-training school of King's College Hospital, London. Nursing was still viewed in some circles as not entirely respectable. It represented a courageous choice for a late-nineteenth-century woman; but Kate seems to have pursued her training with the same enthusiasm and dedication she was later to bring to her wartime work.

In June 1900 she offered her skills to the Army Nursing Service, and spent two years caring for British casualties of the Second Anglo-Boer War in South Africa. Her letters home are alive with both compassion for her patients and a sense of fun and adventure and give an early indication of her journalistic skills. In April 1902 she wrote to her sister Rose from No. 7 General Hospital, Pretoria, inviting her to share the letter with the rest of the family.

When the afternoon sister comes on at 3, I tear up and change and get on to Ginger. We jump the trench and then go bucketing over the veldt to the tops of Angel Kopjes with heaven born views and Transvaal colours. When you go back on duty at 6 you feel a new man...

Major Holt*, of the Royal Army Medical Corps, often features in Kate's Boer War letters, normally appearing under the initials MPH or H. As well as being a senior colleague at work, he goes riding with her and they play the organ together in local churches. 'I may mention he has a fond wife and small boy so you needn't bother to smell a rat,' she tells her sisters. 'But he's a ripping little man with a rather sad refined face'.

A letter written by Kate from France fourteen years after those first meetings in South Africa suggests the sad-faced major in fact turned out to be the love of her life. Recently discovered among family papers at the Essex Record Office, the letter is in a small envelope marked as being for the eyes only of her eldest sister, 'G' (Georgina). It is dated October 21st, 1915:

> MPH came in this evening to say Goodbye. He is going to ————
> tomorrow. Directly I heard that 3 Divisions were going I knew in my
> bones that he would... He didn't seem to think we should ever see
> each other again, but you never know. He said he would have been
> happy all his life with me. He hasn't forgotten a single minute of the
> last fourteen years – that is ours – and the 10 years dead silence was
> no separation – nor will 50 years be, if he gets killed... He called at the
> O.H. but I was in the Surgical and met him coming out. So I took him
> into my little fire-lit office – Goodnight. KEL.

It is not known if he and Kate ever saw each other again.

Apparently undaunted by her experiences in South Africa, Kate joined the Reserve of the Queen Alexandra's Imperial Military Nursing Service on August 6, 1914, two days after the British government declared war against Germany. At the time she was working as Matron of the Berks and Bucks County Sanatorium, having previously been night superintendent to the Charing Cross Hospital, London. Now aged 42, Kate was immediately mobilised and posted to France on August 12, 1914. Her subsequent experience of military service was similar to that

---

* Sir Maurice Percy Cue Holt (1862-1954), in 1902 a Major in the RAMC in South Africa, then a Colonel in France during the First World War, went on to become a much decorated Major General.

of other army nurses: she was moved many times during the war, usually at very little notice. Once a nurse had enlisted she was on 'active service' and subject to military-style discipline. Leave was granted at the discretion of her seniors, and her work and movements were governed by the demands of the service.

In the autumn of 1914, Kate was posted, first to a British general hospital, then to one of the earliest Allied hospital trains, and finally to a series of casualty clearing stations (CCSs). Her *Diary of a Nursing Sister on the Western Front,* published anonymously in 1915, recounts these early experiences of the war. The content was drawn from extensive letters, which often took the form of diaries – or 'journals' as she called them – and were sent home at intervals to her family as round robins. These were written as if she was speaking to her siblings and were kept throughout her time on the Western Front.

Following Kate's voyage out to France in a troopship, the SS *City of Benares,* on 18 August 1914, there was a frustrating period of waiting for orders in Le Havre. But her skills were already in demand, not only as a briskly efficient organiser of nursing staff, billets and equipment (later in the war she would do a spell as a Railway Transport Officer) but also as a linguist.

In due course she was granted her wish to be where the action was. She was moved to Le Mans to attend to the wounded from the Aisne, and, on the crowded ambulance trains she had to deal with the awful results of early battles at Ypres and Neuve Chapelle. Whatever she may have felt at her first sight of such a scene, her actions and descriptions remained calm and measured:

> You boarded a cattle-truck, armed with a tray of dressings and a pail; the men were lying on straw; had been in trains for several days; most had only been dressed once, and many were gangrenous... No one grumbled or made any fuss.

There is much in Kate's letters that is heart-rending, but they never make for grim reading for long. From the horrors of the trenches they move on swiftly: perhaps to the hidden charms of a nearby wood, as their author heads out behind the lines on a rare afternoon off to gather orchids; or, if within range of a new city to explore, she takes us along with her to see the wonders of a French cathedral, where she invariably succeeds in 'resting her soul'. Sometimes awfulness and beauty complement each other in successive sentences.

She has a genuine interest in and empathy with people for their own sake, whatever their creed, caste or rank. She speaks to wounded German prisoners in their own language, as she does to the French children who are brought in after losing limbs playing with bombs. She is at her ease at a tea party held by the top brass, and equally happy to attend bawdy sketch shows put on by 'other ranks'. Her letters are alive with direct speech, allowing her to display her ear for dialect and slang.

Even when Kate becomes a Sister-in-Charge and her natural qualities as a 'no-nonsense' hospital matron come to the fore, she remains true to the best nursing tradition of getting to know and showing caring affection for every patient. It is clear that the very presence at the Front of British women, sharing the same harsh conditions as themselves, came as a great surprise to almost all the men and afforded them much comfort. While it is true that the nurses were not sharing the extreme danger of actual trench warfare, their units came under frequent shellfire and aerial attack. They often showed great individual courage – as can be seen from a small incident casually recounted in one of Kate's letters:

> A boy with his face nearly in half, who couldn't talk, and whom I was feeding, was trying to explain that he was lying on something hard in his trouser pocket. It was a live Mills bomb! I extracted it with some care as the pins catch easily.

On October 17, 1915, after four months at a base hospital, Kate was moved to Casualty Clearing Station No. 6, much closer to the battle-lines. By the end of 1916, she had accumulated a wealth of experience in both base hospitals and casualty clearing stations, and was ready to shoulder the responsibility of a position as Head Sister to No. 32 Casualty Clearing Station. The supervision of the nursing care at any CCS was difficult and challenging, but in No. 32 the work was made harder by the fact that the unit specialised in the treatment of abdominal wounds. Such injuries were particularly intractable and, until the middle years of the war, the vast majority of patients who received them died. Indeed, until the spring of 1915 men with severe abdominal wounds had simply been given morphine and put to one side to permit the time and expertise of surgeons to be devoted to cases considered more likely to survive. Now, Kate was in charge of the nursing care in the most important 'Advanced Abdominal Centre' of the war. It also became one of the most dangerous when the unit was relocated, in late July 1917, to an area in Brandhoek to serve the 'push' that was to become known as the Battle of Passchendaele.

At the height of the Battle of Passchendaele, Kate had a staff of forty nurses and nearly 100 nursing orderlies (the normal nursing workforce for a CCS was 7). As well as doing her rounds of the wards and generally keeping up standards and spirits in the face of floods, mud and shells crossing overhead, a matron had a limitless number of other tasks to attend to. Her duties included organising the Mess, which involved tracking down supplies of such things as fresh milk in the war-ravaged and largely abandoned countryside that surrounded most of the temporary clearing stations. She also took it upon herself to write daily letters to many of the patients' families. Occasionally these ended on a joyful note of recovery but all too often they involved the breaking of bad news.

Kate's time in the Ypres Salient was clearly an intensely stressful one, and the comfort she gained from her visits to Talbot House, a rest home for soldiers in Poperinge on the Western Front, made a huge impression on her. Kate was one of the first communicants, climbing the steep, almost perpendicular wooden stairs to the tiny chapel built into the roof of the house. Her friendship with its founder Chaplain 'Tubby' Clayton outlasted the war and in 1922 she set up, with others, the 'Toc H League of Women Helpers'. Religion was clearly an important element of her life. Although Christianity is not prominent in her writings there can be little doubt that her faith sustained her. As the military nursing historian, Sue Light, has commented, 'believing that a dying man was going on to a better life, or that your own death was a beginning and not an end, must have been extremely comforting and supportive during such dangerous and stressful years'.

Kate's commanding officer later wrote that the work done by her unit in 1917 was perhaps the hardest of any clearing station in France.

Having already been Mentioned in Despatches and awarded the Royal Red Cross, K. E. Luard became one of the few nurses to receive a bar to her RRC. She was decorated by the King at Buckingham Palace on May 8, 1919.

Kate Luard was an independent woman, who travelled to the zone of war, at a time when a woman's place was believed to be in the home. She was both a professional and an author in a world where female roles were still constrained and feminine voices were almost silent. Yet through the confusion of this world, in which men were sent apparently so casually to their deaths and women were denied professional recognition and political roles, Kate's voice resonates with truth and clarity. A remarkable piece of witness-testimony, *Unknown Warriors* is both a vivid and honest portrait of war's wounded, and a chronicle of women's work, revealing the true significance of nurses' frontline contributions. It is also a remarkable portrait of family affection and trust in a world of conflict.

Readers of today will be accustomed to viewing the First World War as something in hazy black and white or muted tones of sepia. Kate Luard's writing allows us to see it as she did, in vivid colour. She shows us the blues of the periwinkles and the French soldiers' uniforms; the red and white of the church tent; the pink ribbons from a chocolate box that were used to strap a 'Flying boy's' broken leg. She even has a colour – yellowish-green – to describe the sound of a shell as it screams towards you.

Kate Luard's ability both to capture reality and reveal her own personality through her writing is impressive. Although the content of *Unknown Warriors* is often harrowing, its style is cheerful and buoyant. Kate's consummate skill as a writer permits her to offer a portrayal of suffering which, whilst presented through a brightly-coloured lens, is, nonetheless, a genuine and respectful tribute to the heroism of those who suffered, were disabled and died in the Great War.

Christine Hallett
Professor of Nursing History, The University of Manchester

Tim Luard
Former BBC Correspondent and great-nephew of the author

'And some there be, which have no memorial; who are perished, as though they had never been . . .
With their seed shall continually remain a good inheritance, and their children are within the covenant . . .
Their seed shall remain for ever, and their glory shall not be blotted out.
Their bodies are buried in peace; but their name liveth for evermore.'

Ecclesiasticus XLIV

By Field-Marshal Viscount Allenby gcb gcmc

These extracts from letters written by a Nursing Sister serving in France from 1914 to 1918 give a stirring account of her experiences in the War Zone.

It is a tale of heroism, modestly told, but unsurpassed in interest by any War novel yet written.

When I commanded the Third Army I had the good fortune to meet the Author on a visit paid to her Casualty Clearing Station during the later stages of the battle of Arras.

I remember well those days and nights of bitter fighting, and how crushing was the burden which fell upon the gentle women who tended our wounded. I look back, still, with admiration on the amazing endurance and self-sacrificing devotion of those Nursing Sisters in their work of mercy.

The Author describes this work in simple unaffected language – language which nevertheless reveals the strength of character that enabled her to bear the strain.

Miss Luard does not hide from us the pain and the cruelty of War; but there is no attempt to shock or horrify. Rather, she attracts our interest in her work at the same time as she enlists our sympathy for the broken heroes to whom she ministered with such loving care.

And, in all the misery of her surroundings, a golden vein of humour sustains her; an appreciation of what is good in life, though standing under the Shadow of Death.

Here are two extracts from the Letters:

May 8th
'I am engaged in a losing battle with gas gangrene . . . a particularly fine man too . . . it is horribly disheartening. When they have been lying out so long G.G. is practically a certainty.'

May 9th
'And what do you think we've been busy over this morning? A large and Festive Picnic in the woods, far from gas gangrene and amputations . . . my chosen spot – on a slope of the wood, above the babbling brook, literally carpeted with periwinkles, oxlips and anemones. . . . When we got back . . . we took the places of the Sisters who had been minding the wards and they went to hear the Band. My dear man was dying. At the exact moment that he took his first breath in Heaven at 7.30 the Band was playing 'There will be such wonderful things to do' to that particularly plaintive little tune. His only attempt at a complaint was to say once when I said good-night to him, 'I wish you were going to stay with me all night.' '

Again, in the year of Victory – 1918 – on the 9th August, at 4 a.m., is this entry:

'All is ready for Berlin. I'm hoping breathlessly that they hold back my leave to see this through.'

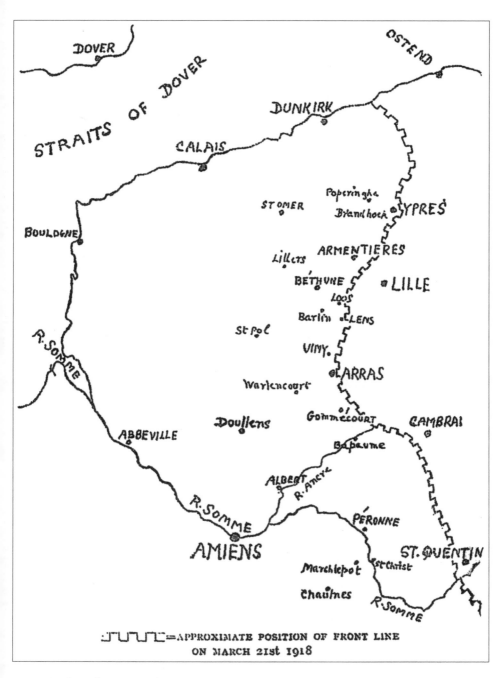

:⌐⌐⌐⌐⌐=APPROXIMATE POSITION OF FRONT LINE
ON MARCH 21st 1918

Map drawn by K.E. Luard

I

WINTER UP THE LINE

OCTOBER 17TH 1915 TO APRIL 25TH 1916
WITH THE 1ST ARMY (SIR DOUGLAS HAIG)

LETTERS FROM LILLERS

During the early months of the War, from August 1914 to May 1915, the writer was engaged in Hospital Train and Field Ambulance work in different parts of the Western Front.

In October 1915, after four months at a Base Hospital, she was sent up the line to take charge of a Casualty Clearing Station. The following letters begin at this date.

Sunday, 9 p.m. October 17th 1915. Lillers, France. This is written by a lovely fire, in an empty Officers' Ward, in an Orphanage, after a hot water wash, my hot bottle filled, the bed made and turned down by an attentive orderly who nearly waited to clean my teeth for me! I am sleeping here to-night, as the departing Sister in Charge from whom I am taking over this Casualty Clearing Station, and whose billet I shall have in the town, does not leave till to-morrow.

The *Orphelin's* French bed looks very inviting.

October 18th. The Sister has been showing me round and handing over her books and keys of office, and has been telling me the ins and outs of it all. There is an Officers' Hospital in this Orphanage, which I do myself – with a Staff Nurse and two good orderlies. This is up a cobbly slum, full of soldiers' billets, leading into the usual Square – called the *Grand Place*. Then there's another branch in another street, where the operating theatre and the surgical wards are: School Rooms, with the stretchers on trestles. Now only the worst cases are left, who can't be moved. The trains 'clear' the movables and walking cases every day. There's another place like it for the Medicals, and yet another building where the C.O.'s office is, and my office next door and the dispensary, etc. The Sisters are billeted about in ones and twos, and mess together in a little squashy house, where the people also do laundry work.

This town is rather like Béthune, only not quite so big and rather farther away from the trenches. It is packed with troops and various Headquarter Staffs.

After the yards of red tape one has been tied up in lately at the Base, there is a refreshing sense of freedom and common sense about this sort of work, but I expect it has its own difficulties. The poor lads in their brown blankets and stretchers looked only too familiar. When there is a rush, the theatre Sister and I stay up at night as well. After the 25th (Loos) they overflowed into all the yards and places. The C.O., the Padre and myself are the only people allowed to do the censoring. I do it for the Sisters. I shall have to be very careful myself, not to mention names, numbers passing through, regiments, plans, or anything interesting. We take it in turns to 'take in' with Béthune, Choques, and another C.C.S. here – one in four turns.

Monday, 10.30 p.m. October 18th. Just got to bed after my last round. The same old murderous thud, thud, thudding is going on still, along the same old spot, but we aren't near enough to hear the crackle of the rifle-firing, or see the star-shells and the searchlights and the flashes of the guns, as we used to do.

I spent the morning in the Officers' Hospital and the afternoon and evening in the Infant School, where the men are; they are busy there to-day – with new bad cases, old bad cases and operations. It seems to be quite as well done as it could be in existing circumstances, but it makes you all the time wonder, more than ever, the Why of it all, and the When it will end.

One officer of the 3rd Grenadier Guards, with an absolutely stricken, haunted face and a monotonous, toneless voice, has been telling me things that make you see the horror of War, and smell it and feel it, over and beyond the wreckage that one handles in the Infant School. He was crawling along a four-foot trench, close to the enemy lines, when they heard a weak voice calling, 'Come and help me.' They reached him at last – a man wounded in the thigh, who had been there since Tuesday and this was Sunday. While they were dragging him back, he was all the time apologising for giving so much trouble! These are the people from the Hohenzollern Redoubt.

Went round the Sergeant-Major's Walking Case Divisions this evening – rows and rows of stretchers, with quite a cheery lot, drinking hot cocoa and reading where there was enough light: they were in class-rooms and places round an open yard, where they cook and brew in large boilers. All the stretcher cases, i.e. lying-down cases, are in my charge, and are called Sisters' Divisions.

Thursday, October 21st. All last night a Division was entraining at the station and rumbling unceasingly over the cobblestones past the house. A boy is lying smiling all day with his head, right hand and both legs wounded, and his left arm off. When asked 'Are you happy?' he said with a beam 'Tryin' to be.' To-day he is humming 'Sister Susie's sewing shirts for soldiers.'

I happened to go into the Infant' School this morning, just in time to see a delirious boy, with a bad head-wound, with a large brain hernia, tear off all his dressings and throw a handful of his brains on to the floor. This is literally true, and he was talking all the time we re-dressed the hole in his head. Then we picked up the handful of brains, and the boy was quiet for a little while. He is very delirious and will not get better.

Thursday, October 28th. The weather is beyond description vile, and the little cobbled streets I wear out my shoe-leather on, are a Slough of Despond and a quagmire. The King has been about here yesterday and to-day, and was to have held a very sodden and damp Review a mile away, only he had an accident riding and had to be carried away instead: no one knows if it was much or not. They didn't bring him to my Officers' Hospital anyway.

Saturday, October 30th. A boy came in at 6 p.m. with his right arm blown clean off in its sleeve at 2 p.m. He was very collapsed when he came in, but revived a bit later. 'Mustn't make a fuss about trifles,' he explained. 'We got to stick it.' What a trifle! He ran from the first to the second trench unaided. The boy who threw his brains on the floor died yesterday, and another is dying.

Sunday, October 31st. This afternoon we took a lot of lovely flowers to the Cemetery for our graves for All Saints' Day. We had enough for General Capper's grave and a few other officers, about ten of our last men and three French soldiers. It took all the afternoon doing them up with Union Jack ribbon, and finding the graves. There are hundreds. It was a swamp of sticky mud, and pouring with rain at first.

All Saints' Day 1915, November 1st. This is the festival of the *Tous Saints*, when *tout le monde* follows the Procession from the Church to the Cemetery and puts flowers on all the graves, and there are services and bells ringing all day. There is also rain. It has been coming down in streams and the streets run rivers: but though it damped, it did not check the piety of the bereaved. Anyone old or young who can claim the remotest share in any tomb – however obscure the relationship or however many years ago – does so in deepest black. The orderlies were much distressed at the weather for them. 'This is a great day for France,' they said. 'The French take these things so serious.'

We have had a busy day – still taking in and also evacuating, and then taking in again. They seem to be getting a lot of bomb wounds. The officers were talking about the trenches in the Hohenzollern Redoubt, that begin British and finish up German, and you never know which you're in. 'I came round a corner,' said a Gunner Officer from Essex, 'and I met a Hun. I had only a map-case – he had a bomb.' 'What did you both do?' I asked. 'I didn't wait to see what he did, but I ran the fastest I ever went in my life.' A Scotch R.A.M.C. officer, who was with his Regiment all through, was talking about the early morning of the 14th, after we had tried to take the H.R. on the 13th. Our dead and wounded were lying so thick on the ground, that he had to pick his way among them with a box of morphia tabloids, and give them to anyone who was alive: tie up what broken limbs he could with rifles for splints, and leave them there: there were no stretchers, and the trenches too narrow if they'd had any. The Guards made three sorties to bring them in, but in getting three, lost so many men, they couldn't go on. They are taking the Divisions into the Line and out again so quickly that nobody gets on with making the trenches habitable, and in this weather you can imagine the result.

Tuesday, November 2nd. It has rained again all day without stopping. We are wondering who has been sent to the Château to nurse a certain august patient. The 'damned good boy' (Prince of Wales) has made himself a great name with everybody. They all call him 'a stout fellow.' He visits dug-outs when they're being heavily shelled, and when he at last says, 'I think we'll go back now,' the rapidly ageing officer in charge of him heaves a sigh of relief and gets him away. He has a passion for exercise and scorches about on a swagger new cycle, with his officer panting after him on an old Government one.

Wednesday, November 3rd. There are signs of another *Tag* coming, but they are vague as yet. I hope my department won't break down anywhere if it comes: one has an unwonted sense of responsibility for people and things. You wonder if you have got all your men on the board in their right places: both Sisters and orderlies have had to be rearranged a bit this week.

A lad had to have his leg off this morning for gas gangrene. He says he 'feels all right' and hasn't had to have any morphia all day. You'd think he'd merely had his boot taken off. Some of them are such infants to be fighting for their country. One has a bullet through his liver and tried to say through his tears 'there's some much worse than what I am.'

Sunday, November 7th. A little Night Sister in the Medical last night pulled a man round who was at the point of death, in the most splendid way. He had bronchitis and acute Bright's Disease, and Captain S. and the Day Sister had all but given him up; but at 10.30 p.m., as a last resource, Captain S. talked about a Vapour Bath, and the little Sister got hold of a Primus and some tubing and a kettle and cradles, and got it going, and did it again later, and this morning the man was speaking and swallowing, and back to earth again. He is still alive to-night, but not much more. It will give me something good to put in her Confidential Report to-morrow. You have to send one in to our H.Q. when anyone leaves.

Monday, November 8th, 10 p.m. Dazzling, sunny clear day, but no time to take much notice of it. We began to take in again this afternoon. A dangerously wounded officer among them this time, badly wounded – abdominal – operated on immediately, before he was washed or changed – have only just left him; he may do, but it is doubtful.

There is a very blithe and babbling boy in to-night. He was in the Argentine when the War broke out – now in the Grenadier Guards. 'I shall always bless the Kaiser,' he said, 'getting me home for this. I wouldn't have missed it for anything: jolly hard luck on you Sisters though – always having to walk so quietly and all that – we can laugh and shout and swear – it's not so bad for us.' I assured him we could do all that out of the wards!

Wednesday, November 10th. It poured terribly yesterday and all last night, and must have made mud pies of the trenches. There are generally about fifteen officers in now, sick – and a few wounded – who are sent down on the trains, except, of course, my abdominal officer, Captain D., who really seems to be going to do. He's got over the first two days and nothing has gone wrong – and considering the dangerousness of his wounds and the tremendous operation, everyone is very much bucked about him – but it is reckless to boast as early as this.

Thursday, November 11th. The First Brigade sent me two tickets for their concert to-night. Two of the others went, and I and another looked in after the Night Sisters came on. Concerts are funny things, when all the performers and all the audience are soldiers and officers waiting their turn to go and get killed, or kill other men – one wonders how much they think about it.

Friday, November 12th. Another bomb accident here to-day – a Highlander officer was brought in at tea-time with a lung wound bleeding badly; if he lives, we shall have him in a long time, like Captain D.

Saturday, November 13th. This week has gone by like greased lightning, I suppose because one's been busy. Have had an anxious day with my two bad officers downstairs and a ward full of sick and convalescent ones upstairs. The one with the lung has Black Watch officers coming in all day to know how he is, and three Padres have been in to see him. We had very bad news yesterday. You remember the boy whose arm was blown off, and who didn't want to 'make a fuss about trifles.' He was kept here as long as possible, and then put on to an Ambulance Train. Unluckily it took him all the way to Havre – about 30 hours – he had a hæmorrhage an hour after he got there, and died next morning. The Sister wrote and told me. He, of all people, one wanted to hear of being petted at his own home. The 1st Division, who have been resting here five weeks, are going up to the trenches to-morrow, and another Division will come down.

Sunday night, November 14th. The town is full of outgoing and incoming people all day, and a lot of Indians on mules and horses. We have been 'Taking in' to-day; the Medical is full up with worn-out people, who have broken down after fifteen days in the trenches, and also with rows of trench feet. Special reports have to be filled in by the M.O. about these – in great detail – how long they were in the trench – how long in water – what foot-gear, etc., etc. Last night, on my way up, I looked into the mortuary to see poor Jock lying under his Union Jack, at the foot of the Cross and flowers. It is a whitewashed sort of coach-house: I do the flowers. The Corporal and the boy in charge of it (and the P.M.'s and funerals) were preparing placidly to sleep there, too! on their stretchers.

They prefer it to sleeping in the billet with the rest and don't mind how many corpses they share it with.

Monday, November 15th. The town is full of troops to-day – a Division down from Loos, with happy faces and indescribable clothes, khaki showing here and there through a thick layer of caked dry mud: there's not a shed or a house that isn't packed with them.

The Train has not come, and yesterday's lot are still thick on the floors; by now the floors, the stretchers and the men are all the same tone of trench mud. One, who is slightly lunatic, wandered out in his socks after tea, and was found an hour later by a search party, somewhere outside. My poor officer is going downhill to-day, I'm afraid. His mother and the girl he is engaged to write piteous letters every day. The Padre and I write to them on alternate days, so that they hear every day.

Tuesday, November 16th. We have an officer in, of this Division, that has just been relieved from holding a bit of our new line next the French. There are no dug-outs of any sort, because, in this wet weather, when they go to sleep in one, the roof falls in and buries them alive: a lot have been killed in this way. And they can't get the R.E. up to get on with planking and draining them because of the heavy shelling that goes on all the time, just when only 'holding the line.' So they have been standing, because you can't walk in it, over their waists in mud, and they can't lie down to sleep or they would be drowned. He can't think how the men stick it and live without the dry change the officers can have. His own company has been standing like this, heavily shelled – the killed and wounded left where they're hit till night, and then taken down the only communication trench there is there. 'The ones left alive just cried at last,' he said, 'but they're absolutely marvellous.' 'What did you do?' I asked. 'Oh, I wasn't far off crying, too,' he said, 'but responsibility keeps your nerves together a bit – though mine wouldn't have stood any more of it.' They are resting for a month – some going home on leave and all as happy as larks now. He said the French in the next trenches were splendid and didn't mind anything, and were 'playing about with their machine-guns as merry as grigs.' He watched the Guards' Division at Loos in their historic charge, in solid separate companies, as if at a Review. He saw one big shell drop into one platoon – wipe out every man except two. These two got up and went on alone without turning a hair.

My Scotch officer with the lung is getting better, and Captain D. is about the same – having a black time. People with such terrible injuries as his generally don't survive; when they do, it seems hardly worth it, unless they get home and see their own people. He may, but he may not. He always tries to smile when he says good-night, and says 'Thank you, for everything.' Captain T. helped me with him to-night, as gently and cleverly as a nurse, because his pet orderly was off, and the other is too hodgy to be of any use for bad people. The Train took some away to-day, but not nearly all. In the Medical Ward they've been having hot baths in front of the fire, and then clean shirts.

Wednesday. They have nearly all gone to-day from the Surgical, and some from the Medical. The queer barn-like wards looked so nice to-night – big fires glowing – floors scrubbed – and snoring, red-blanketed figures all comfortably tucked up.

We have had a very sad day at the O.H., although Captain D., the worst one, has been happier. About one o'clock, a six-foot, broad-shouldered, strapping man was brought in pulseless – wounded yesterday. Captain T. happened to be there at the time, and we gave him a subcutaneous saline and then another and various hypodermics, but he died at 4.15 p.m., on his stretcher by the fire in the Receiving Room. The wound was a smashed elbow; he ought not to have died, unless he lay out a long time, but his clothes weren't like that. He was an Artist. He told me his mother's address, and when he was asked his religion (for getting the Padre) he said, 'Am I going to die? I don't mind being told.' Captain T. funked telling him, but I expect he knew. The Padre came just as he lost consciousness, about five minutes before he died, just in time to say the Committal Prayer. He said once, 'I'm trying to be plucky, but I shall have to give in soon.' Now I must try and tell his mother what I can.

Friday, November 26th. There is an officer in who went into the Loos battle as junior officer of the Battalion, and came out in command of it with 70 men! He said a great many of the men, N.C.O.'s and officers who were killed, had written farewell letters to their wives overnight: 'very pathetic letters they were,' he said. He was a fine, modest little man himself – new Army, Welsh. 'I wouldn't miss a bit of it for anything, but there are certainly some discomforts attached to it'; this after standing in water-logged trenches with no dug-outs, because they all fall in. 'But you get used to it all right, and the men sit on wet ledges, drenched, cold and hungry and actually sing! They're great.' He hated being home on leave – felt like a fish out of water, and said nobody cared about the War. (This was Wales.)

Very cold again. The train cleared a good many this morning.

Monday, November 29th. Captain D. is much worse. Another big gun is to be wired for from G.H.Q. to-morrow to see him. His chances, with or without further opinion, are very bad, and after this three weeks' struggle it is very hard luck. Four Sergeant-Majors and a Staff Sergeant and the Company Cook of his Regiment, came to see him yesterday and all saluted round his bed; they are devoted to him and have served with him in many other climates.

The first Sister starts on her eight days' leave to-morrow.

Tuesday, November 30th. All leave has been stopped for everybody, so my Sister didn't get off. Sir Wilmot Herringham (whom I had met at No. 4 Field Ambulance) turned up this morning – located Captain D.'s trouble, and Captain R. operated at once. He now has a new wound – this time in his back, which will be a difficulty, but he stuck it all like a soldier and is really better this evening. It has been an anxious day, but he stood it amazingly well.

I must tell you about an infant boy servant to one of the sick officers – too young to be allowed to do anything but officers' servant. When they got over the parapet at Loos, the officer found him at every turn, two yards behind, pounding on, not taking the smallest notice of shells, or of men dropping all round him. 'Get out – go back,' he ordered – with more force than can be written, but in vain. Afterwards the boy explained that he'd been told that when your officer was wounded you went to hospital with him, and that you had a jolly good time there: so it was worth risking your life on the chance that your officer got wounded!

Friday, December 3rd. Captain D. is a scrap better to-day, able to emerge from bromides, and talk a little. He told me that when they were holding the Hohenzollern trenches in that worst weather, when they stood up waist-high in liquid mud, two of his men slipped under it when asleep and their bodies were dug out next day. Their food was sodden, the men kept themselves alive on rum, and the officers on whisky. He went one night to a man he knew in another trench to see if he could give him anything to eat, and this other one said how awful his trench was. 'Come and see mine,' he said, and he showed him a place where three men were sitting in it nearly to their arm-pits, huddled together, moaning in their sleep. He went later, in the early morning, with three sound men and found them sunk a little deeper, and woke them and got them out, and set a man to each, to shake them and rub them and put them up in the dry, outside the trench, till the morning mists had cleared, and they had to get into it again.

He met some young boys getting about in their socks with black swollen feet that couldn't be got into boots, saying, 'They were going to stick it, they weren't going to report sick!' Of course he sent them down. They lost very few sick because they made the men rub their feet every day. Some who didn't bother lost 300. Kitchener's 1st Army, all highly trained men, with ten months' hard training, were too valuable to lose in this way.

Monday, December 13th. Captain D. has at last taken a real turn for the better – this is his sixth week, a record in a C.C.S. He is being weaned from sleeping-draughts and only dressed once a day, and gradually coming to life again, temperature coming down and wounds clearing up. He does deserve to get well if anybody did.

The Hospital is very empty.

Wednesday, December 15th. The town is overflowing with weary trench-worn Jocks to-day. They came in to billets last night from the Line with drawn, haggard, unsmiling faces. To-day they are clean and cheery, and you hear the Glasgow brogue everywhere. It is the 15th Division that got farther than anyone else beyond Loos and Hill 70, and would have chased the flying Boches back to Lille if 'the Staff Work' had backed them up. Now their dead are far out beyond the German front lines.

All is quiet here; you wouldn't know there was a War; no guns, no fighting; both sides busy trying to keep dry and taking off their trench boots to rub their feet.

Nothing doing in the Base Hospitals or up here; Sisters going home on leave everywhere.

Sunday, December 19th. A little more activity the last few days, and the hospital nearly full – wounded, mostly not severe in the Surgical, and high temperatures and kidney trouble in the Medical. Very few trench feet; one officer boasts proudly that there's not been a single case in his battalion the last two times they've been in the trenches. If the Platoon Commander, goaded by the Company Officer, sees that every man takes off his boots and socks twice a day and rubs in trench grease, they keep all right. They're rubbed with whale oil before they go up.

The guns are making a bit of a noise again but nothing to write home about. Captain D. is really recovering and enjoying his new hold on the simple facts of existence like a child.

Thursday, December 30th. This morning, a glorious day, the town was lined all through with troops waiting for Sir John French to come through. Some of us went to Sister B.'s billet, which overlooks the *Grand Place*, and had a lovely view. They all presented arms in companies, like a trickle down the long lines as his car came through with a second car behind. The old man was saluting away. He must have felt sad, leaving his dear B.E.F.

'One of our officers went raving mad on May 16th,' said a Wykehamist boy to-day. 'Was he old or young?' I asked. 'Oh, old compared to me,' he said, 'he was twenty-one!'

Saturday, January 15th 1916. 10 p.m. Found everything very quiet when I got back from leave on Wednesday night. They hadn't taken in all the time. We started taking in yesterday and are pretty full up now, nothing very bad except a few poor medicals, one appendix in the Surgical and a poor little boy officer, D. F., unconscious with his brains blown out. He was operated on to-day and it was a terrible sight – quite hopeless. Another Black Watch officer, Captain R., with a fearful abdominal wound, is slowly recovering.

This morning the Jocks' Division marched out with the pipes for the trenches after their month's rest. They looked much fitter than they did a month ago. The 1st Division has come in covered with mud, but not so worn out and trench-looking as the Jocks were. The 15th were so hung round with packs, steel helmets, sacks and parcels and clothes for their extra comfort that I doubt if they'll ever get there.

There is very little War doing just now, but a lot of Schools for this and Schools for that, and manoeuvres of all sorts. The British Army is a busy little feller!

Sunday, January 16th. D. F., the boy with the head wound, has been peacefully dying all day; his hand closes less tightly over mine to-day, but his beautiful brown eyes look less inscrutable as he gets farther from this crooked world. His total silence and absolute stillness and unconsciousness have already given him the marble statue look.

Tuesday, January 18th. He was buried to-day. I got there late, just as the Padre finished. The Medical has been busy to-day with some bad cases, but everywhere else is quiet.

Wednesday, January 19th. A Padre from the trenches turned up at 11 last night to see D. F., his sister's only child, but he had been buried that afternoon. He'd got a wire from her to say he was here seriously wounded. The boy had only been out two months, and had been medically refused originally for being hopelessly under chest measurement, but he did extension exercises till they passed him. He was six foot and as thin as a stick.

Friday, January 21st. Last night three small children were brought in wounded. They had found an unexploded bomb in a field and took it home to play with – one was killed in this game of play, one severely wounded and two more wounded. The third was dressed here and taken home. The two we have in the Surgical Division are Gustav, aged 1¾, hit in the leg and hand, and Robert, aged 3, hit in the tummy, thigh and foot, very white and quiet, poor lamb. The baby is round and rosy and both are very good. Everybody adores them, of course. The orderly stands at the foot of their beds, and shows them off with pride: the little Robert is not out of the wood yet. They were both taken to the theatre to have their bits of bomb looked for this morning.

This afternoon I went to Béthune in my car! It was an official visit to see the C.C.S., and incidentally I had tea with C. at my own beloved Officers' Dressing Station. It was absolutely thrilling to see the big Tower and the Armada Belfry a long way off, and to see the Château of No. 1 C.C.S. on the way, where we heard the nightingales and the guns in May, and coped with the Canadians. C. was very busy, so the Sister in Charge showed me all over.

After seeing over No. 1, I dived into the big Church and was struck all of a fresh heap by its extraordinary beauty and atmosphere. In the *Grand Place* under the Belfry, the R.F.A. Band was playing 'A Wandering Minstrel I' to a vast khaki crowd. Then I dashed into my old billet and embraced Marie Thérèse and her mother, and looked at the shell-hole in the roof of Sister J.'s room in our billet, and had a look at Marie's Château, our first billet, where we had Eau-de-Cologne in the bath and satin quilts and oak staircases. All the big lower windows were heavily sand-bagged.

The two babies are better. The three-year-old demands beer and refuses everything else, so he's had some and has gone to sleep. The baby looks like a Raphael baby, and looks absolutely adorable asleep.

Wednesday, January 26th. We've been busy with a bombing accident to-day. A Sergeant-Major was killed, and two officers, and two men wounded, who have now been operated on. The baby has gone home, but the boy is still here.

Thursday, January 27th. One of the bombed men died this evening on the operating table. He was the one who threw it: it exploded in two seconds instead of five, when it had only left his hand a yard. The poor little officer who got badly bombed went down on the train this morning dressed in bandages. He is an Australian, and knows no one in England, so I gave him G's address at the last minute in the Ambulance; perhaps she can get someone to hold his hand a little, when he gets to London. He clutched the envelope gratefully.

An order has come round that the Sisters in charge of C.C.S's are to lecture the orderlies on Nursing and Ward duties.

Sir Almroth Wright is with No. 1 C.C.S., making researches in gas gangrene. This has nothing to do with Poison Gas. It is the name given to the condition set up by the presence in the wound, in the deep tissues, of a very virulent microbe, which is introduced into wounds on battle-fields by the bits of dirty clothing, mud, etc., driven in with the missile. It generates gas bubbles, and is quickly fatal unless scientifically dealt with at a very early stage.

Friday, January 28th. One very nice feature of being here is that one gets to know some children: on the Ambulance Train and at No. 16 one never saw any. There are two tiny *gamins* about three and four, in the slummy alley I go up and down some dozen times a day, who sight one afar off, and immediately 'line the street,' wherever they happen to be, stiffen themselves with their infant heels clicked together, and fling their little black hands to their little black foreheads, long before and long after one has gone by. They only get washed on Sundays apparently, like the children in Dublin. And there is a dazzling baby of four called Adrienne, who disports herself in front of our Mess all day. Then there is a boy of about seven in a pink pinny outside my office, who goes nearly mad when any drilling is going on. He rushes into the line of men and does all the drill, echoing all the words of command with loud yells, apparently because he can't contain himself. And if you meet the tiny *orphelin* boys being herded to bed, they cluster round you, like ants, and say, '*Bon soir*, Sister,' and wait for '*le petit Raymond*,' aged two, to be kissed.

Wednesday, February 2nd. It has set in for a cold spell, and has been freez-ing since Monday. Coming on the top of dry weather it's not so bad for the trench people as it is when it catches them with soaked feet. Now they get the braziers going everywhere and brew extra hot drinks, and thaw themselves without getting so wet.

This German activity in the West has so far done themselves more harm than it has us; unless an Attack is, in the long run, a success it is the Attackers who lose more than the Attacked.

The last two days I've had to give a lecture to the Orderlies, half the Company one day and half the next. They are all roped in by the Sergeant-Major, and held in subjection by a Sergeant who takes their names, while I hold forth in an empty ward. They've even dug out the post boy, and the deaf man, who dishes out the rations, and the mortuary corporal and the runners and the other clerks, as well as all the ward orderlies. I had to stop the Sergeant-Major from waking up the night duty men! Except for their being such a mixture of skilled and unskilled, senior and junior, it was quite easy, and they were breathlessly attentive, and ready to answer questions. The last half-hour is a bandaging class, which they thoroughly enjoy. I get the Lance-Corporals and Corporals to teach the duffers, which saves their dignity and the situation.

Tuesday, February 15th, 10 p.m. It has been pouring cats and dogs for hours, and the streets are rivers of slush and just an hour ago the 1st Division marched into the front line trenches to relieve the − th, who all got out to-day except those left to hold the line.

One of the officers' servants, a voluble innocent boy, who would be with them to-night if his officer hadn't had his head bombed a week ago, stood this evening with a dish cloth in one hand and a plate in the other, describing with shining eyes what it was like taking over in the wet. 'It has always served us like that,' he said, 'every time. And now you mayn't even put your water-proof sheets up across the trench to keep the rain out, and you stand on the fire-step doing sentry when you're wet through and then you don't care whether you get a bullet or whether you don't. Back in October it was dry and the nights were warm. Up around Hulluch, we could a-stopped up there till the end o' the War. We was enjoying it!' He said they had one Company Officer who always took them up over the top instead of along the communication trenches if it was extra dark or there was a bit of a mist, 'and we never 'ad no casualties,' he finished proudly.

There is an officer of the 1st Camerons left behind sick, who was brought in to-night with a temperature of 104.6, possible pneumonia. He promised his mother never to take off his identity disc, because his brother was killed without his. This one was knocked over in March, 200 yards from his brother's grave, and was laid up till September. He has a brother of 6 ft. 2 ins. 'who is only 15, the little devil, and he's run away from Rossall three times to enlist, and been caught each time – shows the right spirit though.' This one is only twenty.

A dying boy in the Medical is putting up a tremendous fight and Captain S. and Sister J. and Craig the Orderly are slaving over him. He has Vapour Baths, and Oxygen-through-Absolute-Alcohol, and Atropin and Digitalin and Pilocarpin and Eserin and everything ending in 'in' that could floor the various diseases that have got him in their grip: nephritis, uræmic fits, œdema of lungs and pneumonia.

Friday, February 18th. The fight for the boy's life still rages against terrible odds. He has now added paralysis of the transverse colon to his other diseases – which of the heroic remedies it is due to no one knows. Anyway, I'm afraid it is beating us, and he will not struggle much longer.

Last night an aeroplane began buzzing round with an unfamiliar whirr and then came the bomb – through a house a little farther down this street. The explosion shook my bed. It completely smashed up the house (not mine), killed a boy in bed, wounded a woman who died to-day, and a baby, and wounded three soldiers. The bombed baby is with the Nuns at the Hospice; Captain T. and I are looking after it there; it is called Leopold; its father is *à la guerre*, its *grandmère* killed and its mother a *vilaine femme* (no better than she should be). Our boy in the Medical had Sir Wilmot Herringham to see him yesterday. He gives some hope, and things look a little better already.

Tuesday, February 22nd, 10.30 p.m. It has been snowing inches deep all day and now there is a sharp frost and stars, and you tread on crackling slush. It is not the night one would choose to stay out in the garden all night, still less in a trench of any sort – I'm afraid there'll be some frozen men in the morning.

We are very full everywhere to-night – I've had to post another night orderly. Yesterday, or rather last night, the Boche made an attack and used gas, after a din of a day of bombardment on both sides. The strafing was mostly from our side: we came off very well. But a thing happened yesterday which I must tell you. At two o'clock in the afternoon a Hun anti-aircraft shell hit one of our fighting machines at a height of 7,000 feet. It blew the left leg off the pilot, M. H., who then landed his machine safely, close to our front trenches. The enemy shelled it furiously, with poison gas shells among others. A Medical Officer who saw the hit in the air was waiting for them, and was the first man to reach them: he finished cutting off the leg then and there (it was 'just slush' the boy told me) and then the observer (unhurt) seized one of the precious machine-guns and the boy with his leg off seized the other under his arm, and, supported by the Doctor, hopped 20 yards with it to the nearest trench. The aeroplane was shelled beyond help. Then they got him dressed and to a Field Ambulance, and he arrived at my Officers' Hospital at 5 p.m., three hours after he was hit, as cheery as ever.

He had a very bad night from shock, but revived this morning and had a big operation on his ghastly remains of a leg – just below the knee, and has been very bad since. But he must be pulled round somehow. All sorts of flying people come to ask how he is. His Wing Commander came again and the C.O. of his Squadron, who said sadly, 'And I got him into the Flying Corps.' The Colonel told him he'd been recommended for the V.C. 'Oh, that's absolutely childish,' he said.

We talked this morning about the wonderful new leg he would have. 'Perhaps I shall fly again,' he said hopefully.* And he was telling another boy who went down to-day, that he'd just got 'an expensive pair of new boots that he'd never worn – just my luck.'

There's a boy of *sixteen* in the Surgical with bad wounds from a rifle grenade. The bombed baby of the other night is a hero. He sits on the operating table with a long forceps through his shoulder, blowing his tin

---

* He became a Flying Instructor at home later, at Oxford.

trumpet and squeaking his woolly lamb in between all sorts of frightful-
ness of having bits of bomb picked out of his small person. He is about
four. The boy in the Medical is worse again, and poor Sister J. is nearly in
tears. He looks terrible to-night.

Wednesday, February 23rd, 11.30 p.m. It is late and I've just finished doing
the Pay Sheet after a busy day everywhere. The boy in the Medical is
giving up the fight to-night; he has never once been cross or naughty
over anything. Both Sister J. and the Night Sister have slaved over him,
and it seems all for nothing as far as his mother and sisters go.

A man who came yesterday with a headache died to-day of cerebro-
spinal meningitis; it was extraordinarily rapid.

The Flying boy is very ill; gas gangrene has set in and he is not in a
condition to survive another amputation higher up – so all we can do is
to try and arrest the gangrene by the saline drip open method treatment.
He cannot be left, so there has been a lot to do – with ten other officers
upstairs and the bombed baby Leopold from the Hospice; he is pretty
bad, too – bless him.

The flying men still come in, and there is nothing to make their anxious faces any happier.

The Surgical is quite full to-night.

Thursday morning. The Medical boy was breathing his last at 12.0 last
night, and this morning he is not only still in this world but better!!
Atropin every hour has done it.

Thursday, February 24th. The world is still fast bound in frost and snow
and we have some very sick men in. The poor boy in the Medical succeeded in dying this afternoon after a hideous illness of a fortnight.

The Flying boy is better, thank Heaven. The drip treatment is doing
wonders with his leg, and he is getting over the shock. He's a tall, hefty
lad, over twelve stone and has a strong and innocent face of peculiar
charm, age 24. When I showed him the bit in the C. in Chief's communiqué about him in *The Times* to-day he said: 'If Mother sees that
I expect she'll feel bucked.' Poor Mother – she writes such jolly letters to

him, which he insists on my reading to him – anxious one day because he hasn't written, and relieved the next because he has. Evidently she thinks each day he may have to be looked for or not have come home. The other day his petrol ran out when he was over the German lines and he only just got back to our trenches.

Saturday night. Sir Charles Monro came in to-day to see the Flying boy. He looks a fine old man. He saluted and greeted me first and then was most awfully nice to the boy. He said outside, 'What a fine face, I shall come and see him again.' He said it had gone up as a V.C. to Sir Douglas Haig, but it didn't fulfil the exact conditions for a V.C., and nor does it, of course, though it was a superhuman feat of endurance. When someone asked him something about the shell that hit him, he said, 'I want to forget that part of it.'

The Wing Commander who comes every day invited me down to Headquarters to see the air photographs. I explained that joy-rides in Staff cars were, alas, not in our programme, so he is going to bring them up to-morrow for me to see.

Monday, February 28th. The Flying boy is not enjoying himself, it is a bad bit, and is not over yet: the rest of his leg is to come off on Wednesday, when Capt. R. comes back.

A wire came through to-day to his Corps, from the C. in Chief to say that 'by authority from his Majesty the King the Distinguished Service Order had been awarded to Lt. H. of the R.F.C. Please inform Lt. H.'

The weather is still unmentionable, and the world carpeted with slush.

Tuesday, February 29th. A nice spring morning to-day at last; it must cheer the people up a bit after the horrors of weather the last ten days. It seems to have been a bit deeper snow at home – here it alternately froze and then thawed and froze again. Sir Anthony Bowlby came to see the Flying boy's leg again to-day, and was so pleased with it as it is doing, that he said, 'Don't operate – carry on, and he may yet keep his knee-joint.'

It is a great score, as it was bubbling with the gas bug. The boy is finding it a hard job to stick the treatment, but it has got to be done. Three Generals have been to see him to-day.

While I was finishing Leopold's dressing to-day, he solemnly whistled 'Keep the Home Fires Burning' and 'Who's your Lady Friend' all through without a wrong note, to the amazement of everyone! He smiles a divine smile when you ask if he is a *petit Anglais*.

The nuns at the Hospice have wards full of doddery, smelly old men and women, like a Workhouse and an Idiot Asylum in one. They slave after them from 3.30 in the morning when they get up to *faire* the *cuisine*, till nine at night, and laugh and rollick as only Holy Nuns can all the time. They told me four of them are in the town to-night – two sitting up with two *très malades*, and two with two *morts*. 'On veille et on prie,' they said when I asked what they did. There must be some special Heaven waiting for them one day.

Friday, March 3rd. Snowing again to-day, horrible slush on the ground. If our wounded are lying out to-night in this, God help them. What horrors those masses of Germans attacking Verdun must have gone through in the snow last week.

Sunday, March 5th. Still snowing; it's a bad world. We have been very busy to-day. The Flying boy is about the same; he showed me with loud cackles the man in Punch who said one of the compensations of having a wooden leg was that you could keep up your socks with drawing-pins! Letters about his D.S.O. are pouring in, much to his amusement.

Monday, March 6th. We had a convoy of very contented, dirty, wet wounded in to-day, and have all been on all day. For efficiency in this sort of work give me the average British trained nurse, Scotch, English or Irish. When there's work to be done she goes about it without any noise or fuss or flurry, gets unemployed patients or orderlies to work, has eyes all over her head, and brains behind them, and her hands and feet never stop. By 8 p.m., when the Night Sisters come on, the men are all bathed, fed, dressed and tucked up and everything is got out of the Medical Officers that is needed, and the Sisters go, hungry, tired and cheerful, to a hearty supper at the billet and then out again to bed.

The Flying boy is not so well.

Tuesday, March 7th. Snowing all last night and all to-day, slush indescribable. The train cleared off all the bad Medicals except three pneumonias, and all the possible movable wounded. They have a good scheme here of putting the compound fractured femurs up into a new self-contained form of Thomas splint, and putting them back after operation, not to bed, but on to the stretcher with a special bar on it for slinging the leg, ready for the train in the morning, to save moving them again. While we were snoring in our cushy beds last night, a man (Corporal Cottar) brought in to-day, was lying out in the snow all night, with one leg blown off, and the other wounded. Considering all things he is rallying wonderfully well, and will have some more of the leg off to-morrow; it is full of cinders and things.

An officer with a very stricken face came this morning and asked to see an officer who had just been killed by a bomb accident. I hadn't got him, but he was then in our Mortuary, taken straight there. This one then went to the Colonel and asked to see him, so the Colonel took him to the stretcher and lifted the blanket and made some remark that it must have been instantaneous, and asked if he knew him. 'He was my brother,' he said. Isn't this bombing business horrible? The thing exploded instantaneously instead of in the 5 seconds. Wasn't that last V.C., Lt. Victor Smith in the Dardanelles, who threw his own body on to the bomb he had dropped, the most wonderful thing in the War?

Sunday, March 12th. Early service in the Ward. The Flying boy went off to-day at 11, comfortably packed up on his stretcher, looking a radiant picture. Unfortunately the Officers' bunks on the train were full and he had to stay on the stretcher on the floor of a wagon full of slung stretchers. I hope they'll have the sense to turn another officer less disabled on to the floor and give him a bed at the next stop. His leg is still in the raw-meat stage, and his pulse is rapid.

They sent for me in the Surgical this evening to fix up Corporal Cottar on M.H.'s special drip splint; their arrangements were not succeeding.

Wednesday, March 15th. How this month is galloping; these last two days have been real warm sunny spring. There is a story to tell you about the quiet determined-looking little man in the Surgical with the glass eye – Corporal Cottar, of the Buffs – who came in with his leg bombed off. Yesterday morning he was so much better he was able to talk a little more. He told me (only when asked how he got it) that he was leading a bombing attack at the Hohenzollern Redoubt and took his men up a wrong turning, and came on to 'thousands of Germans.' He somehow got his men away again but minus his leg. 'It was dark, and I didn't know me leg was gone – so I kep' on throwing the bombs and little Wood he kep' by me and took out the pins for me.' (His hand was badly wounded as well.) At last 'little Wood' got him into a dug-out in a crater and stayed with him all night.

Yesterday morning General Gough – Corps Commander – and two other Generals turned up and asked to see Corporal Cottar of the Buffs, to tell him he was recommended for the V.C. General Gough told me he was a marvellous man, known throughout the Division as the 'Corporal of the Buffs with one eye,' famed for bravery and scouting at night for snipers by himself. They were awfully nice to him, and Captain R. told them all about the leg and the drip treatment, etc.

Later that day the Corporal had a severe hæmorrhage and so nearly died that they daren't give him an anæsthetic, but Captain R. took his gangrenous leg off through the knee as he was, without his feeling it as he was unconscious. We slaved at him all the evening but he died at 8 p.m. Wasn't it horribly tragic? But he did know about his V.C. General Gough said he was throwing bombs and cheering the men on for hours after he was hit. We sent a lovely cross of white flowers and pink carnations to his funeral this afternoon.

Thursday, March 23rd. There are two very ill and interesting men in the Surgical, one a chest and the other arm and legs. If either pull through it will be a triumph. They are both the sort you can't do enough for, who say, 'I'm a lot of trouble to you' or 'You all here 'andle me so gentle.' That one has a broken arm in a bath, and a broken knee under continuous drip: bomb wounds. Grenades are truly an invention of the Evil One. The Medical is unwontedly quiet.

My friend the Wing Commander turned up this morning to show me the Air photographs he'd promised. They were very interesting; Loos, Hulluch, the Hohenzollern Redoubt and Lille were wonderful.

Friday, March 24th. Snowing hard this morning and to-night, and men are lying out in the cold slush the better to kill each other. Isn't it insane and immoral beyond description?

I went on to 14 Ambulance Train this morning to see Sister C. It is a most beautiful and luxurious train, as far removed from old No. 5 in cleanness, surgical fittings, space and convenience as Millbank is from No. 6.

Leopold is now reclaimed by the remnants of his bombed and disreputable family, but we are still dressing his little aunt, aged 13.

Monday, March 27th. We had a very young boy in the Medical the other day, cowering and shivering and collapsed from shell-shock. 'Where's my brother?' was the first thing he said, when he could speak. The shell that had knocked him out had blown his brother to bits.

I've got an officer badly wounded by a rifle grenade; the poor child might have sat down in the fire by mistake, by the state his back is in. He is to go down on the train to-morrow.

Tuesday, March 28th. To-day in the *Grand Place* (of which you have the postcard) we saw a fine sight. The 44th Brigade of the famous Scotch 15th Division, who broke themselves on Hill 70 on the '25th' at Loos, were drawn up for General Monro to give decorations to one Lieutenant and seven men. The Square was lined all round, and the 7th Camerons, 10th Gordons, 10th Seaforths and 9th Black Watch stood in solid masses with a space in the middle. We collared a window opposite the Red Hats. When the General arrived they sounded 'General Salute,' and the bands blared and the whole mass became statues. Then he called up '2nd Lieutenant Tom Brown' of the R.E. and read out in a terrific voice the story of his valour and pinned on the ribbon, shook hands, and with much saluting and clicking of heels Lieutenant Tom Brown blushingly retired. Then he read out the deeds of all the others, shook hands, saluted, etc. When that was over, he took a huge breath and bellowed out a very fine and stirring sermon on being a brave man and a Scotsman, and how the eyes of their country were on them and how they would never fail, and whether they were Generals or Privates they were all going to be as gallant, self-sacrificing and devoted as the men just decorated. He looked old, and walked lame, and it must have been a great effort. Then the bands got together and swung round into the middle space near the Red Hats, and struck up with little drums, big drums, fifes and bagpipes for the March Past.

The General went on to open the Y.M.C.A. Hut they've at last managed to get here.

The idea seems to be that we are going to a place S. of Béthune, and about that exact distance from the Line, to a little mining village. It is where we ought to be, instead of bringing them all this way back, stone cold and wet and often bleeding.

Tuesday, April 4th. We have been filling up to-day, both divisions. In the Medical are four boys propped up in a row with pneumonia and complications: two of them look as if they might die – and they are the bravest and most smiling. One gasps out 'très bon' when he is put comfortable.

There is a man in the Surgical with his right calf blown off and both bones fractured and his left arm broken, who beams and chuckles all the time. 'Not so bad, considering,' he says. 'No good making a fuss – it's all for your own good,' he went on (whether the wounds or the dressing, I couldn't quite make out!).

There is also a little Irish boy with a wound in the lung, who's been in some time, who was made permanently happy by a pair of very thick, soft bedroom shoes, packed with treasures in each, which came originally from Sir D. Haig. (We keep them for special boys.) He is always asking for them to be put on the chair by his bed: and one day asked if all the others got shoes like that! We told him they were only kept for the youngest in the ward.

Wednesday, April 5th. No train to-day, and ninety more in, so we are full to bursting, especially in the Surgical. Just come to bed at 12 p.m., after operations.

There is nothing much at the Officers' Hospital just now so I spend my time in the Surgical, where they are a bit short-handed. It is glorious to find that these New Army men and boys are every bit as wonderful in 'sticking it' when their eyes, mouths, hands, legs and arms are blown to bits as the original Army used to be. They wait their turn, and never whine or worry, and 'that feels beautiful' is a far more frequent comment than any complaint.

Thursday, April 6th. More operations to-day, and a good clearance by the train – only the worst left. Two are dying in the Medical and two in the Surgical.

Friday, April 7th. Very cold but fine: very few patients left in each division, only the remaining bad cases, and the very slight. The two medicals died yesterday afternoon, and the two surgicals in the night. All four are now lying under their Union Jacks in the Mortuary, where we have plants and a cross and frontal. Funeral to-morrow. A boy in the Surgical, who had his arm amputated yesterday (and was glad to be rid of it), seemed to be worrying about something this morning. It was a perfectly horrible arm, and he hated it. When I said, 'But you're glad it's off, aren't you?' he said, 'Yes, I am meself, but I'm wonderin' how I'm goin' to keep me family.' He had a wife and two children! I told him what splendid new arms soldiers get now, and how everyone would give them the possible jobs, like messengers and Commissionaires, before civilians, and his brow cleared at the rosy visions. I only hope it is true. Is it?

Tuesday, April 11th. Big take-in to-day, mostly wounded from two mines that went up this morning. A great many were buried altogether, but they dug a good many out. One little man with his eyes and mouth full of mud, his back nearly broken, was buried face downwards for four hours before they dug him out. They are a cheery lot in spite of it all; lots of 1st Division men in this. Got the dressings over by 8 p.m. to-night, which is a blessing, instead of starting at 9 p.m. Only three officers in hospital to-day, and to-morrow there'll be none – a record. What horrible revelations of that typhus camp in Wittenburg. How can there be any conscientious objectors after that?

A man had a very nice snowy white Teddy-bear coat. The Sisters who made his bed said how lovely it would be to go home on leave in it. After he'd been taken to the train the orderly brought this coat to the Sister. 'He said you was to be sure and 'ave it to go 'ome on leave in.' And he was devoted to that coat himself.

We had all the acute surgicals out in their beds in the sun to-day, in the school yard, round the one precious flower-bed, where are wallflowers and pansies. They enjoy it very much, and smoke, and have their meals out and the gramophone, and it does them a lot of good. They say it shortens the night. 'It does be long sometimes,' said a boy from Cork with a horrid wound in the knee. 'That knee is terrible sore on him,' said another Irishman feelingly, whose brain has been coming out through a hole in his head. They are nearly all Jocks and Paddys just now. By the by, we've got our new identity discs with our names, corps, rank and religion, so with two gas helmets each we are well looked after.

We went for a jolly walk after tea in the woods, found violets, cowslips and anemones.

Wednesday, April 19th. Orders came yesterday for us to take in no more patients and to stand by to move.

2

ATTACKS ON VIMY RIDGE

MAY 11TH TO JULY 3RD 1916
WITH THE 1ST ARMY (SIR CHARLES MONRO)

LETTERS FROM BARLIN

Thursday, May 11th. Barlin. We left St. Omer at 2.30 by Motor Ambulance and got here about 4 p.m. It was most interesting getting to new country and leaving behind us all the familiar landmarks that used to be in front of us at Lillers. The officer driving us had some difficulty in finding our C.C.S., but eventually he landed us in the right place, where a Field Ambulance used to be. The Quartermaster met us, and took us on to the Officers' Mess where the Colonel and Captain T. had tea waiting for us which we were very glad of. They were very welcoming and jolly and told us all about it while we had a huge tea of honey and cake. Then the Motor Ambulance, Captain T. and the Motor Ambulance Officer and our four selves had a triumphal progress accompanied by an ever-increasing crowd of excited children, to find our billets. Captain T. had put in a strenuous day fixing them up for us, in miners' cottages. Neat rows of little separate cottages in tiny gardens, quite poky but very clean, and kind people anxious to make one comfortable. I had to come to terms with another one who is going to *faire* our *cuisine*: and she had a nice supper of eggs, coffee and lovely bread and butter for us at 7.30.

They have never seen a female *Anglaise* in uniform before and we caused a terrific sensation: if we stand still a moment the children collect round us and the women rush to their doors and windows.

The M.O.s are enthusiastic about the country and the woods near, and the great excitement is to walk to a ridge about ¾ hour away, leading to Notre Dame de Lorette, and to watch the shells bursting in the trenches. They shelled the next village – Hersin – yesterday. We heard a few bursting this evening but did not see them.

Now about the Hospital. It is on two sides of a central lane: Surgical one side, Medical and Offices the other. The Surgical Division is a theatre building including a good operating theatre and a large ward for acute Surgicals, and four large Red Cross Huts holding 40 stretchers on trestles each. The Medical consists of four, large airy schoolrooms, and the Colonel's Office is a hut in the yard; two small huts are requisitioned for me, one for my Office, and one for Red Cross Stores. I am going round the whole thing with the Colonel to-morrow, and shall then have some idea how best to divide the work. We can take 400 lying-down cases, as we are, and there is a huge attic which can take 400 walking cases if we have a Push. We are possibly going to have three more M.O.s and three more Sisters from the Abdominal Hospital, which is going to be either closed down or transplanted into us. In any case the theatre work will be heavy. We are to begin taking in on Monday, so there's a good deal to do yet, between now and then, as the Field Ambulance occupying the site only left to-day. I can see a captive Balloon from my bed, hovering over the line in the day-time and the flashes of the guns at night, but it is not noisy so far.

Friday, May 12th. We had a most curious and interesting walk after tea, skirting the shelled village, then along an Embankment through Fosse 7, round the Slag heaps through a lovely wood out on to a ridge where there are some sappers and some sort of fortification. From this ridge we saw with the naked eye shells bursting round the one column of what used to be called the Tower Bridge at Loos, and all the landmarks so familiar from the War pictures. A man lent us his field-glasses and we saw parapets of trenches between. The Boche observation balloon was poised just opposite ours. We saw the flash of one of our 6-inch howitzers but couldn't see their bursts. We came back through long streets of miners' cottages for Fosse 7, slummier and townier than ours where we live. We drew large crowds, they darted into each other's houses to call their friends in case they should miss the wonderful sight.

Between the ridge and the mine the way we came back is a vast thick forest where we are going to look for fly orchis to-morrow. We found a white speckled one out and lots of other good flowers.

I am trying to plan out the work, but it will depend really on the sort of convoys we get. There are to be three operating tables going at once, for one thing, and a great many beds for acutes; also infectious tents. It is the Night Duty that will be the difficulty unless we have some more Sisters and Orderlies. Fortunately I know pretty well the dependableness and capability or the reverse of every individual orderly now, and can place them out accordingly.

Saturday, May 13th. It poured cats and dogs all night and all to-day, and the ground is changed into a thick sea of rich creamy mud where it isn't a running stream: we have been wading in it all day between the two Divisions, our billets and our mess billet, and getting through a lot of work, but there is still a great deal to be done.

A Padre belonging to a Battery of my old beloved Division (which is here and goes back to rest to-morrow) came in to say what services he will have to-morrow, but we have our own. He asked if the miner people were getting over their excitement at seeing *Anglaises*. 'It's rather exciting for us too,' he said, 'to speak to an English woman up here,' and he made the most of his opportunity! He says we can pick up bits of shell in a field in Hersin only two miles off, that were put over the day we came, so we're going to explore to-morrow if there's time, and if the mud is fordable.

Sections of R.F.A. clatter by continually with very smart teams of six big mules, and limbers are painted all colours like scenery, as the armoured trains used to be. This reminds me rather more of the taste of

Ypres days than anything else, without the breathlessness of holding up the German rush on Calais. No man is allowed to go about without his gas helmet slung round him, even the schoolchildren have them.

You can follow through the wood on the top of the ridge till you come to Notre Dame de Lorette, the devastated bit the French held in their advance this time last year, when they took the Labyrinth.

Our Mess is a rather hand-to-mouth one at present, but I hope to get it better later on. At present the only pudding the rather noisy grasping Madame can run to is four baked apples. I had to teach her how to *mélanger* a rissole. But she produced some good *potage* to-night.

Tuesday, May 16th. It has been a dazzling blue day at last, so as the other two are recovering from typhoid inoculation of yesterday Sister S. and I took sandwiches in our haversacks and set out to explore the Ridge. We had a great day. The Ridge is a long high plateau which runs at right angles to the trenches (i.e. East and West) and eventually meets them, so the farther along you get on its top level the better view you get of the positions on your left. Our C.C.S. is just below its Northern edge. Two officers who happened to be there after weeks in the Loos salient and who know every Fosse, town, village and landmark, showed us everything. You could see the communication trenches and the whole front line of trenches with the historic battered villages and mines, and shells bursting on them. It was a great sight. The trenches are lines of whitish clay. We had all sorts of adventures getting to that point and found ourselves exactly under the captive sausage observation balloon. There were successive displays of peppering of aeroplanes all the time as it was airmen's weather and a great many were out, but none got hit. On the way back we came on to some empty French gun emplacements and lovely dug-outs, in a jolly good position. We also found a lot more Fly Orchis.

We were attacked by some huge mosquitoes with hooked noses in the wood, and had to swathe our ankles and necks in the sandwich wrappings.

They are being very leisurely in the alterations to the theatre, and there's not a great deal left that we can do just now in the hospital. We shall be too busy for expeditions when we've begun to take in, so it is a good thing to take advantage of the opportunity.

Sister S. and I had another ten-mile ramble to-day over new ground. It was again a blue day and the forest was lovely beyond words, full of purple orchis and delicate green and the songs of little birds, and ferns. We tracked up through it over the ridge and down the other side South of the ridge looking over Vimy with a spreading view of a peaceful kind like Hampshire, not a Fosse or a mining village or a slag-heap to be seen that side. We had our tea under some pines and then took to the forest again along the top of the ridge towards our old observation point.

We'd forgotten to bring the map and had to trust to the light of nature (mine only, as S. follows me blindly) to find our way anywhere. Then we struck a road and held up a galloping gun team to ask where we were. They were very polite but didn't know themselves), and referred us to some men a little farther up the wood. This was a section of a Battery, living in extraordinary French dug-outs; there was also the smell of dead animals or dead men. They were most interested to see us, and the Sergeant and Sergeant-Major eagerly asked us if we would come into their lair and have some tea 'if we would so honour their humble abode'! Of course we did, and they bustled about and gave us lovely hot tea in enamel mugs, and showed us their beds made of wire netting and branches of trees like children's cribs, exactly as the French left them. The men sleep in rows on shelves made of branches. And there was a huge brick open stove in the middle. They said how exciting it was to see 'English ladies' and told us a lot about their guns. Then we went on to a village packed with men who also 'passed the word' that we were English and did a great deal of beaming and saluting.

After that village we fetched up at Observation Point at 7.15 and a lively Evening Hate was going on. What looks like summer lightning at night is by daylight or twilight a dazzling flash of flames and in the miles of map spread out before you from this place to beyond the German lines, we could see these points of flame every time our guns loosed off, and far ahead we could see the Boche guns also, and bursts of shell all along the lines of trenches. Poor lambs.

Thursday, May 18th. The other three Sisters came back to the fold to-day and are much pleased with the place. The theatre is the only part that

hangs fire as the engineers are being such a long time over the alterations, but the other Surgical huts and the Medical Schoolroom are
looking very smart and ready. We shall be taking-in every fourth day
from Convoys, evacuating by train once for each take-in; we shall also
take bad cases, abdominal or chest, any hour of any day or night.

It has been another brilliant hot day. Sister S. and I sallied forth after
lunch with our haversacks as usual. Our objective was to track down
towards some reserve trenches we had seen from the ridge if possible.
We kept on the level below the ridge as it was shorter though hotter, but
were stopped by a sentry under a railway arch, who said he could let no
one through into the 'forward area' without a permit or a *laisser-passer*.
He was very obstinate and only let us pass on my producing my identity
disc from round my neck. We then traversed a new wood and came
out on some cornfields behind another lower ridge between us and the
firing-line. There was a little house on the skyline with the windows all
sand-bagged and a hole in the roof which looked promising, and lo and
behold when we reached the skyline there were our reserve trenches
about 200 yards below, and not a soul to be seen except a few girls and
women ploughing behind us. Below us the road curved downhill to a
village nestling against the big ridge. In our innocence and joy we sat
ourselves down on a bank and got out our map and field-glasses and
biscuits and chocolate and had a wonderful survey of the German lines
just opposite us.

At one spot in Lens where we had shelled their mines to rags it looked
a ghastly wreck. We watched our shells bursting on their lines but they
didn't seem to be doing much to ours. We remarked on the complete
absence of any Tommies on that road or anywhere in sight and then
decided as we'd got so far we'd have a shot at seeing a ruined mill just
past the beginning of the trenches. We started down the empty road to
all this and then discovered a sentry at the bottom. He looked surprised
and pleased so we asked him if he could take us to see the ruined mill on
the rising ground in front. He called a Corporal who said the road we'd
come down was kept strictly closed as it was in full view of the German
lines and our people were most anxious for it not to be known to be
used! However, as we were there he took us round their dug-outs, some

very deep ones, and as far as the barbed wire entanglement, but it was too daylight to go to the ruined mill.

Then we went up the devastated pretty curling village Bouvigny with hardly one sound house left standing. Tommies filled the place in barns and smashed-up rooms, and a few French people still kept on their little village shops and sold beer, living in their cellars. The Church was a fine one but had big holes in it. There were a good many officers about the houses, who looked as if they would like to have trotted us round, but we were firmly taken possession of by this Corporal first. It was a pitiful-looking place, and must have been an exceptionally pretty village.

Friday, May 19th, 10 p.m. The D.M.S. came to see the Wards to-day and said he never expected to see things so well forward. Certainly the spirit of competition has done wonders, I never should have thought the men had it in them to be so keen: they have been most industrious and ingenious. The other three Sisters have been a great help to-day, and we are beginning to look like a Base Hospital with lots of beds instead of stretchers, and nice clean sheets and red blankets. The theatre will be as good as any Stationary Hospital and runs a Base very close.

Our Mess is still a bit of a problem as the woman is no help and there are no shops and the rations don't amount to much, and the Sisters seem to eat an awful lot! Our dear Madame at L. was an angel. I shall have to find some way of improving things.

Sunday, May 21st. Boiling hot day and our first take in here: not a very bad lot, only two who look as if they wouldn't pull through. They are not from our old part of the line (Hohenzollern Redoubt, etc.) but from farther S. towards Vimy. We've had two sensations this afternoon, first a gas attack signalled – Church Bells rung, and every man, woman and child to his helmet, but no whiffs came that I could make out. Then they fell to shelling Hersin only 1½ miles away, great explosions that sounded close enough to make you look round to find them: some people were killed, and four casualties brought in to us, one a French miner with his hand blown off.

Monday 22nd, and a Black Day. This German intense bombardment and occupation of our front trenches here at Vimy Ridge, and our desperate attempts to get them back have filled all the C.C.S. and all the worst cases have been scurried up to us as the nearest C.C.S. and the Special Hospital for Abdominals and Chests (which we are now). Just finished in the theatre at midnight – six have died and more will die, and they are still bringing them in – English and French.

They are all being angels of patience and silence, only asking for things, even drinks, when they're absolutely obliged. One who died to-day said yesterday he had 'nothing to complain about', and he was afraid he was a great trouble! We've had three officers in – one nearly died when he was having his foot taken off. One who had his arm blown off was laid in a dugout and then that was blown in on him and it took two hours to dig him out – he was the most cheery of all. Another one was buried for 15 hours – he died this evening. A boy who was trephined on Saturday night here, and has one eye destroyed and the other covered up, never speaks, but kicks every stitch of clothing off and breaks out into 'Lead Kindly Light' and 'God Save the King.' To-night, when a Frenchman in the next bed was raving, he trilled out, 'Thy Kingdom Come, O Lord' in a very sweet voice!

Tuesday night, May 23rd. The boy is now singing his hymns in Heaven. Captain R. was called up directly we dispersed at midnight last night and was operating all night and doing his dressings this morning till 1. Operating continuously a day and a night takes a lot out of you – and he had to be ordered off duty for 12 hours after that. Two men died in the night and two more to-day, besides an officer who died just after he was taken out of the Ambulance.

The big ward with beds all round and two lines down the middle is a very sad place – quite full of wrecks – and not one of them ever well enough even to speak to any other one. The next acute hut with beds also is very busy with compound fractures, heads and amputations, and some chests; but the worst chests, and the abdominals and the bombed people with several serious wounds, are in the big ward. Then there's an overflow hut with stretchers, and I have to plant my foot firmly down to prevent the Medical Officers sending heads and amputations there instead of to the bed wards.

We are rather short of men in the detachment, and when eight have to be taken off to dig graves it doesn't add to the simplicity of the work. I've had a night staff put on to the theatre so that the day ones shall not break themselves by doing day and night, but everyone is needed, so it is difficult not to despoil one place in propping up another. The C.O. came and had a long consultation with me to-day over the placing of the work generally. So far it is running pretty well, but at a great pressure, and I don't know how long the Orderlies and Sisters will last out. The Colonel says he thinks we shall always have this rush because we are so near the Line, but of course since Sunday's attack it has been much worse than usual, and violent and desperate fighting is still going on. I'll be able to tell you more about it later on when it is history: but a whole line of our front trench has been buried with men in it, under thousands and thousands of shells bursting at once dead on to it – and the after events have been neither pretty nor cheering. We are doing a lot of heavy howitzer work to-night very close, which is very distracting.

Last night we were woken up by a great shelling of Hersin again, from about 2 a.m. It was very jumpy. This is supposed to be going to be a busy night. I am going to be called, if so.

We went a few minutes up the road to Hersin after dinner at 9.30 to-night to get a breather, and to see the flashes and hear the lions roaring. It's an incredibly murderous noise.

Good-night.

Wednesday, May 24th. It has been a bad day and a bad night. I wonder if next May will be the same. And the whole thing seems the same utter waste of life and suffering as it was last May – and the same story of wasted self-sacrifice. There is very little left of the brave 47th Division. Those London men are such gentlemen all the time. They have all the old tradition of sticking it that belongs to the original B.E.F. without the funny vernacular of the 'Old Soldier.' The City Man, though he is an unbeatable soldier, goes on being a City man all the time. A boy who had to have his arm off to-day used to be a London School Teacher. They ought to be proud of him.

We have four badly wounded officers screened off at one end of a hut – all charming and patient and battered. One who had to lie for many hours face downwards on his dirty stretcher till it was safe to move him, said all the time 'I'm most comfy, thank you, don't worry about me – it's all very funny.' Another, wounded in the chest, said what really worried him going over the parapet was having his Sunday tunic on, because he happened to be dining with the Colonel when the order came. Another, the bad one with his leg off, dictated in his letter to his father, 'We had a bit of a scrap last night and I came into rather violent contact with a bomb.' He is very ill today.

The sad ward is very sad still. Two more deaths, and there will be more in all the wards to-night. Six abdominals were done to-day. It is all made much harder to run by our being a special Hospital for abdominals and all critical cases, and an ordinary Clearing Station as well, with only enough personnel and equipment for one. It is packed to-night. I have been mostly in a ghastly hut full of head cases (falling off their stretchers), compound fractures, chests, two amputations and five compound fractured femurs. It is only equipped for walking cases and has no beds, but has had to take these as the rest were full. Two Orderlies, snatches of a M.O. and I have ramped in it all day, when I could get away from the abdominal ward. The others ramp in theirs, and we meet for snatchy meals at intervals. We had tea out of a glass jam pot this afternoon from the cook-house – a hasty lap each. Between 9 and 10 p.m. we have handed over to the Night Sisters, and linger over supper at the billet, and tell each other all the funny and all the brave things of the day.

Some of the wounds this time are, for some reason, crawling with a seething, wriggling mass of live maggots. I've never seen it before.* Many of the men are stuck fast to their stretchers – blood is like glue if you leave it long enough. They have to have an anæsthetic before you can try to unstick them.

---

* Sometimes, when a man is badly hit, and unconscious, he may lie for some hours without even a field dressing. Bluebottles settle on the wounds and lay eggs.

Thursday, May 25th. The train cleared an enormous number of wounds and fractures, leaving the heads, chests, abdominals and amputations – so we still have our hands full. We are all getting a bit tired. If, at the end of this week, there seems no prospect of anyone getting any off-duty time, I shall apply for another Sister.

I must tell you about a boy who died to-day, aged 17. 'I fought I was too big to be walkin' about the streets wivout joinin',' he explained. He was fatally wounded in the chest, brought in last evening, blue and gasping. This morning when I was washing him he could barely speak plainly, and only in gasps, but he said (after asking for more soap on his face): 'I fought a lot of fings – when that – shell hit me. I fought about – goin' over the water again – and I fought about seein' mother – and I fought about dyin'. Will they let her come and see me quick when I get to a Hospital in London? – I fink I'll write to her this afternoon.' Later on, with great difficulty, he gave me her address, so I wrote to-night. He died at 5 o'clock. His gasping recital of his 'foughts' was the most upsetting thing that has happened of all the upsetting things.

It is raining cats and dogs, and their first field dressings will now be full of wet mud instead of dry mud.

Friday, May 26th. No regular Convoy in to-day – only the bad cases dribbling in – so there's been a little more time to attend to our four wards of poor bad ones. They still go on dying, but some of the abdominals are pulling round by inches, and more of the chests. I have three gas gangrenes in my hut. Some of the up patients in the fifth hut are marvels of helpfulness and obedience. Two have added themselves to the Staff all day – and they carry out instructions as if on parade – which is more than some Orderlies do.

Tuesday's *Times* gives the *German* Official Report of the taking of our trenches at Vimy Ridge and it is word for word true. They call it 'quite extraordinarily sanguinary losses' (on our side) and that is what the survivors here say. In one of these attempted counter-attacks the order to attack was cancelled at the last minute, and this failed to reach two Companies of one Battalion, so they went over alone into a perfect hell of machine-guns, and were absolutely done in with 'quite extraordinarily sanguinary losses.'

Sunday, May 28th, 10.30 p.m. The train cleared a good many stretcher cases to-day. We have five bad officers in. I see very little of them. The abdominals are taken to the theatre within half an hour if they seem to have a dog's chance of surviving. So far, only one has lived as long as four days afterwards. The boys stand it very badly. About one in every three comes in too far gone for operation.

Monday, May 29th. Poor Hersin has been getting it all day, since daylight; refugees are coming along piled in carts. Ten civilians have been killed to-day, and that mine we went to where we picked up the bits of shell has been powdered. Each shell-burst makes a most distracting noise. A soldier on leave from Verdun had just opened his front door and met his wife when his leg was blown off. Our old French ploughing man from another village had to have his most horrible leg amputated to-day.

We had a rush of in-extremis cases in this morning – three have died to-day. There seems to be an unusual number of charming boys, who have joined in tremendous keenness and are now filling the cemetery. One called Reggie something, who talks like a gentleman, is slowly losing the fight with a lung wound. And another called Jack is paralysed from a fractured spine. He says wonderingly, 'What is it, Sister? I can't move my legs – will it be all right?'

My two gas gangrene boys side by side with continuous drips on their arm and leg stumps have never once lost their mental balance or fussed or cried or fretted. Their chief anxiety is to say 'thank you' and to smile and to say, 'What should we do without you?'

Wednesday, May 31st. The last two days we have been able to slip away to the nearest Slag Heap, ten minutes off, and sit on the grass and feel the breeze and see the British Front spread out below. The ox-eye daisies are out, very big ones.

Jack is dying to-night, paralysed from a wound in the spine. He doesn't know what is the matter with him and can't feel anything, so he goes on smiling and making polite little jokes, and thanking and apologizing till we could all cry. Reggie is worse to-night. He holds out his small hand and says, 'Will you come and sit by me for a little while and hold my hand – it encourages me.' A boy who has lost one eye and can't see out of the other said this evening, 'I do feel bad, will you come and talk to me?' and you hardly ever can.

The London School Teacher boy with his arm blown off, and his foot nearly, is an extraordinary example of fortitude with a large F. I should like to meet him again in Peace time, if there ever is such a thing.

Ascension Day. A great Fête Day in France. All the little girls in white frocks to their feet, and veils and wreaths, and the boys with white bows on their arms made their First Communion to-day, and there has been a lot of church-going and processing all day. It has been a day of deaths, two in the night and four to-day.

Jack is alive still but very weak and wandering, asking us all day to take off his boots; we scrabble about with his bare feet and he is happy for a moment, and then begins again. The train has not cleared for a week and we are getting heaped up.

All your letters about the garden are so otherworldly from the place we live in, and it is going to be worse before long. We have got to take the top of this Vimy Ridge.

Friday, June 2nd. The bombarding yesterday afternoon and evening was an attack by my old Division, and when we came on this morning the wards were filled up with wrecks. It has been a ghastly day. The train came in the afternoon and all who could possibly get to the Base alive, and all who had been waiting for the train were packed up and put on. It must have been a bad load. But of course the trains will know by now that they're in for a bad load from here.

Jack died at half-past ten last night, and three abdominals: this time they have been about the most appalling shell wounds I've ever seen – how they get here alive I don't know.

They shelled the Observation Balloon to-day, but it did not get hit.

The French Bishop came round the wards to-day after the Confirmation (which seems to follow the First Communion) and blessed the *Blessés*. A lovely old man like Moses in gold tassels.

Saturday, June 3rd. There is nothing new or cheering to write about. A battery of 4.5's has planted itself immediately at the end of our row of billets. Sister G. and I were admiring the guns to-day, and the Staff Sergeant came up and did showman of their shining and intricate insides, till our brains reeled. He adjusted the sights and made us look through and do everything but fire a shell. They can put in 6 a minute, which is not quite so fast as a *soixante-quinze.*

Four gigantic crocodiles puffed heavily past to-day, with their empty truck things, on their way back from taking a Grandmother.

Captain W. is dying to-night of gas gangrene. His younger brother was a posthumous V.C. and I think another brother has been killed, so it won't make a pretty letter to write to his mother to-morrow. He is a particularly charming boy.

Enormous shells were bursting on our lines this evening when we went to the Slag Heap. It is a beastly sight.

Sunday, June 4th. The day began with the early morning papers giving the news of the Naval Battle and the first (exaggerated) account of the British losses. Later we got more cheering news. It is difficult to think of anything else.

Sister S. and I got off at 6 this evening and walked to Hersin which is not being shelled to-day for once. The mine is much more smashed and there are a lot more houses gone. Some desolate stricken-looking families went by this morning on carts, sitting on their mattresses and beds, mothers hugging their babies and fathers their small sons, in silent misery, all the voluble French clack knocked out of them.

We went to the cemetery and counted the graves since Sunday week – 50 in a fortnight died of wounds at this one little C.C.S. Captain W. died this evening, the third son killed, I believe.

General B. commanding the 23rd Division came round to-day, and talked to every patient, especially an infant boy called Billy.

You should see my Reggie, Walter, Joseph, Harry and Billy, and the armless, legless ones, who won't tell their mothers. Walter said when I was washing him, 'Mother, thinks the world o' me, I'm the eldest, I'm glad she can't see me now.'

There's an old worn-out Newcastle man with a wound in his liver who when he is uncomfortable wails, 'I can't find a resting place. I shouldn't mind nothin' if I could find a resting place.'

Monday, June 5th, 11 p.m. What do you think? This place and H. are full of Marines. Some of the Anson Battalion too are in hospital. I only found it out to-night, one was awake and told me he was in support of the action of July 13th in Gallipoli and 'heard all about it.' He'd seen F. 'He was well liked,' the boy said. And a Padre with them was asking for me to-day, but I couldn't be found, and he couldn't wait. There were a lot of them in Church yesterday, the Night Sisters said.

Haven't seen Sunday's paper yet but it is said to be cheering, and that the Battle Cruiser Squadron by attacking the monsters saved the day; it will buck us all up, all over the world.

It has been quieter to-day, the first day with no deaths, and we are all getting a little bit of off duty. The poor old Newcastle man who couldn't find a resting place is soon going to find one with the other 52. He asked me to write and 'send his love to the Missis and the three bairns.'

Our Mess is improving a bit; Madame cooks better and gets decent things for us: we had green peas to-night.

I want some packs of cards badly for the convalescents.

Some men from the Ypres salient say it is much worse on this Vimy Ridge business than anywhere they've been.

Tuesday, June 6th. We have had a lull this evening since the train cleared.

The men here from Gallipoli say they'd rather be there than here. You could fight there; here you can only sit and be killed, or smashed up.

Whit-Sunday. All is quiet here, the fighting has entirely died down; we hear no guns. Hersin is left in peace and Motor Ambulances have ceased their long procession. Even on taking-in days we get very little and only the very worst cases are brought in at other times. So there is plenty of time to spoil and pet the bad ones left, whom we all get very fond of.

There is a field full of bee-orchis on the ridge, close to some new machine-gun emplacements; it is being fortified in case of a German advance.

Our big acute Surgical Ward looks, and is, exactly like a Base Hospital now, with red blankets, red jackets, red screens and white sheets and white trollies – such a contrast to the dirty old school-rooms at Lillers, with stretchers and brown blankets and only a very few beds. The Medical Acute Ward here is spacious, light and airy, with trees looking in at the big windows on two sides and lovely beds, and green mats on the floor. It is so awfully nice being really able to do them well up here – the standard of comfort goes up and up, and everything we want we get eventually.

Whit-Monday, June 12th. Icy cold and soaking wet as usual. The mud out-muds itself everywhere, and the men have come in to-day starved with cold and wet on their stretchers. Two very young boys of the Naval Division were only just alive; one died in an hour. The other is warming up and may do.

A gunner who had one leg amputated two days ago had to decide this morning whether he would have the other one off or die. At first he wanted to die because he 'couldn't face his wife with both legs gone' and what was he to do for a living? He lay there with white lips looking into a black future out of a hideous present. It seemed almost too big and grim a question to persuade a man about, but we told him what his wife would say. Now it is over and he is quite brave and a wee bit better and if he lives through to-night he may do.

There's a little Lancashire lad in the big ward who came in with the wreckage of Friday week's attack and was expected to die of one or all of his many injuries. But he 'took and lived' and has had two operations. He is half dotty still and calls out 'Howd on, Mother' when you are going to touch him. He calls us all Mother – 'Give over, Mother' is his favourite way of saying he's had enough. His name is Joe.

Reggie is going to be put on the train to-morrow. His mother will cry when she sees the little panting skeleton who was a marching soldier when she last saw him. But it's a wonder that she sees him at all: it didn't seem possible he could live with such holes in his lung.

There's a boy called Bob with awful wounds in his side who is creeping back to life. He has an illuminating smile all the time and says he has 'nothing at all to grumble about if only I can get to sleep, everything's champion.'

The R.F.A. invited us to a scratch concert the other night: three sisters who were off went, and said they were thoroughly fussed over and spoilt. This afternoon the Adjutant of that battery turned up at our Mess at tea-time with a gorgeous bunch of roses, a huge basket of cherries and a box of cakes. He'd brought them back from St. Omer for us. Of course we asked him to tea, and he told us much uncensored information, as Gunners always do, which I'd love to hand on to you.

Saturday, 6 p.m. At last a lovely, June day, no rain, no icy wind. Two Hun aeroplanes came over this afternoon. I heard a great commotion and popping of Archies but didn't see them from where I was. There has been a good deal of noise one way and another. The band struck up an overture last night, *tutti*, big guns and little guns for half an hour on end and made the world shake. To-day Hersin has been getting it again.

You can see aeroplanes for miles from here, and the big sausage Observation Balloon wags foolishly on its rope in the wind, and at night there are the Verey lights going up and looping down.

I don't think I told you that the Gunner Adjutant who brought us roses and cherries came again carefully at tea-time and this time brought me the maps he promised me. And yesterday his battery went back to a hot spot for three months, but he thinks he'll be able to ride out to tea with us again one day!

Our map is the ordinary squared large scale map they all have, which may go on the wall. The other two are wonderful elaborate maps, which may not be shown to anyone, of the Hun trenches, and the front line of ours – made from Air photographs, which he also showed me. They look like photos of skin diseases with Greek pattern trenches scored all over them, and every shell hole like a pock mark. We compared one with its bit of the map and it was exact.

We have had some bad cases in, chiefly boys; some have died. Reggie has been safely packed on to the train and I've written to the Sister of whatever ward he gets to, to get him sent home if she can before he gets any worse. Joey's 'Howd on, Mother' is getting less forcible and frequent and it won't be long before he leaves off saying it at all.

I never told you about Bob, the very badly wounded boy from Yorkshire. He has a weary painful existence, but he dictated to me this letter to his mother: 'Dear Mother – This is to tell you I am doing grand – the wound in my side is healing fine (It isn't; it is a colotomy and also has a broken rib sticking out of it). You are well looked after here – it is as good as being at home – bar kin – You live on the best of everything. I had chicken and jelly for dinner to-day. And there is a gramophone and the best of company. Tell Dad and Daisy not to worry about me at all. I hope I shall soon be with you all. Your loving son, Bob.'

I said, 'Well, you've told her all the nice things, Bob, what about all the nasty things?' He looked me deliberately in the face and said, 'And what are the nasty things, Sister?' And he has very bad nights, a racking cough from the rib, a helpless right arm lying on a cushion, a septic wound through his cheek which gives him a horrible taste in his mouth, and the broken rib and the colotomy.

Joey said one day in a detached way, of his left foot, 'I reckon that foot's a little 'ero the way 'e sticks it.' He is wounded in both legs, both arms, and his neck, and has a lump of brain sticking out of his forehead.

Tuesday, June 13th. This War is sitting very heavily on one's chest to-night, perhaps because (*a*) it is still raining and the squelch is of a depth unbelievable and they are brought in sodden and clammy with it, (that is what the British Army's French bed is to-night), and (*b*) the guns are talking again and machine-guns yapping viciously, and (*c*) there's a rumour of another Naval Battle, glorious of course, if so, but so much more wholesale killing.

A man here died the other day of his fifth set of wounds.

A band was playing the people up to the trenches to-day with 'Keep the Home Fires Burning'; they plodded meanwhile through the squelch to a worse squelch with shells to keep them from going to sleep in it. And yet they don't look sulky or rebellious – every face and every type of face has a definite expression of purpose in it – from the youngest to the oldest. They are very thin and were very bronzed, but they look paler this month since the wet. We are all thinner too, except the 'Heavy-weight.'

Thursday, June 22nd. We have had what one of the Scotch Sisters calls a 'norful' day, the Acute Ward is packed with poor groaning boys in all stages of distress. They ought not to live through their awful injuries and operations, but they do, for a few days or a few weeks sometimes.

In the middle of it all a Hun aeroplane dropped bombs on one of our two mines in this village and a woman and a girl of fifteen, her stepdaughter, were brought in to us dying. Both died in the anæsthetic room with the stricken father wandering dimly between the two. It was a terrible business. He came this evening and I had to take him to the mortuary with three nice nuns who prayed over them, and then he took them both to his desolate home in an ambulance. The child Lucienne was washing soldiers' clothes and the mother was mending them in the yard – the father was in bed in the house and escaped unhurt.

An old man was also brought in with a compound fractured femur, and a wee boy of nine with a bit through his head.

Friday, June 23rd. We've had a busy day again: among other events two legs got secondary hæmorrhage and had to be rescued in a hurry with tourniquets and then taken to the theatre. One was first spotted by an orderly who was very prompt with the T. and saved the man's life before he had time to call anybody. We always keep a T. hanging over the bed of anyone likely to get a hæmorrhage, and this man's had been ready for days.

There was a heavy thunderstorm to-day and it is wet again now. Joey died this evening. The little French boy Batiste has been bad all day, very sick and wailing.

Captain – of the Suffolks, who died here two days ago from a bombing accident, picked up a live bomb which had fallen short to throw it again, but he was just too late and it got him; he was buried yesterday; the Suffolks lined the road with their band, and followed 4 deep finishing up with 30 officers marching behind. They were awfully cut up about it.

Saturday, June 24th. The affair of last night was a wash-out because the Boche got wind of it and nipped it in the bud by an awful dose of Minnenwerfers and rifle grenades before we got a chance to get to work. The results have trickled in to-day all with the same story. One officer got a jagged piece of shell three inches long in his neck harmlessly tucked away alongside his carotid artery, now safely removed.

Saturday night, July 1st. It has been the first summer day for weeks, and good news has filtered through from the Somme, that we are advancing and that they are on the run – it's not official yet but we shall see what we shall see. I wonder if 'the spirit of the British Army' that has mushroomed out of the Contemptible Little Army into all these new boys in their millions, is going to be the factor which will win the War after all?

The Boche aeroplanes have been very inquisitive here lately. All our marquees have had to be scene painted, and the Battery wagons round about are all covered with branches like Xmas decorations.

We have had 97 deaths since May 21st.

Sunday, 11.30 p.m. This has been a strenuous day, all the wards packed. Only four have died to-day, and the others have got the feel of 'Advance' in them and don't seem to mind how much wounded they are. So it has been a rather happy day really.

The number of German prisoners taken on the Somme varies with the reporter; if an orderly, it is 47,000, and they are all at the Station here; if the Colonel, it is 6,000. Anyway, we have one wounded Saxon boy in this ward who says continually, '*Ganz gut,*' when you ask, '*Wie geht es?*'

It has been a dazzling day, and is now a dazzling night. The – th Essex is here in many beds: bandaged but cheery. They did last night's raid at Vimy quite successfully but it always means casualties.

Poor Bob who asked me, 'And what are the bad things?' is going steadily downhill.

Monday, July 3rd. He died to-day suddenly clutching my hand and saying, 'Is it all right? Don't leave me.'

We have that ward full of abdominals in all stages, recovering, hovering, and going to die or dying. It is sometimes rather overwhelming to all our nerves. The Sister (Miss D.) who runs it is made of real gold of a quite rare kind, and was made especially for it, but it will wear her out in time.

We cleared a lot by the train to-day, and were taking in at the same time which makes things more difficult.

Last night was decidedly interesting though fatiguing. I couldn't leave the wards till 1 o'clock (and could have found plenty to do all night). I was enjoying a very poppy sort of a dream at 4.15 a.m. which gradually resolved itself into a Scrap in the sky immediately overhead with innumerable Archies popping like corks round a humming Taube just above us. Then came a horrid whizz of a bomb coming down and the inevitable crash, followed quickly by two more, and I got to the window just in time to see the third burst, apparently in the garden of Sister D.'s cottage billet a few houses up. There was a great commotion, and Madame ran up to tell me there were no *blessés*, so I breathed again, and we had some coffee. The Boche was meanwhile making off through a hail of Archie shells. He dropped five but two failed to explode. They seem to have been trying for the Ammunition wagons and stores about. It is always a jumpy business and you immediately think they've bombed the wards, but I'm getting quite used to it now.

3

Vimy Ridge – Continued

July 11th to October 12th 1916

Tuesday, July 11th. Two months ago to-day since we came up here, and it seems months and months ago.

There is a little Bantam in the Medical, aged 47, height 5 ft. 1, who has just not died of double pneumonia, a sporting soldier, isn't he?

One mother wrote back, 'Will you tell me by return of post which day he will be buried, as I should like to see him buried.'

They almost invariably write and ask if he 'said anything under the operation' or if he 'left any message' when you've carefully told them he was unconscious from the time he was brought in. And when you've said the Chaplain took the funeral they write and ask, 'If he was buried respectable?' Some of them write most touching and heart-broken letters.

We had another Taube last night, or rather 4.30 this morning. He dropped five bombs a little way out and then got away. I watched him dodging our shells which were bursting with a 'whang' just overhead.

Wednesday, July 12th. A very badly wounded man in Hut 3 suddenly went off his head this afternoon and roared like a lion just when Col. – , the 1st Army Consulting Surgeon, was doing a round. His bed had to be carried out of the ward till he finished bellowing. To-night he said, 'If you give me an orange I may go to sleep' – which was done, and he did.

Saturday, July 15th. There is a very young boy, in yesterday, who is going to die – with a chest wound. He said to-day, 'Do you think I stand a chance of getting to Blighty with this?' meaning, 'Is it bad enough?' He had morphia at 2 p.m. after a troubled morning, and when he roused after tea he said with a smile of peace, 'I *have* had a lovely half a day. I feel as fresh as a daisy!' He died at 8 o'clock this morning, Sunday.

The boy who fell on to a bayonet bringing his prisoners in, has got the Military Medal. He said, 'Mother and Father and my sister will open the letter at breakfast, but they won't be able to eat any, it will go out again! And they'll go and tell all the neighbours.' And now he's got to have another operation because the bayonet, after going through his stomach, pricked his pleura and he has an empyema. The wee lad from Glasgow – who has a hole in his side, which, now his lung is collapsed, gives a spacious view of his ribs as far as his breast bone – is to be tightly bound up and packed up for the Base. The hole holds a *quart* jug of lotion and then you sit him up and tip it all out into a receiver! He's the boy who was told one frantic night not to call Sister so often. Some hours after, he was found awake and was asked why not asleep? 'I canna sleep, but I can keep quiet,' he said proudly. I don't know what we shall do when Jock has gone.

Sunday, July 16th, 10 p.m. Three Battalions are going over the top to-night. Our artillery has been tickling up that area all day and last night, but unluckily it is wet to-night which is a bad handicap. We have an officer of the Anson Battalion who had his arm blown off by a shell this morning. He is making less fuss than if he'd had a tooth out. When he asked me to tell his mother he said: 'She's not panicky – she'll take it all right.' I said: 'If she's anything like her son, she certainly will,' and he said apologetically, 'Oh, I think the worst is over now.' He is at this moment having it trimmed up in the theatre. And there is another officer with gas gangrene in his leg; he is having it taken off to-night, too.

The Boche is making a great noise at this moment (and also between 7 and 8 p.m.) dropping heavy shells into Nœux les Mines between two and three miles from here. The Gunner Adjutant brought us the evening wire from his H.Q. to see: Attack begun on 3rd Line – 4 Boche aeroplanes down – lots of heavy guns – more prisoners, woods and villages, and an unsuccessful shot at Pozières. I wish it was my luck to be with the British Army in their elated moments, though of course I'm humbly thankful to be allowed to be with it in any moments.

Monday, July 17th. We all come on duty now with our faces ornamented with mosquito bites, and the M.O.'s too. I have just bayoneted three, but they are counter-attacking heavily, and being a great interruption to my pen.

We have got some very shattered men in to-day, three are going to die in one ward, and all our officers' beds are full – one got stuck in the chest by a bayonet by one of our own men who mistook him for a Boche.

Wednesday, July 19th. Yesterday the hospital was fairly slack, so Sister D. and I went off for a 12-mile tramp (there and round and back over the most thrilling country): we walked from 2.30 to 9 p.m. with only three rests of 20 minutes each.

We got up to the end of the wood where a sentry stands with fixed bayonet, and beyond are hundreds of French and German skeletons of May 1915, and no one may be seen above ground. The wood edge we came back by is full of shell holes and dead trees and empty gun emplacements – and deep trenches with traverses and hundreds of dug-outs. We had got about a mile beyond the ruined village of the forbidden cross roads, and came back through it from its worst end; it is the most frightful deserted desolation especially at that end. Near the gaping Church is what was once a beautiful Château, now a Brigade H.Q. of the Naval Divisions. We were just going through the archway to get a better view of the gaping holes in the beautiful rooms when a Marine warned us off because this gateway was under direct observation by the enemy, but said we might see it through another.

The 'billets' in that further (skeletons) wood were a marvellous picture of War: every conceivable kind of dug-out, thatched and sandbagged, sheds and huts and lean-tos and bomb stores, and all swarming with men, washing or working or lying about. They smiled politely at us, and no one attempted to challenge our right to go on, so on we went. A Padre stopped us eventually, showing us where we were on his big scale map, and saying 'it would not be wise' to go further. We knew we could not get past that last sentry. It was a great afternoon; we went quite warily and always take care that we are not getting ourselves or anybody else into any trouble.

Our wee Jock has gone down to the Base on the Barge and we miss him horribly.

We've had three funerals to-day; one was a boy who said in his delirium about an hour before he died, 'Let us rest in Peace.' Then the gramophone outside struck up, and he began conducting the 'Mikado' with both hands!

Sunday, July 23rd. Nothing of importance to report on this front. We have got a good many old Daddies in, who ought never to have been allowed to come out. It is so jolly knowing them all in every ward. Some new 60 pounders bustled up the other evening and billeted themselves at the end of our lane. Two of their officers showed us the insides of their guns under their landscape painted dressing-gowns, and down their muzzles. They warmly offered us their mess-cart to drive up to their gun positions later on to see and hear them speak! I don't think we shall see them speak, but we may some others – you never know.

Wednesday, July 26th. We are not a bit busy, only three wards full and plenty of us to look after them. There is something extraordinarily attractive about these men and boys who go through so much and become such friends with us. In their letters when they go down to the Base they say such lovely things about the C.C.S.

Our Gunner Adjutant has gone south with his Division; we shall miss his cheery company at tea, and bringing us the evening wires, and sending the Mess cart round, and the large consignments of roses. He writes: 'Apart from leave, Barlin was the one bright spot of this beastly War'!

We are moving our Mess to a more homely, but less noisy and dusty spot: the house belongs to a soldier's wife, who has a boy of five called

Eugene who already haunts the Hospital. Though our actual Messing has lately been quite excellent, it was very expensive, and we were being badly cheated by the very unpleasant woman who ran it, and we had to pay a servant as well.

Friday, July 28th. It is a lovely, sunny day, and we had their beds out in rows under improvised awnings. They are always carried out as soon as their dressings are done if there's any hope of a fine day. We have some very bad new ones in just now, and five officers. Miss McCarthy is also going to put in for further charge pay for Sisters-in-Charge of the more important C.C.S.'s, of which this is one.

It is so clear and bright to-day that we could see into the German lines from our local slag heap with the naked eye. The blue sky has been an aerial battlefield all day.

Sunday, July 30th. Our new Mess Lady is not a success, so I am going to abandon French cooking and have a soldier cook, and see how it works out. The house is all right, and she will lay the table and wait and wash up, while the batman cooks – in her kitchen.

Not being the beginning of a cook myself, my attempts to explain to her in French how to do things I don't know how to do myself have ended in disaster.

It has been almost tropically hot yesterday and to-day; I expect you have had the same. We have only 42 patients in just now – 4 died yesterday. One was a boy who, in the night before he died, insisted on knowing the Christian name of the Night Sister. 'I'm Sister S.,' she said. 'But what's your *Christian* name?' he kept on. 'Betty,' she said. 'Betty, get me a drink,' said the boy.

An older man who was dying, and was off his head, said: 'I'm going now, but I can't manage my pack and my rifle and my overcoat; that'd be a bit too much. I'm sorry I'm leavin' yer just when I've got used to yer.' He was in the most *awful* difficulties of breathing, but hadn't an idea of it, and said he was feeling nicely! Large hole in his lung at the back. It is a mercy they so often have all their distress completely veiled either by morphia or shock.

Monday, 10 p.m., and a boiling night. The Sergeant-Major brought my new cook up this evening. Her name is not Eliza or Mrs. Jones, but Lance-Corporal Keeling of the 1st Devons. He has been in the Cook-house in the Medical Division. He clicked and saluted and said, 'I will do my utmost to give satisfaction, Matron; a man cannot say more'! So we hope for the best and start to-morrow.

Wednesday, August 2nd, 10 p.m. The heat continues. It is very trying to the patients but I like it.

Our new cook is doing well. He talks broad Devon and knows no pidgeon French at all, so he bawls his instructions to the speechless Madame at the top of his own dialect and fondly imagines she understands. She is very nice indeed to us, and very wroth with the French shops who charge us exactly double for fruit, etc., what they charge the French. 'Ce n'est pas juste – ils sont voleurs,' she says – so they are.

Two fine men of the Naval Division were brought in this evening, and both, I am afraid, will die.

Monday, August 7th. This morning between 11 and 1 we were shaken and made to sit up by the loosing off of some Grandmothers* near by. The rumbling of the big shell as it travels away is a unique noise, and the actual firing of the gun is like a mine explosion. It must have stirred something up at the other end, because between 1 and 3 o'clock this afternoon they suddenly landed eleven 15-inch shells in Béthune, plumb in the middle of the town – lots of casualties of course. Our Padre has just ridden in there. It is the first time they've put anything over there since November, and Marie Thérèse and her mother told me the other day they never shell the place, so it must have been a rude awakening. The C.C.S. there was not hit, but it was a nasty jar for them all. Talking of nasty jars, since I wrote that (10.30) the most appalling explosion shot me out of bed to turn my light out, and then hang out of the window. But there are no Taubes overhead and nothing to be seen. The French are putting their heads out and calling out: 'Qu'est ce que c'est?' It must

---

* 15-inch naval guns.

be one of their 15-inch pets coming a bit nearer, perhaps into Nœux les Mines, but I thought it was in the garden! This is not the most soothing place to live in.

Tuesday, August 8th. The C.C.S. people at Béthune have all been evacuated. The Chapel of the College they were in was hit, and some Motor Ambulances, and six of the A.S.C. drivers killed. No one actually in the Hospital was hit, but it was a matter of yards that they weren't. I know the place well, the yard of our Officers' Dressing Station opened on to it.

Sister S. and I got leave to-day from the Colonel to go with Major W. (whom I used to meet at Béthune when he was in charge of No. 3 Field Ambulance) on one of the cars of his Motor Ambulance Convoy to the Main Dressing Station of the Naval Field Ambulance. A Naval Surgeon showed us over: it was at some Mine buildings, where the mine only works at night.

Then Major W. and his car had to go back, but these Naval Surgeons took possession of us, and trotted us off with them in their cars to Bully Grenay to see their Advanced Dressing Station, at a place about a mile and a half back from Loos. There emerged some more Naval Surgeons who in their turn did the honours of their extraordinary spot.

The front was bodged up with sandbags, and the back was more or less open to the air. The dressing-room and places for patients were all in the cellars, very neatly arranged, and their one room in which they messed and slept (their pyjamas and towels were hanging on a line in it) was a room opening on to the shattered yard. They took us upstairs and we had a good view of everything that was left of the village, through the walls and roof, of which only a few lathes remained. Our batteries were all round us and were making an awful din.

Then we said good-bye to these, and our original Surgeon whirled us off to another Advanced Dressing Station, Aix Noulette, at the one place we'd always longed to get to with not a single house with a roof and not a stray hen living in it. The grey stone Church has one solitary pillar left standing and a bit of the tower and part of the walls. This Advanced D.S. was in the remains of a Brewery – also all business underground. This they took us all round, and invited us to tea; but Surgeon B. said tea was being got ready at his Field Ambulance for us, and we were driven back to the Mine Dressing Station to their Mess in a very comfortable house belonging to the Mine Manager, full of carved oak furniture. Tea was laid in a big dining-room – very good tea and English cake, and the Staff swarmed in. Then the C.O. sent us in the car to the top of the Ridge where we wanted to finish up. In the course of our travels we were taken to a battery in action, and shown a beautiful shining gun with a H.E. shell all ready in the breech. The sweating shirt-sleeved gunners were frightfully proud to show it off to us. They had a lot of flowers in the dug-out of the ruined gardens, in jam tins hideously arranged, and face-tious messages were chalked on the shells. 'Must liven 'em up a bit,' they explained. The road skirted the communication trenches leading to the front line, up which the rations are taken every night – and the parapets just now are a wonderful blaze of poppies, cornflowers and big daisies! Of course there was the chance of a shell coming the whole time, but these Gallipoli people were so keen to show us all their Dressing Stations they thought we might chance that. At the top of the ridge, about a mile to our right and on the same level we saw a place in the trees (presum-ably one of our gun positions) being badly strafed. Shells were bursting on it, one on the top of the other.

Wednesday, August 9th. This has been one of the hottest days, and we've had a convoy in, the first for a long time. The flies are a great torment and always collect round the worst cases.

Thursday, August 10th. This morning General Paris sent a note asking me to come to Divisional H.Q. to tea and to bring a friend. So Sister G. came with me. We were led round the corner of the house on to the lawn which was carpeted with Brass Hats and Red Hats. Sir Henry Wilson,* 4th Corps Commander, was there, and we were introduced by General Paris to him and to Lord Dundonald, Wilson's A.D.C. Then we went in to tea round the big table. I was between General Paris and Sir Henry Wilson. He is about 7 feet high, very thin, with two rows of

---

* Later Field-Marshal and Chief of the Imperial General Staff.

ribbons, and a pretty wit. Another young General came in and gradually the big table filled up with a great buzzing of chaff and jokes and pulling of legs about craters and sandbags and barbed wire, led uproariously by Sir Henry Wilson who would call Prezymzysl 'Chemise' and said it was the real way to pronounce the word. Then they all got buried in a big trench map, and while this was going on Major S. told me all about F. on the 13th, about which I am writing separately. They all gradually melted away and then General Paris** and Major S. saw us off at the gate.

It was jolly altogether and a far cry from our poky little piggery of a Mess and our own eternal topics. Wil son said that the day before Béthune was shelled they were having a massed Open Air Service in the Square with 6,000 troops – and the Square is now mincemeat.

Monday, August 14th. The crash last Monday night was a 15-inch shell and it fell on the railway.

A man of the Seaforths (in here sick) up from the Somme, was telling me, with a trench map he'd picked up, all about the 9 days of Longuéval and Delville Wood; the Argylls had the middle of the village to take, and they swept up the street playing the pipes – with the South Africans on the left and the Seaforths on the right. Then they had to pile up the British and German dead in heaps each side of the street to get a passage clear for traffic. He said that in the last big Boche counter-attack to try to retake the wood, the Seaforths held the edge, and nine and a half Battalions of Germans came on at once with spiked helmets, but our guns were ready and they only got half-way.

Tuesday, August 15th. It seems some time since I wrote but nothing has been happening. We have been taking Convoys again, no special fighting but the daily wastage of casualties and sick that goes from a specified area to four Clearing Stations on four successive days, so we have been more busy. This hot weather has sent a good many sick, but few considering the numbers of men there are. We are one Sister short just now. The

---

** A few weeks afterwards these two were doing a round of some trenches when the only shell on that trench that day came over, and killed Major S. and severely wounded General Paris.

King and the Prince of Wales did not visit us, alas – we are a little bit off the track.

Friday, August 18th. But they went to my beloved old town, Béthune, which has just been shelled on our left, and to a point just the other side of our Ridge, on our right, overlooking Vimy and Arras.

There is a Capt. M. of the R.M.L.I. in with a compound fractured ankle, who knew both F. and T. well.* He has been recommended for an M.C. He was telling us about an old Salvation Army Captain who is one of his men, and for whom he has got a Military Medal. There was a badly wounded man in the trench and Captain M. was giving him a drink of water while the S.A. man was bandaging him up with great skill, a rifle for a splint for the leg and a bayonet for the arm. He saw another Minnenwerfer coming and shouted 'Look out' to the S.A. man. The S.A. man was blown clean up into the air by the blast of the explosion, and came down smiling, saying, 'Praise the Lord for all His Mercies!' and finished bandaging the man!

We had a batch of three abdominals in together this evening: a boy Lance-Corporal, a Sergeant-Major and a Scotsman. The boy had 14 wounds in his tummy, his right arm broken, his left hand off and a hole in his forehead. He could only just speak and felt nothing. 'Is it serious?' he asked, and answered the question himself in the next world five minutes afterwards. He struggled to tell me his father's address in that five minutes, but I found a letter from him in his pocket afterwards. To-morrow I shall have to write and tell him. I'm afraid the Sergeant-Major is going to die too, and another boy with a leg.

It has actually rained heavily to-day, which is a blessing for the dust.

Wednesday, August 23rd. There has been no time to write just lately: we have been very full up, and only cleared to-day – rows and rows and rows of our lambs lay packed on their stretchers waiting for the train to-day, with their heads on the pretty, gay, soft cushions from Witham; spotless splints and dressings and clean pyjamas and gowns on. One Sister on a

---

* Kate's brothers, Frank and Trant, both in the Royal Marines.

Barge wrote to Sister D. that they always knew which came from here because they were so clean, happy, and well-clad, and talking lovingly of their wards. That's a good testimonial, isn't it? It is keeping them so long that does it, there is time for affection to grow on both sides. We've just had a great upheaval in the Staff, five leaving and five new arrivals. They all seem quite good, so I hope the same traditions will carry on: thank Heaven Sister D (the Mother of the Abdominals) remains.

Those five Sisters in the Casualty List were the ones who got scratched by the 15-inch stuff that came into Béthune. They attended the wounded well under fire: and for this they have all got the Military Medal (the only one open to us, and the one that you can only earn under fire), so it is jolly good.

The D.M.S., General P., told me yesterday that there is to be a great function at Army H.Q. on Tuesday to pin their ribbons on, and that all the C.O.'s and Sisters in Charge of C.C.S.'s and all the world are to come too, and have a sort of garden party afterwards at the Château. So the C.O. and Sister D. and I are to gad over on Tuesday. It will be amusing.

I was in Béthune the other day meeting new Sisters and went to see the damage. It is bad: the Armada Belfry is still standing, but the block of houses it belongs to is knocked out and another block exactly behind my Marie Thérèse billet. And the poor Chapel in the C.C.S. School is a ruin.

Friday, August 25th. The A.D.M.S. of the 9th Div. (of Longuéval and Delville Wood) came strolling in to-day to look round – I knew him in Festubert days at the C.C.S. where we took refuge and I met him last on the platform at Victoria Station. He is a good man, and rather an old friend, so we had a most pleasant meeting.** They have the pleasing job of taking Vimy Ridge of all poisonous spots, and he says they will be giving us some work. If it is anything like the last attempt, when we first came here, they will have more than they want of it, but I expect after overcoming the difficulties of Longuéval and Delville Wood they will be the people to overcome this. Every lot that tries says the French knew what they were about when they gave us over this bit of their line.

** Very soon afterwards he was killed by a stray shell.

My five new Sisters are settling down happily and efficiently so far, but it means a lot of supervision at first, and in many directions. If it wasn't that one was well supported by the C.O. and had got the right side of the Sergeant-Major, charge of a C.C.S. would be even more harassing than it is. It is equally easy – and fatal – to be too fussy, or not fussy enough with such queer fish as orderlies are. You have to know the possibilities and the limitations of practically each individual one to place them all to the best advantage.

There are just now in the Abdominal Ward two or three almost miraculous recoveries: their lives went down to the lowest possible ebb with all the signs of death on them, but they just hung on and flickered back, and now instead of being in their coffins they are among the row of recovering wrecks outside listening to the raucous strains of the gramophone! The Surgeon and Sister D. are shaking hands with each other over them.

Sunday morning. Was waked at 4 a.m. by bursting of big shells at Hersin and the sky in a blaze from Boche guns at Lens – lit up my room. Rather alarming, but beautiful.

Tuesday, August 29th. Rumours last night that Rumania is in, and it's in to-day's French paper. Now Greece has seen which way the cat jumps, perhaps she'll come in too. 'Ça avancera la guerre,' as my miner's wife says hopefully.

They're bombarding Béthune again heavily and the C.C.S. has again had to be dispersed. We are to get all their emergency work now as well as from our own area, so we shall have a lot to do.

Friday, September 8th. The Sports went off very well and gave enormous enjoyment to the men and the N.C.O.'s, and incidentally to a vast audience of French infancy from the age of 2. There has been an absolute din of guns going all day. The wards are pretty full, but we were able to let most of the orderlies go to the sports.

I'm glad the German airman had a decent military funeral with R.F.C. Officers to carry the officer. For a taste of Hell before the next life I should think to be in a burning Zeppelin in the air would be the most realistic.

I am now looking after the gas gangrene cases, who, according to a new regulation, have to be in a separate Ward. It is a job that just suits me, and the Ward is close to my office so I can do both, as well as my rounds. They are necessarily always very ill and want a great deal of care and elaboration of exposed dressings, but it is a paying job when they pull round after heading straight for the mortuary.

We are getting a good many serious casualties in from the usual spot, but very little else except some chills, rheumatism, and a little paratyphoid and dysentery. A man was brought in yesterday evening wounded all over with bits of shell, but not too badly. In his left breast pocket was a fat little Testament with a bit of shell wedged safely in as far as the Epistle to Titus!

There is a lecture this afternoon by Colonel Galloway (Consulting Physician, 1st Army) on gas poisoning, which all M.O.'s, Sisters, and Orderlies are to attend. To-morrow the R.A.M.C. are having their long-deferred sports, if it turns out fine.

The officer with a bullet still in his brain is perfectly charming, though off his head: his adorable manners always show through his madness, and you never know whether he is going to be normal or mad. Yesterday he was interviewing the Kaiser all day. And when he has answered quite rationally about his food or his position in bed, he says, 'What time do we get in?' and you find he thinks he is landing at Southampton. He also told me the War was over, and asked if the Kaiser was still there (in the ward). When I said, 'No,' he said, 'I'm glad he's gone – did you see him?' I said, 'No, what was he like?' 'Oh, he's a tall chap,' he said. I write to his Mother every day, but have only had a wire from her yet.

A man who died yesterday had a letter to his wife in his pay-book – to be sent to her in case of his death in action – left open for the Censor. I sent it to her with the news.

One mother wrote to me in answer to a break-the-news letter: 'It must have been a mortal wound'!

Tuesday, September 12th. We are having heavenly weather and rather busy times. You'll have seen that our part of the world and the areas just north and just south of us have been locally 'active' and it is bringing us, nightly and daily, small batches of poor things. One has both arms broken, and one has both legs broken; three have one leg off and the other tottering; and there are some sad people already dead to this world from injuries to the head. Everyone has been kept pretty close to it, but I got two of the Juniors off for a trip to Lillers to-day, in the lorry that goes in every week for beer, coffins and medicines. They went to tea with Madame F. and enjoyed themselves very much. Two more will go off somewhere to-morrow, and after that we are to get some more work. I have two gas gangrenes who are slowly emerging to life and an approach to recovery; they are out in the sun all day.

Thursday, September 14th, and I have a third to-day who will not be here many more hours. The wards have been very heavy lately with wrecks, horrors and heroes in every bed. The worst has now happened. Sister D., the Mother of all the Abdominals, has her marching orders and goes down to Rouen to a General Hospital to-morrow. Her loss is irreparable: the place will never be the same again. It will be my turn next, as I have been here eleven months.

Saturday, September 16th. Only time for a scrawl; still very busy. The man with two broken arms has also a wound in the knee – joint in a splint – and has had his left eye removed to-day. He is nearly crazy. Another man has compound fractures of both legs, one arm, and head, and is quite sensible. Another has both legs amputated, and a compound fracture of arm. These people – as you may imagine – need very special nursing.

Monday, September 18th. We are all grappling with work all day now; some of it is wonderful, but much of it is nothing but black. There is a boy dying who has his Will in his Pay-book made out 'to my beloved mother.' He looks about 17; he said when I asked him what he'd like me to say to her, 'Tell her I'm all right; I don't know what to say; I don't want her to be worried, and give her my love!' My three resuscitated gas gangrene heroes would all have been going down on the train to-morrow, packed to the eyes in splints and rings and slings and pillows, but a cerebro-spinal meningitis was put into my ward and now the whole ward is in quarantine for a week (except me for some illogical reason) and they may not go.

There is a mad boy who is very funny; when you feed him he says, '1, 2, 3 a cup of tea, bread and butter 4, 5, 6, it's 238 now, and 915.' All his thoughts are in numbers. Another boy beckons me to talk to him as I go by, and after the conversation I heard him say, 'Kind owld sowl, ain't she?' The blind boy with both legs off is dying; he doesn't know his legs are off, and is cheerfully delirious most of the time. He calls us 'Teacher' and says, 'Look sharp, dear, go and get it now'! He was murmuring 'Such is life' just now.

Tuesday, September 19th. The blind legless boy died this evening. I had him at the last in a tent, as he had developed gas gangrene. He also said, 'Tell Mother I'm only slightly wounded.'

Friday, September 22nd. One of our new M.O.'s has come from fifteen months with the Irish Rifles in the front line; they were wiped out on July 1st at Gommécourt, and all his friends were killed or wounded. The enemy batteries were massed there and we never got beyond our own front lines. He said we were treading on our own dead four or five deep in a communication trench that was pulped by 8-inch shells.

Glorious Tank stories are going about. They've thoroughly cheered up the whole British Army in the Field.

It has been appallingly wet and slushy lately, but to-day was lovely and we had all the beds out and a great treat happened after tea. The – th Division Band came and sat down in front of the beds and played for an hour and a half, a good big Regimental Band, with lots of wood-wind. It was lovely in this gramophone existence. They played Gluck, Rachmaninoff, Gondoliers and lots of things the men know. A man in one of the wards, whom I always go and say good-night to (one leg off and just hanging on with the other), said solemnly 'Good-night, Mother' to me to-night.

It is a long time since any of us went for a walk now, but we may be able to occasionally when the two new Sisters come. My new Staff is settling down quite happily, and working well on the whole. They all say our orderlies are very good. Certainly they are very keen, and extraordinarily good to the patients. They have come on tremendously since we've been here, and even some of the raw young ones who knew nothing beyond scrubbing and counting kit and drawing rations can now go round the worst cases and lift them and turn them and do their backs and wash them like any Sister. Of course we ourselves have learnt a great deal. There is no form of horror imaginable, on any part of the human body, that we can't tackle ourselves now, and no extreme of shock or collapse is considered too hopeless to cope with, except the few who die in a few minutes after admission. Some of the most impossibly pulseless people have 'done' (the slang word for recover) after hours of coping with every known means of restoration, most of which can be got going in five minutes as we have everything ready for these efforts in every ward.

Saturday, September 23rd. There is a man in with both eyes and the top of his nose scooped out by a bit of shell. When I was cleaning him up he told me he was 49, but he'd given his age in as 38 to join the Army. Then he said, without any sort of comment, 'I think I've lost my eyesight,' as if it had been his rifle or his boots.

Tuesday, September 26th. Great news of two Zepps brought down in Essex and one of them near Colchester! I wonder did you see any of it? Proud moment for the Special Constable who took the 22 Germans prisoner in the middle of the night!

All my three gas gangrenes are packed up ready for the train to-day, a real triumph, as they did their best to die at one time. One of them, the Marine, is very ill still, and clothed in splints. Yesterday Sister G. and I achieved a long walk to our old haunts. It was the first breather out of the wards for a long time, and tasted very good. We reached Bouvigny, the deserted ruined village, where a soldier, after some minutes' conversation with us, said, 'And do you both speak English as well as French?' He thought the place so far beyond the reach of English women that we must be French, and he didn't happen to know the uniform! Then we struck up the Ridge into Bouvigny Wood, where the Hut billets are. There a Staff Officer on a horse caught us up, and walked a mile with us, greatly excited at finding us there. 'I suppose you are the first English ladies who've been up on this road for two years,' he said. From the ridge we saw clouds of gas being liberated in the trenches, and travelling South to North with a bias towards the enemy, most interesting to watch. At 11 p.m. just as I was settling down to sleep after the 10-mile walk and then a late round, the mine hooter began to wail and the Church bell to clang and the dogs to bark for a Gas attack. My cottage door was violently banged and a summons came for me to go to the Hospital. When I got there, all the gas helmets were put round the wards and the Sergeant-Major was running round excitedly, but there was no gas at all, and the alarm was then called off, and I went back to bed again, after tea with the Night Sisters.

September 29th. We have a man in who fell out of an aeroplane! or in one, yesterday morning. They were brought down by a Boche Archie, and then the plane was shelled to bits on the ground, but the officer and the man got away. The man is delirious from head and face injuries, but the officer only had a broken wrist.

October 1st. The man with no eyes and no nose mercifully died yesterday. My friend who says 'Good-night, Mother' to me and is going on the train to-day, said this morning he 'would think of me in terms of love till his dying day!' and he looked as if that day wasn't very far off, poor old thing.

The Aeroplane man seems to be going to die. A baby Flying officer who came to see him to-night fainted gracefully into my arms at the foot of the bed, on to the floor, overcome by general fatigue, hot day, and ward air after The Air.

We are trying to do a special rescue of a brave boy, H., hovering on the edge of gas gangrene; I have him in a marquee and have to put him into an iodine bath to-morrow. He dictated this afternoon, 'Dear Mother, just a few lines to let you know I am in the pink of health, hoping it finds you the same.' ('Mustn't let her worry,' he explained.) When asked if he had a best girl he said, 'No, only Mother'!

October 2nd. We have a sudden and unprecedented lull just now, very few wounded coming in. I believe they are taking the casualties we have always had to the nearest C.C.S. of the 3rd Army, which adjoins us to our right. As we are eight Sisters now instead of ten, this does no one any harm, while it lasts.

The rescue of my boy H. is a tragic failure. He is dying of septic pneumonia from a clot from his knee wound, after a triumphantly successful cleaning up of the other wounds by the hip bath treatment. He sat in it smoking cigarettes as happy as anything, and now he is unconscious and babbling and quite hopeless. He is a very gallant boy in the Drake Battalion. Three of his officers and his Chief Petty Officer have been to see him.

Wednesday, October 4th. H. died yesterday morning.

In the afternoon J. and I went to Lillers in the lorry to fetch the beer and coffins. It is a pleasant drive; about 15 miles. We did a little shopping and looked up my various billet ladies (who were most welcoming and voluble) and then went to tea with Mme. F. She was very hospitable and affectionate. The house and garden and tea seemed very civilised and clean and spacious after our piggeries here. She had had Prince Arthur billeted in her best bedroom for three weeks. She had to give him breakfast. Great commotion was caused one morning by his servant hitting hers, a boy called Marcelle, who stopped Prince Arthur in the hall and said he was not going to be hit by his servant!

Thursday, October 12th. Still busy, with increasing demand for coffins. My two new Gas Gangrenes have been solemnly visited this afternoon by all three Padres, C. of E., Presbyterian and R.C. The two patients have each lost an arm through the shoulder joint, and instead of a clean stump each has a black evil-smelling crater. But the M.O. gives me a free hand in dressing them, and one is showing signs of clearing up: the other is still very ill, but I have hopes of him too. Both have the main artery exposed, and pulsating in the wound. They have both been within as near a view of their graves as you can get to without getting in, so it will be fine if they pull through. A boy who died in the night said, 'Tell them I died like a soldier.' He would always apologise when he was sick all over you. Another boy was brought in yesterday evening, face downwards, on his stretcher, with an un-set compound fractured thigh, and wounds in his head and shoulder. He asked in a thick far-away voice, 'Is it very bad?' He has had the leg off to-day, and I'm afraid he is going to die. (He did.)

There have been a few cases of Shell Shock in; they have no wound, but tremble violently at the least noise, and don't speak. There is a 'Specialist' to whom they are all sent, who treats them by suggestion and hypnotism.

During the third Winter the writer was in charge of another C.C.S. stationed behind a quiet sector of the Line. In March 1917 this Unit was transferred to the Third Army south of Arras in readiness for General Allenby's attack which began on April 9th.

4

BATTLE OF ARRAS

MARCH 3RD TO JUNE 3RD 1917
WITH THE 3RD ARMY (SIR EDMUND ALLENBY)

LETTERS FROM WARLENCOURT

Warlencourt. Saturday, March 3rd 1917. We left St. Omer on Thursday morning and travelled all day round by Calais and Boulogne to Étaples, and then to 3rd Army H.Q., where we were put up for the night at a Stationary Hospital there, high up on a race-course with a lovely view.

From there, yesterday, we came here by Motor Ambulance, a 25-mile run up and down hills, over roads like young earthquakes sometimes. Some curious action of deep frost and thaw has upheaved them in places and it is a breathless toss up whether you stick fast or go up into the air. Eventually we found the Camp at a place called Warlencourt, on the top of a ridge, about six miles from the line, behind Gommécourt. This area hums with work: R.E. Dumps with every description of War material; Ammunition Dumps; 2 Aerodromes; Kaffirs making new roads and German Prisoners building our huts. They are the new Nissen pattern, like enormous drain-pipes, lit and ventilated from the ceiling, with windows and doors at each end but not on the sides. Already huge tents are up, and six big huts.

The Colonel has made a little compound for us, walled in with canvas all round, including a Kitchen [*sic*], Armstrong huts to sleep in and a small Nissen hut about 24 feet long and 18 wide for a Mess Room in the middle, with a Cook and a Batman. The kitchen is not finished yet and the Nissen hut not up, so we slept on stretchers in the Mess Hut of another C.C.S. just over the road, where we have our meals, and to-night we are to put up our beds in our own huts and come back for meals. As soon as ours is ready we shall send for the other five Sisters and get to work.

Sister R. and I are going to search the country round for a cottage to take our laundry, and to look for possibilities of milk, eggs, and butter, as we are ten miles from shops.

A place a mile away is shelled every day, and they once had to evacuate the patients in the C.C.S. across the road for shelling. The guns sound very close, and last night one heard again the big shells reverberating through the air as they travelled. The German retirement will make a difference here. There was a very sharp frost again last night and it was hard, or rather impossible, to get warm.

Sunday, March 4th. Still hard frost; ice all night, and a bright sun all day, reducing the top layer to an indescribable stickiness. We had a lively night last night. We were cosily tucked up in bed with dozens of blankets, and our oil stoves burning in our canvas huts and I'd just put my lamp out, when big enemy shells came whizzing overhead from two directions. They burst a long way past us, but made a tremendous noise being fired (from a big naval gun they run up close to their line), and loud screams overhead. Our 9.2's and 12-inch in the wood here kept it up all night with lions' roars.

Had a busy morning in the Camp with the Sergeant-Major and then with the C.O. over important details that are apt to crop up afterwards, when it's too late to get them done. The scheme of action for a 'Strafe' can be modified for 'Peace-times', and you have to provide for both. I'm getting him to put in for another Sister, anyhow, for Peace-times, and three more will arrive for a Strafe, and the men will have to expand accordingly. You have four theatre tables going in a Strafe, and they are worked all the 24 hours, either in day and night shifts, or in shifts of 16 hours on and 8 off. There's a tremendous lot to be done yet, everywhere.

They have a lot of badly wounded across the road. Two poor boys from the Flying Squadron a mile back were brought in dead to-day. They were killed flying; smashed to atoms near here.

It is very difficult to sleep at nights, the heavy guns are so close on the one side, and on the other we touch the main road to Arras that runs N.E. from Doullens, and all the work is done by night on it. Coming back from Doullens this evening, where I went to-day for the Red Cross Stores, we had to leap the chasms in the road without lights: nothing but small red lights are allowed on the last few miles as it is often shelled.

It will be a blessing when this frost is done with, but we seem to have got into another anticyclone and may keep it up again for weeks.

The country round looks inviting to explore, but I don't see when we shall have any time. We have accommodation for about 700 beds already.

Monday, March 5th. Woke up this morning with ½ inch of snow on our beds *inside* our huts, and 6 inches outside. Melting now and a terrible mess.

We shan't see what our weak points are till we begin, but if unity is strength it ought to pull well, as no one is clashing anywhere.

Tuesday, March 6th. Had a busy morning putting in for extra surgical equipment that we shall need, with the C.O. and the Dispensary Sergeant. No one here except the C.O. and myself has had any experience of a Strafe, and people have the vaguest ideas about numbers, and how quickly your stuff of all sorts gets used up. I am having a surgical stock marquee for cutting dressings and padding splints. The Technique of Modern Field Surgery has become so elaborate that you need quantities of special plant and apparatus, and some of the kinds in vogue vary in the different Armies.

We are also to take gassed cases, and there seem to be a good many bad ones. Some came into the other C.C.S. last night, including an old Frenchman and his daughter, from a village a few miles off. He died, and his daughter looks as if she would, too. (She did.)

Our group of Casualty Clearing Stations (3) is nearest to Gommécourt, and there is a great deal doing just here.

Boche prisoners are putting up our Nissen huts; they are quite a young lot and look clean, healthy and unconcerned.

Here are two boy-officer stories. In the July strafe, one night in the middle of it all, a boy brought in at his last gasp heard the Sister and Medical Officer talking. 'Whose voice is that?' he asked. 'Didn't I hear a woman speaking?' 'Yes,' said the Sister. 'Oh, how ripping,' said the boy, and died an hour later.

Another, a Jock, very badly hit, was crying. 'Here, Sister,' he said, 'I'm one of the Seaforths and I'm blub-blub-blubbering like a wee wean. What are you going to do about it? Can't you stop it?'

Our gunners are making an awful din to-night.

Wednesday, March 7th. A biting N.E. wind to-day verging on the blizzard.

My new cook is a promising boy called Simmonds, and Savins is our batman. He is so attentive he almost does our hair for us. His first question this morning on bringing my early tea to my bedside was, 'Are you going to put on your ammunition boots first thing? I've got them dubbined ready.' I thought lovingly of indoor slippers and the dining-room fire. What with the wind bashing your canvas walls in massed formation, and the 9.2's roaring their loudest, and the lorries and caterpillars lorrying incessantly on the high road, it is not exactly soothing; but you soon get used to it, and when you're working hard you can sleep through anything.

Saturday, March 10th. The frost has broken and left us in a quagmire, but the icy blast has gone. The roads are bad enough, but our Camp is unspeakable. The original field sticks to your feet and gradually works towards your knees, and if your shoes are not anchored on by puttie straps you leave them behind. To-morrow I shall tackle it in my ammunition boots. We have been very busy getting straight the last two days, but managed a short walk up the main road the day before yesterday afternoon. You never see a French man, woman, or child, but only British, Kaffirs, and Boche prisoners, horses, mules, lorries and all that goes to make up a Somme film, and all out for the same set purpose – to finish the War. There's a wonderful unity of feeling in that common aim through every department from top to bottom.

The Sergeant-Major in his shirt sleeves with a fork and shovel had a lot of men on path-making all day, but even laying down thousands of empty tins bottom upwards makes little impression, as they get trodden out of sight almost at once.

Sunday, March 11th. The D.M.S. rang up the Colonel last night to say that we should have to be ready to take in patients in three days, so things have had to get a hustle on to-day. The Engineers have sent 60 men to finish the Wards and get on with the Theatre, the Kitchen and the road for evacuation. Neither the Water supply, nor the lighting are done, so both will have to be improvised at first. It takes a lot of labour to bring up water by man-handling and to store it in tanks.

There is to be a new Surgical Specialist, who coped with the Somme last summer, so we ought to do well. We've had a busy day equipping one of the Acute Surgical Huts and putting finishing touches to the Mess arrangements. The others will probably be here to-morrow night. I shall be glad to set them all to work, there's so much to be done.

Monday, March 12th. It poured cats and dogs all night and you can't imagine the state of the Camp. No one could who hasn't wallowed in it. The others haven't turned up. Feeding them is going to weigh heavily on my chest. It is one person's job to run a Mess at the Back of Beyond, and I have this Hospital (700 beds) to run for night and day, with the peculiar difficulties of a new-born unfinished Camp, and emergency work. For the Mess you settle a rice pudding, but there is no rice, and the cows have anthrax, so there's no fresh milk, and the Canteen has run out of Ideal milk. Well, have a jam tart; lots of jam in the British Army, but no flour, no suet, no tinned fruits, no eggs, no beans or dried peas, not one potato each. But there is bacon, ration bread and tinned butter (when you can get it), jam, marmalade sometimes, cheese, stew, Army biscuits, tea, some sugar, and sometimes mustard, and sometimes oatmeal and cornflour.

Also we have only 1½ lbs. of coal per head per day, so when that is used up you have to go and look for wood, to cook your dinner and boil your water. Everybody is ravenous in this high air and outdoor life, and so as long as there's enough of it, you can eat anything. None of them I hope will grumble if we can work up the true Active Service spirit, but it is an anxiety.

The guns have been very quiet the last few days. Colonel Gray (of Aberdeen), the Consulting Surgeon for the 3rd Army, came and looked round yesterday and asked how we liked being shelled.

We have got to build and run our own Hospital laundry with 7 Permanent Base men as laundresses – when the water is laid on. So far we have only 70 beds and mattresses – all the rest will have to be on stretchers. I've bagged some lovely crates that the pneumatic-wheel stretchers came in, as linen cupboards. The C.O. and the Sergeant-Major go and steal planks from the road when I want boards for ward-tables, and I have stolen the trestles myself. The days aren't nearly long enough for all the scrounging that has to be done and prevented.

Tuesday, March 13th, 10 p.m. The mud is still a great hindrance, but we are getting on.

This evening Sister and I strolled down to the flying sheds – about a mile behind us. An infant pilot showed us over and we saw all the lovely shining creatures, the newest pattern just out, bristling with uncanny inventions and guns. Then he took us to see one of his friends land from a patrol; he made a very pretty landing, but it was dusk and he didn't see us, and to the undisguised horror of about 15 men round, the excited boy in the pilot's seat burst into a torrent of ruddy language about three Huns he'd met. They coughed and talked and tried in vain to shut him up. Then he suddenly saw their red faces and caught sight of us, and in a hopeless roar of laughter from everyone he said to us, 'I *beg* your pardon.' It was quite funny.

Wednesday, March 14th. Pouring cats and dogs all night and most of the day; quagmires everywhere. I have got officer's gumboots now from Ordnance, big enough for me to wear two pairs of men's socks over my stockings, and therefore possible to wear all day without getting trench feet. Went round with the new Surgeon this morning and learnt his requirements.

The other five sisters arrived to-day and we are now running our own Mess instead of going over the road for meals. They are good children and are only amused at the mud, and the ration butter, and lamps instead of fires, and no baths, that are the chief things that hit you in the eye at present. They have dug themselves in cosily into their halves of their Armstrong huts – they are all old campaigners – and to-morrow they will get through a lot of work in the Hospital.

Saturday, March 17th, and no sign of any buds out anywhere in these parts. I've got a plate of moss with a celandine plant in the middle, and a few sprouting twigs of honeysuckle that you generally find in January, and also a bluebell bulb in a jam tin.

We have got some flour to-day and a cauliflower, also some more coal.

The Hospital is developing daily in every direction. The D.M.S. yesterday thought it had got on well since his last visit. Now the mud is drying up and the roads beginning to be under control again.

Sunday, March 18th. We worked all the morning and all knocked off at lunch to-day as it was a dazzling day, and the new-comers had had no time off since they came. It seemed a good chance to do some exploring if we're going to be busy, so G. and R. and I armed ourselves with our identity discs and gas-helmets, and my field-glasses and a map and some chocolate and biscuits (as S. and I used to do at Barlin), and set off East. We went through three villages, all packed with men doing the four days in and four days out of the trenches, and at the third village, we asked a woman if she could give us some coffee. She did, with zeal, and refused to be paid, and then came a stroke of luck I've been looking for all through this War. I asked her if there were any 'Grandmothers' about. 'Yes,' said little Louise of 13 eagerly, 'there is one,' and she took us to it. There was the painted monster with a team of R.M.A. and a R.M.A. officer, who was most kind and introduced us to his little pet, with the enormous shells in a row alongside.

He told us the Germans had gone back 15 miles in the night, and he was in the act of arranging for her to be disintegrated and moved on to-morrow, he didn't know where to. It takes five traction engines to heave her on her way. The heavy traffic going up the main road has been deafening the last two days and nights. The other C.C.S. has been warned to-night to be ready for lots of work. The R.M.A. officer said the cavalry were out now.

The village had been shelled up to yesterday. We were in the region where you hear the men say after you've passed, 'Why, they're English!' The R.M.A. officer said the Marines had been having a very bad time the last six weeks, and told me where they are.

Monday, March 19th, 10 p.m. The Flying people say the Germans are leaving huge black clouds of smoke behind their burning trail. Our high road has been like a live Somme film all day and a roar all night. It has been blowing hard, and to-night is a roaring tempest with floods and raging wind. The little canvas huts are standing it all right so far, but in the worst bursts you look round and wonder at which moment it will crash in on you and your lamp and your belongings. The camp is very much exposed with nothing to break the wind. No guns, of course, now, to add to the noises. No wounded came in to the other C.C.S. last night. The Stunt came off all right but met with no resistance, the Germans having gone back so far.

Tuesday, March 20th. The gale last night was terrific – our compound was a wreck this morning. In spite of the wind deliberately picking up wooden posts and heavy canvas tenting (which yesterday were the walls of the compound) and bashing them savagely and regularly against the part of the hut next the head of my bed, it didn't succeed in keeping me awake. I knew it couldn't be stopped, and intended to sleep in spite of it, and did.

Sheets of rain all day and more mud.

Orders came this morning to be ready to take in large numbers of wounded at short notice, and guns are busy again. All departments immediately got a hustle on and this evening the C.O. wired that we were ready. The kitchen is not going – some water laid on – wards equipped and Theatre improvised in one of the Dressing Huts, as the real new one isn't quite finished; 1000's of lbs. of dressings are stocked, but they soon run out. Lotions, dressings and clothing will all run out, I believe, because things take so long coming up and have so much red tape to get through first.

Our official strength is 7 Sisters – far too few for any battle, but that will become obvious.

Wednesday, March 21st, and it is still snowing and yesterday was the first day of Spring. It is *unspeakably* vile – biting wind – driving snow and deep slush. We can still hear the guns but nothing like so close as before. I believe this group of C.C.S.'s clear the wounded now from the Arras area. The R.E. are still building the Theatre and Laundry etc., here, and until they clear out altogether we are only to take any overflow from the other two C.C.S.'s, which has not yet occurred, so we go on improving the detail of the Hospital all day – and expecting to be – but not being – called up all night.

Robinson, V.C., has joined our Squadron here, and the boys fly madly round and round us, rapping their Lewis guns for no other reason, apparently, than to say, 'Look at me!' There is one who loops the loop till you feel giddy watching him – he does it like a street-boy turning somersaults.

Friday, March 23rd. The three C.O.'s of the three C.C.S.'s here were summoned to 3rd Army H.Q. to-day to a Conference with the D.M.S. The Colonel was only just back when I went to bed, so I don't know our fate for certain, but their Mess Waiter reports to ours that we remain here when the Attack begins.

Heavy distant growling going on.

The Sapper Officer working for us told me he was sent to prospect over all the evacuated ground on this sector yesterday. There is a crater at every cross-road, and every main road is exploded every 300 yards. The wells are poisoned, the apple-trees cut down and the houses wrecked and burnt: bridges and railways destroyed.

We have been living on bully and beans for three days – it is rather good; bacon, jam, margarine and milk are all tinned, but we have very good meals out of them.

Sunday, March 25th. We start taking Convoys probably to-morrow, so as the Hospital is now almost boiling over with readiness, we all set forth with our lunch this morning in twos and threes to explore. We walked altogether 15 miles and got a bit footsore, but we have been over No-Man's Land and down into the deep German dug-outs on the scene of the tragedy of last July at Gommécourt. It is all indescribable. Bairnsfather has drawn it, but no one can ever, in words, make anyone realise what it is like. A big village, Fonquevillers, beyond the one where we went last Sunday (which was then teeming with British and is now absolutely deserted except for the few French inhabitants and a few clearing-up parties left behind), lies, or rather used to lie, the other side of a wide plain packed with guns, across which we walked; now there are only the empty gun-pits, the shell-holes, and a few men guarding a few shells round the dug-outs. This village is shelled to pieces by both sides; it was *on* our front line for two years. One of the huge Church bells was lying upside down half buried under the remains of the tower. A big crucifix on one lonely wall is untouched.

Then you come to what was Gommécourt. It must have been, when it existed, full of orchards, and half in and half out of a wood. Now there is one wall of one house left. The wood and the orchards are blackened spikes sticking up out of what looks now like a mad confusion of deep trenches and deep dug-outs battered to bits. We went with an electric torch down two staircases of one and stepped into a pond at the bottom. Some are dry and clean and have the beds still in them. You step over unexploded shells, bombs and grenades of every description – and we saw one aerial torpedo – an ugly brute. I picked up a nose-cap; and the sapper who was with us said hastily, 'That's no good,' snatched it out of my hand and threw it out of sight; it still had the detonator in it. Then he picked one up without its detonator and gave it to me.

On the right of this wood, the other side of the Germans' wire, is the No-Man's Land, where the Salvage men are busy burying our skeletons who have been there since July 1st. The Prince of Wales and every Brass Hat have been to see the awful place. The village we and the Germans have been shelling for 2 years made you feel dazed. But the battlefield made you feel sick. We got some snowdrop roots with the flowers out, from under a boulder at Gommécourt.

Here you get to the culmination of destruction for which all civilised nations are still straining all their resources. Isn't it hopelessly mad? A few poor French civilians who lived there before the War and have now for the first time been allowed to creep back, were sadly poking about the ruins. The two Mademoiselles de G., to whom the Château belonged, were there a few days ago. They found only the two gate-posts, which look as if somebody had picked them up and stuck them where they thought the Château might have been. The miles of German wire stretching N. and S. is rusted deep brown and looks like burnt gorse. It is much more savage and prickly than ours – longer spikes and closer together.

Some London Territorial N.C.O.'s who inhabit a dug-out in the village, insisted on giving us tea among the ruins. They produced a chair, packing-cases, and some glorious tea and toast: we were thirsty and grateful.

I was amazed to see how, since last Sunday, we have got every one of the hundreds of guns away; they are now thundering in their new positions. As we passed the 6-inch howitzer gun-pits a man appeared with a polite message from his Sergeant-Major, who would be very glad to give us tea. As we'd just had some and it was getting late and we had nearly five miles to go, we reluctantly declined.

At the next village a Major and two other officers invited us to tea, but again we had to hurry on. We had shed some of our clothing on the way at the house of the kind woman who gave us coffee last Sunday. When we picked them up she had hot coffee and three cups waiting for us, so we didn't do badly. They look very dull and lost without the British soldiers, who have been in and out of their houses so long, but as the shells have also ceased they seem to think the War is over.

The D.M.S. was very pleased with the Hospital yesterday, especially with our arrangement of the Dressing Ward.

Monday night, March 26th. The Quarter-Master paddled me round all his soak-pits, incinerators, thresh disinfectors, ablution huts, bath huts, laundry, etc., etc., this morning. They are primitive but clever.

Tuesday. Convoys arriving.

Tuesday, March 27th. At last we've taken in our first convoy, no hitch so far. The two new Sisters arrived in the nick of time, and the posting of Sisters and Orderlies seems to be working out all right. We have a particularly nice set of Medical Officers. The C.O. and I and the Sergeant-Major meet and compare notes in our endless rounds and severally help each other out of holes. Sometimes I want a fatigue party from the Sergeant-Major or he wants one from my men, or the C.O. claims both lots or the Q.M. wants them for unloading lorries, but we all get it done in the end.

It has been the usual poisonous weather again, biting N.E. wind, driving storms and deep slush. The two new Sisters are tucked into their bell tent, and I hope won't be too cold. We take in from 6 a.m. to-day to 6 a.m. to-morrow – in rotation with the other two in this Group.

A Flying Officer said to-day that the Germans in one place got away so far that our Cavalry after them lost touch with their rations. The R.F.C. then dropped sacks of bully down to them! Our bombardment is still going on, and they also are shelling hard round the Arras pivot, into us in their old trenches.

Wednesday, March 28th. We are bombarding them harder than ever; it is a continual din. We took in another Convoy in the night and had a busy morning, but a train came before tea, so our first venture is admitted, operated on, treated and evacuated within 36 hours; all but the worst Surgicals and Medicals unfit to travel, and a handful of walking-cases, soon fit for duty. One of last night's is dying of shock, in spite of strenuous efforts to pull him back. I've already had to begin writing the Break-the-News Letters to the wives and mothers. It is so much worse for them; the man or boy who dies nearly always knows nothing about it till he wakes in Heaven. The Hospital is to be kept as empty as possible for the Strafe.

Friday, March 30th, 10 p.m. It stopped raining in the afternoon and changed back to the beautiful icy wind we get so much of. There are ten new officers in to-night, all very quiet and trenchy and glad to be warm and dry and out of the shells. The men, too, are very quiet and done up; and there is no talk among either officers or men except about the trenches and the fighting.

We haven't quite got into the right mechanism yet between Wards and Receiving Room, and when some wards are filled up one is always finding the overflow sent to the wrong places – stretchers to tents where there are no Sisters and very little equipment and no fires, and walking-cases to the huts where there are Sisters, etc. Then you have to get this reversed.

The C.O. and Q.M. are making preparations for possible thousands: so am I.

I managed to get a sack of potatoes for 17 francs to-day for our Mess; great rejoicings; tinned milk is still very scarce, and cows' milk does not exist. The Minor Scourges of War are everywhere again. I am a victim as usual.

The R.C. Padre has come but not the C. of E. yet. One of my best orderlies is a Lay Brother of the Society of the Divine Compassion. He is helping me fix up the Mortuary and the Church tent.

Tuesday, April 3rd. We are in the middle of terrific work, so I can't write much; all the casualties from the attack on Hainy and Croisilles came to us, we hadn't nearly enough Sisters to go round and it never stopped all day and all night and all to-day till 5 p.m. The D.M.S. came to-day and I asked for more Sisters. He said he was trying to get up to 20 for us for this Strafe and we might get 17. Two more turned up to-night, and are sleeping in a tent for the first time, much thrilled.

So many die that I shan't possibly be able to write to their mothers, and some have no trace of next of kin.

I had to run a ward equipped for 14 officers and had to get 28 in, on stretchers on every inch of floor, some badly wounded; they were all angels of patience and uncomplainingness. And I could spare them very little of my time, but they had good orderlies. The two new Sisters of the other day are running the Theatre magnificently.

Wednesday, April 4th, 10.30 p.m. Reinforcements are coming in – two more Sisters to-day, that is 13 altogether, and there are now 13 M.O.'s and

2 Padres, and 40 men coming to-morrow. 12 Nursing Orderlies came the other day. There is still a 'Team' to come, consisting of four people, one surgeon, one anæsthetist, one Theatre Sister and one Theatre Orderly; a brainy scheme – one Team to each C.C.S.

We've had a very full day getting ready for to-morrow's take-in, opening new lines of tents and getting stock up, and patching up the too-bad-to-travel, of whom there are many.

The two last Sisters seem keen enough – four of my old team work like bricks. I have to help Sister G.'s bad ward a great deal; it becomes too much for her with all her devotion. We are running a Preparation-for-Operation Ward to-morrow, to which all operation cases are to go from the Dressing Hut, and from there to the Theatre and then to the Wards.

The increased Mess makes extra work and catering is appallingly difficult. We all eat whatever comes, whether cold or hot, raw or cooked, nice or nasty, and do very well on it. The kitchen range is made of petrol tins, cement, and draughts. Thank Heaven, it has stopped snowing and blowing, though it still rains a bit.

Thursday, April 5th, Midnight. Just got to bed after my last round. Had a very big take-in, but not so many bad ones; a Gunner Major with his leg off nearly died this morning, but I hope he'll do now. A boy in the Officers' Ward with his right leg off nearly at the hip, and his right arm all to pieces, is not so well to-night. I found three dying ones to-night in one of the wards, and got them into a corner together on their stretchers with a stretcher-bearer to look after them. Two died, but one revived and still lives.

The Preparation-for-Theatre Ward has been working very well. It is to this Ward that every stretcher-case is sent from the Dressing Hut, except those who are so slightly wounded that they can be sent to one of the Evacuation Wards to be dealt with at a Base Hospital. Here the number of battered men, generally from 50 to 60, never seems to grow less, as although they are carried when ready to the operating Teams in the Theatre, their places are continually filled by others.

All the layers of sodden or caked stiff clothing are cut off, pyjamas or long flannel pinafore gowns put on, taken from a blanket and screen enclosure kept heated by a Perfection Lamp. Hot blankets, hot-water bottles, hot drinks, subcutaneous salines and hypodermics are given here, as also in the Resuscitation Ward to which all the apparently hopeless cases are taken.

When the stretcher-bearers come from the operating Teams for their next case, you have to be careful to send the most urgent before the ones who may have been waiting longer.

It often happens that no M.O. can be spared for this tent, so a great deal of responsibility is thrown on to us, and only the Sisters with nerve, experience and sound judgment are any good here. With any luck you may be able to have 2 Sisters to spare for this work and one or two orderlies or convalescent patients.

Once when I was cutting off a split boot of a man wounded in the head, chest, and the other thigh, half his foot came off in it – a detail overlooked in the Dressing Hut and the Field Ambulance with all his other injuries.

General Macpherson (next to the Director General) came round to-day with the D.M.S. The 'Team' have arrived and are at work in the Theatre at this moment. A 15th Sister also turned up to-night, and a week ago we were 7.

A man with his right arm in fragments, a penetrating chest-wound and a piece of shrapnel in his abdomen, said he was 'a bit uncomfortable, but nothing to talk about!' He came to us in the Preparation Ward pulseless, with instructions on his label to 'generally counteract shock.' After six hours we had him fit for operation; they whipped off his arm and dug the shrapnel out of his inside, and the M.O.'s call me an Optimist when I say he is going to do; now he's in bed with a pulse. (Died next day.) Lots of them they said must die have lived and sit up eating boiled eggs!

It has been sunny and windless to-day, a blessed change, and bright moon to-night. It is all a ghastly business, but they take it without a word and it is grand to see the apparently dying men come to life again. And it is bringing out the best of everybody, from the C.O. to the man who does the lamps.

What we have had so far is child's play to what is to come before you get this, so I'd better try and go to sleep, and not think of the amount of things one has to leave undone, owing to the great drawback of having only one brain, two hands and two feet.

Good Friday, and pouring cats and dogs. Had a train to-day, but the whole of one Acute Ward are too bad to go. Sir Anthony Bowlby was here to-day; he took much interest in it all and thought the abdominals were doing well.

A Staff officer said to-day that the men grumble twice as much when it is fine as when they are soaking wet! Haven't I always said the same, and Punch too, about the Incorrigibles?

A boy with his face nearly in half, who couldn't talk, and whom I was feeding, was trying to explain that he was lying on something hard in his trouser pocket. It was a live Mills bomb! I extracted it with some care, as the pins catch easily.

Just had a fatiguing but successful hunt for the Minor Scourges of War (why Minor!?).

I was telling the stretcher-bearers who were taking a man to the Theatre to wait his turn, to put him not facing but back to the operations already going on. It is not exactly encouraging for a man to see operations going on just before he has his own. The man burst into roars of laughter! 'Take more'n that to put the wind up me, Sister, after bein' out here all this time.'

(Battle of Arras. Easter Monday, April 9th 1917)

Easter Tuesday, April 10th. The 3rd Army went over the top yesterday and a wire came through by mid-day that we'd taken Vimy and 4,000 prisoners and, Sir Anthony Bowlby says this morning, 30 guns. The Cavalry are after them, and the Tanks leading the Infantry, and all is splendid, but here are horrors all day and all night. The three C.C.S.'s filled up in turn and then each filled up again, without any break in the Convoys: we take in and evacuate at the same time. The Theatre, Dressing Hut, Preparation Hut and Wards and Tents are all humming – the kitchen goes on cooking with a Day Staff and a Night Staff, and the stretcher-bearers go on stretcher-bearing, and the Mortuary Corporal goes on sewing up corpses in canvas. The Colonel carries the lame walking-cases on his broad back, and I look after the moribunds in every spare second from the Preparation Hut, which is (during take-in) the stiffest corner of all, and Sisters, M.O.'s, N.C.O.'s, Orderlies, Convalescent Men and Permanent Base Men, all peg into it like navvies. We meet for snatching meals and five-minute snacks of rest and begin again. All are doing 16 hours on and 8 off and some of us 18 on and 6 off.

All the organisation is working without a hitch so far, but we are not as tired yet as we shall be. There are 30 officers, some very much smashed up and all as good as gold, like the men.

We ought to have 100 more hot-water bottles, but I can't get them. All the cut gauze and wool is supplied through my dressings-bunk with a convalescent London Division man at work there.

Stretchers on the floor are back-breaking work, and one's feet give out after a certain time, but as long as one's head and nerves hold out, nothing else matters, and we are all very fit.

Evacuation has been held up to-day for some hours and the place is clogged. The wards are like battlefields, with battered wrecks in every bed and on stretchers between the beds and down the middles. What a load the train will have, and how the Home Hospitals will be filling up. I'm afraid about five Officers are going to die. We take in to-night, but there are two trains in to clear.

The Padre is wonderful; he fills hot bottles with his one arm and gives drinks and holds basins for them to be sick, and especially looks after those poor ghastly moribunds. The Theatre teams have done 70 operations in the 24 hours.

These 'battlefields' show up the best in everyone; the Orderlies are splendid and refuse to go to bed, and never lose patience in the most trying moments. There's a Night Duty Staff of M.O.'s; one new one works like an Orderly at night in the Preparation Ward. He is just up from the Base and it is all new to him.

The transport of wounded is extraordinarily well worked out over all these miles. The walking-cases come in lorries and buses and the lying-cases in beautifully electric-lighted Motor Ambulances, which look like the lights on the Embankment as far as you can see down the road, and the stream to the three Hospitals never ceases. It was all worked out in H.Q. Orders weeks ago.

They packed me off to bed to-night when I'd seen that every place was properly staffed, and the right people 'standing to' to be called if wanted (of whom I am one). We are longing to see Monday's and to-day's telegrams in the papers. Of course we've had snowstorms and icy gales all the time.

Wednesday, April 11th. Post just going. We began again admitting, evacu-ating, operating at 1 a.m.

I could tell you for hours, stories of the men and the officers, brave, funny, tragic, ghastly, especially the first and the last, but they'll be lost, because this kind of life allows only work and sleep. An infant 2nd Lt. of 17 (Army age 19) said on the table before his operation in severe tones, 'Let me tell you that I am an Officer, and I wish to go back to the Officers' Ward.' He looks 15, like a drummer-boy. The moribund Ward is (fortunately) indescribable; about 25 have died there to-day, besides others in other Wards, but some have been resurrected and have gone down on the trains.

Friday, April 13th. The D.M.S. came to-day and said the Push was held up by this extraordinarily inopportune burst of bad weather. It blew and raged madly all Wednesday night, and there was deep snow in the morn-ing. Last night and to-day we have been getting the poor boys in who have been lying out in it for two days, and many of them have died since of the exposure and gas gangrene.

The D.M.S. said that Sir Anthony Bowlby (who has been here every day lately) has reported very well of this Unit – that the arrangements were excellent, and things going well, and that the report had gone in to H.Q.

The Strafe is over for the moment, and we are full of the leavings, the most tragic part, though dozens who have been evacuated will die, too.

The Sisters have shown themselves up to all that has been required of them and are doing magnificently.

We have some Germans in; several have died.

Saturday night, April 14th. I've never in my life seen so many aeroplanes or so many dead men or so many German prisoners; they are marched in hundreds down our road. We have a small Hun, named Jan, a baby abdominal of about 17, whom we are trying to pull through; the boy with both legs off died yesterday.

A grey, stiff, frozen man who was wounded on Monday, was brought in to-day – Saturday; he had been kept alive by drinks in a trench and found and brought in last night. We got a pulse into him after some hours, and warmed him till he thawed and felt too hot, but one leg was hopelessly smashed and of course had gas gangrene and he died this evening.

One Cockney boy with both arms smashed said to the Padre, 'Sy a prayer for me, will yer? That would be nahce. Can't yer confirm me?' It's the only time I've seen the Padre laugh. Then the boy offered to sing 'Tooleroolerity, I want to go to Blighty – Blighty is the plice for me.' And then he died.

A magnificent Sergeant with one leg blown off and the other smashed was dying, and the Padre praying with him, when the Sister heard him say, 'That's good.' He told me when I wrote to his wife to 'break it to 'er gently, like.' He had three little girls he longed to see.

An abdominal officer, Lt. S., 1/8th Middlesex, told me a few hours before he died to 'tell them I've got a slight wound.' All the time he thought of us and everybody but himself.

On the other side of the picture there are many glorious 'resurrections' smoking cigarettes and eating chicken and reading magazines. They have lots of champagne and eggs and oranges and jelly, and everything to make them buck up. It has been a fine sunny day at last, but windy.

Sunday, April 15th. Early Service in the Church Tent at 7 a.m. The Padre has made it very nice with a red and white reredos and our own altar-cloth. It has a Communion-rail made of trees, and there is a duckboard with stretcher pillows to kneel on.

The fine day was the usual solo. It has poured all day since 6.30 and the swamp squelches out loud. All the wounded to-night will come in soaking wet.

We've had a very busy day, some of it very disheartening. They haven't yet begun to take-in over the road, so we may have a free night for once. The Theatre people have the longest hours, and for the Surgeons the greatest strain of work, but for the Sisters it is much less harassing and wearing than the work in the Wards, cutting off the caked khaki and the clammy socks and heavy boots, with the incessant cries of 'Give me a drink' or 'Sister, I do feel bad,' and the everlasting saline infusion and men being sick or delirious or groaning or hæmorrhaging. The younger Sisters who are new to this kind of work send for me as if I was a kind of Travelling Rescue Circus. We have been trying to keep a double amputation alive all day; he said to-night after something he liked, 'I was in 'ell and am now in 'eaven.'

Tuesday, April 17th. We have had a lull the last two days, and everybody has been off duty long enough to go for a walk in relays and pick Lent lilies, cowslips, and anemones. Operations and funerals still continue, but the wards are not so full. I believe another Stunt is expected to-morrow.

To-day we have had no bread, but only 'dog-biscuits.' At breakfast, with no porridge, and at tea they are rather a blight, as they are so hard they take hours to eat, but we manage to consume enough to support life!

I got about 60 behind in writing Break-the-News Letters the first few days of last week, and have never caught them up, but manage now to work them off as they occur, every 24 hours.

It poured and galed all last night and most of to-day with the usual alternations of heavy rain, snow and sleet, with a driving bitter wind. What the men in the trenches, and the wounded, are like you can imagine. I have never seen anything like the state they are in, mud caked on their teeth and under their eyelids.

Wednesday, April 18th. Yet another quiet day. I have sent everybody, including the Sister-in-charge, off duty part of the day. Bread to-day instead of brickbats, and duckboards half-way across the swamp (I have sat down in it twice!).

Saturday, April 21st. No rain for once, and the swamp drying up. Went for a walk after tea with P. and found periwinkles, paigles, anemones and a few violets – not a leaf to be seen anywhere. The D.G., Sir Arthur Sloggett, came round this morning. He liked the Hospital very much; said it would make a good nucleus for a Stationary Hospital, so I hope that means we will move up sometime.

Sunday, April 22nd. This continued bombardment is shaking the earth to-night; it is on the same scale as on the day before Easter Monday. The Hospital is almost empty, ready. Four Nursing Orderlies have gone sick, and not one can be spared, but I suppose we shall get through somehow.

Have got a top-hole new square Indian Marquee up for four of the new Sisters; each inhabits a separate quarter – curtained off; it is splendid, with double fly, ventilators, porches and windows, and they are revelling in it. The other four now have a bell-tent each instead of sharing, so all are happy.

I took some Lent lilies to the Cemetery this evening; it is rapidly spreading over a high open field; there must be nearly 2,000 graves there now, since it began last June. I planted some on Major L. J.'s grave, and put the rest on some of our boys'. There was a sunset and a young new moon showing.

No one knows when we shall fill up again but it can't be far off, with this din. If you could hear it for five minutes, you would never forget it.

(2nd phase of the Battle of Arras. April 23rd 1917)

Monday, April 23rd, 10 p.m. Just come up to lie down for an hour before the next take-in. We have filled up twice, and they are hard at it again over the road; we come next. The men say our guns are so thick, they're wheel to wheel and it is 'like playing the planner'; the earth-shaking noise this morning did its work; the wounded Germans tell me there are a great many dead. We have a splendid six-foot officer boy lying silently on his face with a broken back, high up. I hope he won't live long. The D.M.S. came this afternoon to ask me for a Sister to go up to a new Abdominal Special Hospital with a Field Ambulance at a place farther up; out of shell range, but overlooking the whole battlefield.

The men, the blankets and even their moustaches are swarming with J.J.'s and we are getting attacked ourselves – isn't it absolutely beastly? I've been looking after 100 stretcher-cases in the tents to-night; they are all ready now for evacuation – just heard the whistle.

Tuesday morning. The Senior Night Sister came up at 12 to say they were taking-in again – not too bad cases, and no one need be called; so the Dressing Hut Sister and I stayed where we were and slept. Went down early this morning. They were fairly clear as there'd been two Evacs., no deaths. (This new Abdominal Stunt is making a difference there already – it ought to save many lives.) I heard a dying officer (exhilarated by morphia) gaily dictating a letter to the Padre as follows: 'It is not at all serious and I am getting on all right. Don't worry about me. Love to all, your loving Son.' He is cold and pulseless and won't live many hours.

A Captain of the Yorks had his leg off yesterday and makes less of it than some people with a toe-nail off. The glorious boy with the broken back is lying on his back now; he doesn't know about it and says he's all right, only his back is a little stiff and aching.

Some of the men say they were picked up and looked after by Germans, so we are being extra kind to the Germans this time. There is in Hospitals an understood arrangement that all Germans (except when their lives depend on immediate attention) should wait till the last British has been attended to, for dressings, operations, food, blankets, etc. It is only kept up in a very half-hearted way and is generally broken by the M.O.'s, who are most emphatic about it in theory!

Tuesday, 10.30 p.m. It has been a pretty sad day, 12 funerals, including four officers, all fine brave men. The spine boy has found out what is the matter with him and is quite cheery about it; told me to tell his mother he had had Holy Communion this morning and that she was not to worry about him; he called out to the dying officer opposite to him that he was done for, and he was to give his love to the boys.

A young Pilot was brought in this morning with a smashed foot. Went up from here at 6.15, met five Huns at 8.15; they riddled his machine with bullets, but his Observer turned on his Lewis gun and brought one down. Then one of their bullets killed his Observer and caught his foot. He was 12,000 feet up and couldn't use his rudder owing to the smashed foot, but he got down somehow and crashed at the end. The machine was smashed up, with the dead Observer in it, but he crawled out and was just getting ready to set her on fire, thinking he was in the German lines, when some Tommies came up. At 10.15 he was telling me about it while I cut off his boot.

They are not taking-in so fast to-night over the road and we hope to work it through the night with a single Theatre team. They are very tired.

We had butter for tea to-day.

One mother wrote thanking me for writing to tell her about her son, but 'it would relieve the news somewhat if she knew which son it was, as she has three sons in France!'

A German Sergeant-Major died in my Moribunds Tent to-day. Some of the officers hadn't had their clothes or boots off for eight days. I find it bliss to have mine off after only 40 hours.

Two given-up boys whom no effort of yesterday or last night would revive in the Moribund Tent, seemed to me not hopeless this morning, and after more resuscitation they are now both comfortably bedded in one of the Acute Surgicals, each with a leg off and a fair chance of recovery. The others, with torn kidneys and spleens and brains, are no good, I'm afraid. The people who have been coming in all day are the left-outs in German dug-outs, since Monday, starved, cold, and by some miracle still alive, but not much more. This last 300 has taken 16 hours to come in, so the lull is beginning and probably the C.C.S. over the road will be taking-in all to-night and the other all to-morrow, instead of all of us filling up every three hours or so. It is piercingly cold again and looks like rain.

Thursday, April 26th, 10.30 p.m. No take-in and no evac. to-day: just slogging along with the remains. My two resuscitated boys in the Moribund Ward are all right and we've got two more to-day who were pulseless, now operated on and bedded; one, a gas gangrene, is having the new Flavine treatment and stays with me, but he's going to do all right.

The officer boy with the fractured spine isn't going to die yet; though the C.O. and Sir A. B. gave him 24 hours days ago; I got the Colonel to put him on the Evacuation list to-night to give him a chance to get X-rayed at the Base and perhaps recover.

Icy cold wind all day. We shall be due to take-in to-morrow morning, the first that come back from Over the Top.

Friday, 4 p.m., April 27th. The Attack came off all right, but 'he' (as the enemy is frequently called in these parts and in the communiqués) didn't wait for it! He has gone back another five miles, so all those hundreds of our casualties are saved and there's nothing doing. Isn't it splendid? And it shows they didn't think it good enough to get another hammering like Monday's and Tuesday's.*

My dear little resuscitated Suffolk boy got G.G. above the amputation and died this afternoon, and the other boy has had to have the other leg off now. The gas gangrene boy left is going wrong to-day, but the moribund head cases are smoking pipes and eating eggs and bread and butter! The kidney man is being dressed with Flavine and has had a leg off and is nearly convalescent!

In one ward there's hardly a man with two legs; and when one Boche made a noise when he was being dressed, there was a chorus of encouragement from the British beds: 'Hold on, Fritz, soon be done – be all right in a minute,' regardless of any difficulty in language! A head man who hadn't spoken since his operation two days ago began to look as if he was taking notice, and when asked how he was, said gaily, 'Tres Beans, I'd like a smoke.' That is the British Army rendering of a useful French phrase.

The 6 ft. boy wounded in the spine with total paralysis below the chest was safely taken to the train this evening. When I told him he was going down to be X-rayed, he said, 'That'll be better than lying on my back all my life,' and his eyes filled with tears. All these days he has never said one word of complaint or self-pity, though he knew his probable fate from the second day.

An Orderly who has been running the Marquee of 50 stretcher-cases without a Sister, has gone sick with trench fever. He leads one of the

---

* See Ludendorff's remarks in 1919.

most Christlike lives I've ever seen; there is no other word for his selfless devotion, though he is comic beyond words in speech and appearance!

Saturday night. I didn't mean to write tonight as 14 hours a day every day with these wonderful smashed-up soldiers doesn't leave much over at bed-time. They make you feel proud of belonging to the same race. There's a handsome young Scot with one leg off who asked me last night to take his socks off. I took the one off. 'Have you taken the other off, too?' he asked. 'Yes,' I said guiltily; 'they're both off now.' Next day Sister told me he knew his leg was off, but he didn't. To-night he said, 'My feet are hot.' 'Yes,' I said, 'especially the one you haven't got, I suppose?' (It always is the one they feel most.) 'Have I got but one?' he said. I was covered with confusion. 'Ah, well, I see by what ye say I've got but one, but it's no matter. I feel a pain in them whiles, but I can smile between the pains. I've got two daughters and a wee son I've never seen. I know what I'll do when I do see them. Don't I know!' (And I'm afraid he's in for gas gangrene and may not see them.). Then he looked round the ward at all the stumps and splints and heads and said, 'Seems a pity nearly everyone has got to get like this before Peace is declared.'

Two more of my moribunds are marked for Evacuation. The little gas gangrene boy hangs on, but that's all. A very dear polite old South African regular, all through that and all through this, who was longing to see his wife and children, died of gas gangrene to-day. What a life it is!

Monday, April 30th. We have had a whole week without snow or rain – lots of sun and blue sky. I went for a ramble after tea yesterday to a darling narrow wood with a stream at the bottom between two hills, a quarter of an hour's walk from here. Two sets of shy, polite boys thrust their bunches of cowslips and daffodils into my hand with, 'Would these be any use to you?' Also banks of small blue periwinkles like ours, and flowering palm; absolutely no leaves yet anywhere and it's May Day to-morrow.

My two remaining so-called moribunds went gaily on the train this morning – the blind man murmuring, 'Get a move on – I want the train for Blighty – Get a move on,' at intervals. Very few left in the wards to-day, but what there are, nearly all tragedies.

General Babtie, V.C., came round to-day with the D.M.S. He was very much disturbed at the Sisters doing such long hours and asked how many I had, and did they have to get up very early, and could they rest after a rush, etc., etc., till at last I said, 'They're quite happy really, Sir,' and he suddenly laughed and said, 'I'm so glad. Good-bye,' and went away.

A frightful thing happened this evening. You know every morning, mid-day and evening our sky is thick with machines going out and coming back to their meals across the road. At ten minutes past seven a Reconnaissance Biplane crashed into a single-seater Fighting Machine 3,000 feet up. Captain B. and the Colonel saw the R. Biplane drop like a stone with planes hanging, and the other came wobbling slowly down and then crashed. They tore across the field and helped to drag the two crushed heaps from under the first machine, both instantaneously killed, now in our mortuary. The boy in the Fighting Machine did some marvellous evolutions to avoid the collision, and then with one control and a broken plane planed down till he found himself crashing, and then leaned his head and shoulders clear, and managed to get off with only both legs broken. He was brought in a minute afterwards. 'Did you see my little effort?' he said. 'It's only both my legs. I brought my 4th Boche down to-day.' When we had him in the Preparation Ward he had a cigarette. 'Don't you worry about Nervous Shock and all that,' he said. 'I've dropped 10,000 feet to avoid a Hun and then righted myself before now. And I love anæsthetics, had dozens for appendicitis and little things like that!' They've done the operation; both simple fractures by some unique chance; (the engine sat on his legs) and he will be all right; one is in a Thomas and the other in a back splint. It was the fault of the other machine. This boy is a Flight Commander, an M.C. with a bar.

May Day and a dazzling day and very little doing in this Hospital. G. and I celebrated the occasion by going to the woods in the morning, starry with anemones and never a leaf to be seen, but blue sky and fresh breezes and clear sunshine. It is all a tremendous help, physically and psychically.

The Flying boy is better and is taking his broken legs down on the train to-morrow. When I told him how good his pulse was when he was brought in, he said, 'So it was when I got to the ground. I felt it – it was about 84!' His friends say he is unkillable, and has 9 lives over and over. Time he left off playing with them, I think.

My boy with both legs off is safe now and going down, too, and a man dragged back from an imminent death from femoral hæmorrhage has begun to live again. (Died later.)

Some of us and Capt. B. have been having a bad fit of pessimism over them all lately, wondering what is the good of operations, nursing, rescues, or anything, when so many have died in the end. But even a few miraculous recoveries buck one up to begin again.

A Suffolk farmer boy is dying to-night, who has hung on for a week; everyone is so fond of the child. (Died on Wednesday.) Another fine-looking boy is on the extreme edge of dying of shock and internal hæmorrhage. Every conceivable thing has been done that can be done, and I think there is 'the half of a broken hope,' but he has not yet a glimmer of pulse. (Died same night.)

I had a letter from a brave Glasgow mother, full of gratitude and incoherence, ending up, 'And don't forget to let us know how you are keeping.'

Wednesday, May 2nd, and another dazzling day. Hospital almost empty to-night after Evacuation, ready for a Strafe.

The Flying boy went down on the train with pink ribbons off a chocolate box on his broken legs, in great form. He is a glorious creature, very good-looking and always a twinkle over everything. 'Yes, they ache like sin: flying is an overrated pastime in War Time.'

Thursday, May 3rd, 11.30 p.m. They went over the top this morning and have been pouring in all day. We are now taking in for the third time – to-day. The fine weather makes a huge difference to the conditions of the whole thing. Their accounts vary as to success or failure, but Active Operations on a large scale generally include both.

Saturday, May 5th. After tropical heat all day (lovely, but hard to work in) the weather has changed and a cold dusty gale is blowing and sky overcast. A boy was brought in to-day with his leg blown off – 'I wonder what Mother'll say when she hears of this,' he said. 'It's only a little thing really, losing your leg, in this War, but she won't think that.'

A poor old Boche with the lower part of his face missing came in this morning (no tongue or lower jaw); dying of thirst apparently; he nearly went mad with joy when I succeeded in getting two feeders of water and brandy down him, by means of india-rubber tubing on the spout, but he died later.

Tuesday, May 8th. We have had a comparatively slack time the last two days, very little doing. Lots of noise but few casualties. We have begun taking Marquees down with a view to moving. It will be a big business, but we shall be expert at it by the time we've finished.

Fritz is putting up a very big resistance both with Cannon Fodder and big guns, but we are out to keep him busy. The men coming in now are quite cheery about things again.

I am engaged in a losing battle with gas gangrene again – in the Moribund Tent – a particularly fine man, too. I believe the general toxæmia begins long before they get their legs off, because no amount of elaboration in the latest known treatment seems to stop it, unless it is only in the superficial tissues, and then you can floor it. But it is horribly disheartening. When they have been lying out long, G.G. is practically a certainty.

We have had a good healthy rain and some leaves are beginning to show at last.

Wednesday, May 9th (of 1915 black and brave memory). And what do you think we've been busy over this morning, 9th of May, 1917? A large and festive Picnic in the woods, far removed from gas gangrene and amputations. We bought some chocolate biscuits and some sawdusty cakes and some potted meat at the Canteen, and asked the C.O. and six M.O.'s and seven of us; we had an Ambulance and two batmen to bring the tea in urns to my chosen spot – on a slope of the wood, above the babbling brook, literally carpeted with periwinkles, oxlips and anemones. It was a great success and we are going to have it again between the next two take-ins for the seven M.O.'s and seven Sisters who couldn't come to-day.

We had a bowl of brilliant blue periwinkles in the middle of the table-cloth and had a topping good tea. When we got back at 5.30 we found the Divisional Band about to play outside the Y.M.C.A. hut, close to my Moribund Tent; we took the places of the Sisters who'd been minding the Wards and they went to hear the Band. My dear man was dying. At the exact moment that he took his first breath in Heaven at 7.30, the Band was playing 'There will be such wonderful things to do' to that particularly plaintive little tune. His only attempt at a complaint was to say once when I said good-night to him, 'I wish you were going to stay with me all night.' And if he wanted me when I happened to be busy with the dotty head boy on the floor, he'd say: 'All right. I'll wait – she's busy.' He never knew he would die; this morning, when he was having his hair brushed, he said, 'I'll have to have a servant when I get back home.' Capt. B. came in just as we were putting the Flag over him. We had both hoped to keep him.

To-morrow the 3rd Army Commander is coming to inspect the C.C.S.'s, Allenby of the Cavalry of the Contemptible Little Army.

Thursday, May 10th. Sir Anthony Bowlby has been pottering round to-day – he is very interesting, surgically, to listen to. Sir Wilmot Herringham came later to see the charts – and in between came Allenby. We and all the M.O.'s were at our posts in clean aprons and Sam Browne belts. I had to meet him and the Colonel and General Murray Irwin and the A.D.C., and go round with them. He asked lots of questions about how the men stood shock in that arctic weather, and talked to some of the worst of the patients. One little boy a mass of bandages and amputations said he felt 'Champion' and a bad abdominal whispered that he felt 'Very well indeed,' both of which answers pleased him very much. He thanked us charmingly for looking after 'his Army.'

Saturday night, May 12th. We are very light in the way of work – fewer wounded, fewer operations and only about one death daily and one nightly; we don't know ourselves. And invitations are descending upon us. A.S.C. Sports to-day – eight Sisters went and the rest of us minded the Hospital. They were fetched in cars and made much of, and both entertainers and entertained seem to have been very happy. To-morrow is a Garden Party with a Band, among the apple-blossom at a Divisional Rest Station, which is a Château in a lovely orchard.

We shall have a very funny summer if we move up; push work all the time and nothing outside the Hospital for miles but shell-holes, dug-outs, old trenches, old wire, unexploded shells and bombs, blackened tree-stumps and not a leaf to shade under!

Sunday, May 13th. Had a busy day again; bad cases in all the wards. I have a German gas gangrene, a terrible chest wound, that made me more nearly sick than anything in my life before, when I was dressing him this evening. Also one of ours with fearful wounds that Captain B. wants me to put bodily into an iodine bath to-morrow, but I don't think he'll be fit for it. Captain B has great faith in what he calls my stunts in X Ward* for them to be 'returned to stock.'

Monday, May 14th. Sharp thunderstorm last night mixed with a noisy strafe. Had a rather ghastly morning with my three moribunds and then handed them over after lunch to someone else, and Sister G. and I set off in a Motor Ambulance to visit the Abdominal Centre higher up. The driver had not the dimmest notion of the name of the place or how to get there, but I headed him off from various attempts at all other points of the compass with the help of my map, and eventually we got there. It was Gommécourt over again but in newly sprung green this time. I think it made the little hilly, curly orchards and wooded villages look sadder than ever, to see the blossom among the ruins, and the man-gled woods struggling to put their green clothes on to their distorted spikes. And in that country *every* tree along *each* side of *every* road was neatly cut through about three feet from the ground, and lying by its stump. It was a weird sight. And coming back the driver lost himself, and to our joy toured us round and round the country looking for the Arras-Doullens road – so we saw enough to keep a newspaper Special Correspondent going for a week.

---

* Name of the Moribund Ward, called later the Resuscitation Ward.

The Corps Main Dressing Station, where Sister R. is, where they operate on the abdominals, was our objective, and it is close to our new site. It is a splendid little place, of marquees and baby Nissen Huts and is fitted up very well. We had tea with her, and then explored the German trenches and deep dug-outs. Just before we got there we nearly fell out of the Ambulance with excitement on seeing a tank waddling thoughtfully about wiping out wire, 20 yards from the road, and turning round to see if it had done it nicely! It was a priceless sight, half comic and half devilish.

Ficheux, the village, is a cheery collection of bricks and stones. The woody villages before that have one wall of perhaps every third house still sticking up, and skeletons of Churches. No inhabitants for miles and miles.

The view from the Corps Main Dressing Station, which is on high ground, is a vast desert of treeless waste, cut up by trenches and shell-holes and light railways. And just as at Barlin, we could see our own guns spitting sudden flames and the ugly burst of black H.E. over the German lines. The Sausages were hanging overhead and it felt just like this time last year.

Wednesday, May 16th. A splendid Flying boy died to-day. He was one of those people with a spring and a vitality and a laugh and a beam in his eye that takes everybody by storm. His friends loved him terribly. Half an hour before he died he laughed over the champagne, 'bubbling in my chest, you know.' Then came a bad turn and one cry of 'My God' and then unconsciousness and the end – or rather the Beginning. The Padre and I were with him. He had brought his machine in five miles with a shattered leg, afterwards amputated.

My Fritz is dying to-night. A walking German wounded prisoner came to see him yesterday. They clasped each other's hands and the first question of both was, 'Welches Regiment?' We got his address with difficulty this morning; he has a terrible wound in the chest and one arm gone; he wanted to tell us, and then cried because it was so *schwer zu sprechen*. Sister L., who has been in Austria and speaks German fluently, is going to write to his mother for me.

We had a very noisy and rather alarming afternoon. Fritz got his long-range guns on to this direction with the biggest shells I've ever heard burst; they were a few miles away, and we were thankful they were.

In a few days we may be very busy, after that is over we shall be ordered to make a start.

Fritz died this morning. His last word was '*Schlecht*' when I asked him, '*Wie geht es?*'

Sunday, 20th. They began coming in at 3 p.m. It is now 10 p.m.; they are taking in over the road and we expect to begin again about 1 a.m. Lots of Jocks this time. Just off to bed, as I am going to be called when they roll in again. This may be our last 'Take-in,' as we have already begun to pull down.

Monday, 21st. They didn't roll in again till 4 a.m. and lasted till 4 p.m. We had 24 walking, slightly wounded German prisoners, and they looked the worst set of scarecrows I've seen yet.

Friday, May 25th. Dazzling weather and very little doing. The woods are full of bluebells and bugloss and stitchwort, and the fields of buttercups and sorrel. Our wards and own huts and tents are a mass of spring.

There is a boy in with his spinal cord exposed, lying on his face, who was wounded on Sunday and not picked up till Thursday morning. He was in a shell-hole crying to four other wounded in it all the first night. They took no notice and in the morning he saw they had all died.

We've had a lot of Germans lately. I had three in X Ward with gas gangrene and they all got better and have gone down the line.

Monday, May 28th. Still taking in slowly. We have five badly wounded officers. One is coming round now but not quite out of the wood. He has lost one eye and one leg, besides other severe wounds. The –th F.A. invited us yesterday to their place up the line to tea and music. They sent a car for us, three Night Sisters and three Day. It was a Divisional Rest Station, where they keep men and officers up to three weeks to fit them for duty, instead of sending them down the line. It was in some lovely orchards, small brown huts and tents among the trees. The men were all laid out in rows out of doors on wire-netting beds everywhere, and it looked so shady and English and peaceful. Their own Band played and they had an Open-Air Concert with some really clever sketches and things. Some other Sisters were there, too. There were little afternoon tea-tables dotted about, and it was beautifully done. They made splendid hosts, never let anyone feel dull for a moment, and they thanked us earnestly for coming; we tried to put it the other way.

Tuesday, May 29th. We are Taking in, Evacuating, Detaining and Packing up all at once. The C.O. had another message to-day to 'prepare to move to another Area at short notice' and we are to send a 'Team' out of our permanent staff on in advance. He has told me in a whisper where it probably is; of course it is just the exact part I've always longed (and in-tended!) to go to if anything was doing there.* And we shall be near enough to the line to get the men from the Dressing Stations direct, without intermediate long journeys and waits, which is what the C.C.S.'s are out to prevent nowadays.

Friday, June 1st. We are rather full just now, but shall be left with only four unfit to travel after the Evacuation this afternoon. The divine weather is the only thing that seems to matter. There are fields between woods, snowy with the hugest oxeye daisies I ever met, like a field in the Alps in June. Early mornings – high-noons – evenings – nights: all are perfect – we haven't had one death for nearly a week. The Flying officer is just hanging on, and the legs boy has turned the corner and goes on the train.

Sunday, June 3rd. The last patient cleared yesterday and there are only the huts left standing. The tents are packed and waiting by the siding. We are off to-morrow.

---

* The Ypres Sector.

127

Kate's parents Rev. Bixby Garnham Luard and Clara née Bramston. (Caroline Stevens)

The Luard family on Birch Rectory steps. (Caroline Stevens)

Kate (on the right) with her sister Lucy in 1878. (Caroline Stevens)

Kate's brothers Fred (West Indian Regiment), Hugh (Indian Medical Service) and Frank (Royal Marines). Frank was killed at Gallipoli on 13 July 1915. (Caroline Stevens)

Kate in QAIMNSR uniform at Birch Rectory (Caroline Stevens)

Envelope addressed to Kate at No.4 Field Ambulance. (Essex Record Office)

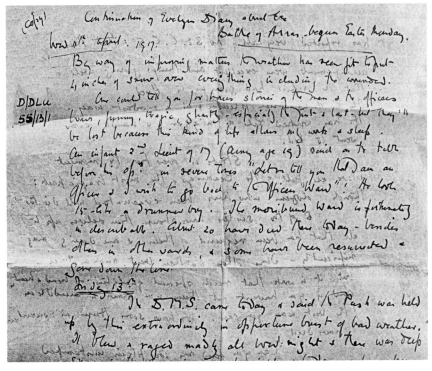

Letter from Kate – Wednesday 11 April, 1917, during the Battle of Arras. (Essex Record Office)

Advanced Dressing Station in a field. The wounded were brought here from the regimental aid posts, which were situated only a few metres behind the front line, often in a support or reserve trench. (Wellcome Library, London)

Gassed: This scene is the aftermath of a mustard attack on the Western Front in August 1918 as witnessed by the artist. The tent ropes of a dressing station are visible on the right of the composition. Oil painting by John Singer Sargent (RA) 1918. (© IWM ART 1460)

'The Work of the RAMC on the Battlefields'. RAMC orderlies are depicted gathering the wounded from a trench after a severe engagement. In a grey and brown wash, by Fortunio Matania. (Wellcome Library, London)

Stretcher cases being carried on a light railway near Feuchy on 29 April 1917, during the Battle of Arras. These French narrow gauge railway systems were easily assembled and normally used to transport munitions and artillery. (The RAMC Muniment Collection, in the care of the Wellcome Library, London)

'Transport of the Wounded', oil painting by Ugo Matania. (Wellcome Library, London)

Wounded soldiers are gathered on their stretchers beside the huts, tents and marquees of a casualty clearing station awaiting medical care. (Archives and Library of the Army Medical Services Museum, Aldershot)

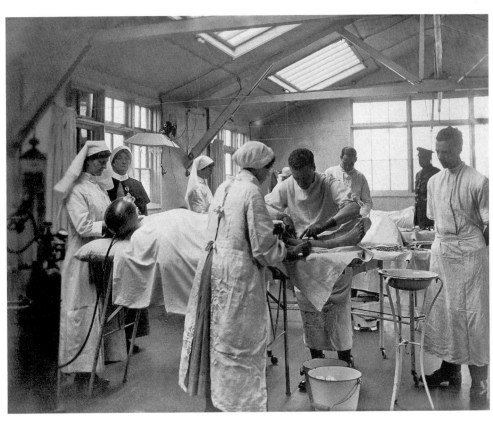

British Army operating theatre at Wimereux, near Boulogne. (Wellcome Library, London)

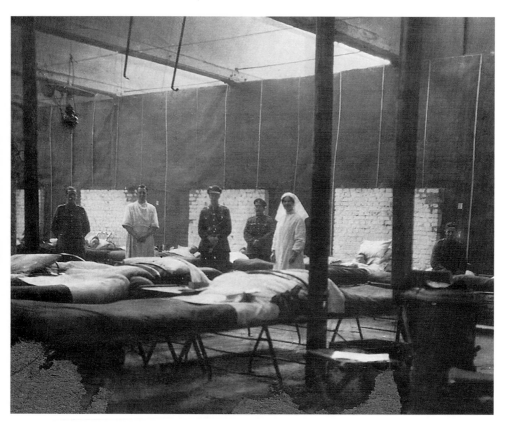

This shows the basic conditions of many improvised CCSs, and in this photograph the trestles on which beds were set. (Sue Light)

Tented nurses' quarters at a casualty clearing station. (Sue Light)

'Wounded at a Casualty Clearing Station'. A wash drawing by D Lindsay, *c.* 1917, from
Medicine and Surgery in the Great War 1914–1918. (Wellcome Library, London)

No. 64 Casualty Clearing Station, Mendinghem, July 1917. (Archives and Library of the
Army Medical Services Museum, Aldershot)

GRAND CONCERT

AND

PANTOMIME

PROGRAMME

GIVEN BY THE

Royal Army Medical Corps

in this town

FRANCE   NEW YEARS EVE 1915.

Come early. — Take your chance. — No seats booked.

DOORS OPEN, **5.30** P. M. — COMMENCE **6** P. M.

Stretcher Bearers

& Ambulances at 8 p. m.

RAMC Grand Concert and Pantomime Programme. (Essex Record Office)

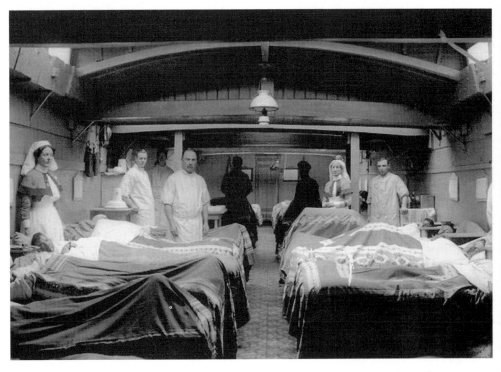

Many wounded were transported from casualty clearing stations by water in hospital barges. Although slow, the journey was smooth and the time allowed the wounded to recuperate. (Sue Light)

Medical orderlies watched by two QAIMNSR nurses lift a stretcher-case, wounded in the capture of Hill 70 (Lens), onto a train departing from a casualty clearing station during the Battle of Passchendaele in August 1917. Photograph by Lt W Rider-Rider (Canadian).
(© Imperial War Museum CO 1801)

Casualty Form—Active Service.

Army Form B. 103.

Kate Evelyn.

Regiment or Corps _QAIMNSR_

Regimental No. _Sister_ Rank _A/N/S/_ Name _Luard K.E._

Enlisted (a)_____ Terms of Service (a)_____ Service reckons from (a)_____

Date of promotion to present rank }_____ Date of appointment to lance rank }_____ Numerical position _Awarded Bar to RRC_

Extended_____ Re-engaged_____ Qualification (b) _Supp to LG No 30111 43 4/16_

Report		Record of promotions, reductions, transfers, casualties, etc., during active service, as reported on Army Form B. 213, Army Form A. 36, or in other official documents. The authority to be quoted in each case.	Place	Date	Remarks taken from Army Form B. 213, Army Form A. 36, or other official documents.
Date	From whom received				
		So 16 Gen HP.		1/4 10/15	
		" 6 C.C.S.			
		" UK - leave		2/5 - 9/5	B213 of 4 5/16
		" Leave 28/10 - 10/11/16			B158 31/10/16
		" 32 CCS		11/11/16	B213 4 11/11/16
		" Leave 8/2 - 16 2/17			
		" 12 Sty HP		6 6/17	B213 16 6/17
		" 10 Sty HP (?)			B158 15 7/17
		" 32 CCS.		25 7/17	B213 29/7/17
		" 37. CCS.			B158 of 30/10/17

Casualty Form – Active Service for K.E. Luard. (Sue Light)

5

THIRD BATTLE OF YPRES

JULY 23RD TO SEPTEMBER 4TH 1917
WITH THE 5TH ARMY (SIR HUBERT GOUGH)

LETTERS FROM BRANDHOEK

July 23rd. St. Omer. Orders came yesterday for us to move and we are just off.

July 25th. Brandhoek. We got to Railhead (Poperinghe) about 5 p.m. The station was busy being shelled. Everyone was turned out of the train about 1½ miles before the station, and we sat on our baggage there for two hours while the R.T.O. telephoned to the D.M.S that we'd arrived, and at last he sent five Ambulances; there were 10 of us, so we all rode outside. The R.T.O. had been shelled-out and had a temporary Hut on the line there. He thought we wouldn't be allowed up any farther, but here we are. We got a rousing welcome from the C.O. and Capt. B. and everybody. Ten other Sisters had arrived to-day, which makes twenty, and six more come to-morrow. I shall probably have 30. There are about 30 Medical Officers, including some of the pick of the B.E.F.; we are for Abdomens and Chests – 8 Theatre Teams.

Our Quarters are very nice: bell-tents (I have my Armstrong Canvas Hut) and two big Marquees for a Mess Tent. I am having a Home Sister so that I shan't have to be bothered with the Mess or the Quarters, and four men. We dined in the Officers' Mess to-night, as we had no rations till to-morrow. It is a brilliant starlight night and the battle line, four miles away, is blazing with every conceivable firework and the noise is *terrific*. Is anyone going to sleep?

The C.O. has been explaining to the new Sisters (some from the Base and some newly out from home!) which noise means a burst beyond you, and which means a burst on your right or left, and that the one that does you in you don't hear! We've been dished out with gas helmets and tin-hats.

Friday, July 27th. Yesterday everything went so well one knew it couldn't last. The hospital had only been pitched since last Saturday and it was already splendid.

This venture so close to the Line is of the nature of an experiment in life-saving, to reduce the mortality rate from abdominal and chest wounds. Their chance of life depends (except where the injuries are such as to be beyond any hope of recovery) mainly on the length of time between the injury and the operation. As modern Field Surgery can now be carried out under conditions of perfect asepsis, the sooner the infection always introduced into every wound with the missile is dealt with, and the internal repairs carried out, the more chance the soldier has of life. Hence this Advanced Abdominal Centre, to which all abdominal and chest wounds are taken from a large attacking area, instead of going on with the rest to the C.C.S.'s six miles back.

We are entirely under Canvas, with huge marquees for Wards, except the Theatre which is a long hut. The Wards are both sides of a long, wide central walk of duckboards. There was a great deal of detail left for me to arrange of course, and we made good progress yesterday. It was also a dazzling day, but incredibly noisy. All the personnel were so pleased to have the Sisters back that everyone's face was a huge beam. Our Mess is shaping into a most comfortable place under the able hands of my new Home Sister, late Home Sister from Reading Hospital, food sketchy and plain at present, solely rations; a nice fat corporal cook.

After tea there was a certain liveliness coming over from Fritz, but nothing into the Camp; then came an order from the C.O. that the road was Out of Bounds – that tin-hats were to be handy; and that if he blew three whistles in the night everyone was to get up and go to an appointed spot. It was a lovely clear evening, and it was very interesting to watch Fritz's efforts to bring down the nearest of the eighteen sausage Observation Balloons, hanging over our heads as far as one could see on both sides of us. Two more Sisters turned up after dinner, making 29. General S. came in the morning and asked for me, and was very pleased with everything. Sir Anthony Bowlby turned up later. 'How d'you like the site this time? Front pew, what? front row dress-circle.' It is his pet scheme getting the operations done up here within an hour or two of getting hit, instead of farther back or at the Base. That is why our 30 Medical Officers include the largest collection of F.R.C.S.'s ever collected at any Hospital in France before, at Base or Front, twelve operating Surgeons with Theatre Teams working on eight tables continuously for the 24 hours, with 16 hours on and 8 off. They have sent some very good Sisters up – all as keen as ninepence.

And then the Blow fell – not the shell but the sentence: Army H.Q. couldn't sleep in its bed for thinking of the 29 precious Sisters exposed to the enemy fire up at Brandhoek, and sent an order at 10 p.m. that all the Sisters were to go off to two Canadian C.C.S.'s about 6 miles back. Utter consternation in both Messes. We packed up and waited for the 14 Cars, and with a great send-off departed, skirting Poperinghe by the Switch Road somewhere about midnight. Eventually we got to bed between 1 and 2 a.m. in a new Nissen Hut, a Ward just opened. The pretty Canadians were full of concern and hospitality for the poor refugees, but we felt most awful frauds.

The C.O. is going to communicate with me to-day about the next proceedings. I think we shall be back in a day or two.

Same day, 9 p.m. The C.O. sent for some of us this morning and we went back to go on getting the Hospital ready. They'd had the quietest night they'd had since they got there! We got back to our Canadian C.C.S. to dinner. All that we see on the way there and back mustn't be written about. As we were coming back through Poperinghe, which is like nothing I've ever seen, though I've seen some crowds of troops before in the same circumstances, a huge shell crashed into the roofs immediately on our right, close to Talbot House; the crowd swayed like bending corn and then continued its conversation and walking. I am sitting in a corn-field a little way from the Hospital to get a few minutes' solitude and to read *The Times* of yesterday, and the shells meant for Poperinghe are squealing over and dropping a few fields away. Flanders is populated by millions of mosquitoes, which are a fearful nuisance.

My Sisters are being very nice. They are now 31. The Theatre Sister and another to help are going in again with me to-morrow. The Colonel thinks we shall all be sent back to him all right when the work begins – so do I.

Saturday morning. Fritz turned up late last night overhead, and dropped a few bombs some way off. Our searchlights turned on and Archie chased him off.

Monday, July 30th, midnight. Brandhoek. Cars came for us at 5 p.m. and here we are. By the time you get this it will be history for better or for worse.* By 6 a.m. our part will have begun and everything is organised and ready up to the brim. That we have 15 Theatre Sisters tells its own tale. We have 33 Sisters altogether, and they are all tucked into their bell-tents with hankies tied on to the ropes of the first ones to be called when the first case comes in.

We have had a Gas Drill to-night from an Irish M.O. from up the Line. It is a beastly job and rather complicated, and has to be done in six seconds to be any good; we all take about six minutes! The signal to put on box helmets is the C.O.'s whistle and a loud banging on the Hospital gong (an iron rail hanging on a sort of gallows). The din is marvellous. Some Grandmothers (15-inch guns) on each side of us are splitting the air and rocking the huts, and everything except the Field Gun drumfire, which hasn't begun yet, is joining in. Fritz is sending his over too, with an ugly whang. The illumination is brighter than

---

* It was far worse; 3rd Battle of Ypres and Passchendaele.

any lightning: dazzling and beautiful. Their new blinding gas is known as mustard-oil gas; it burns your eyes – sounds jolly, doesn't it? – and comes over in shells. I wonder how many hundreds or thousands have got only four more hours to live, and know it?

The first day we came up here we met some prisoners just taken, being marched down. I hope there'll be hundreds to-morrow. Good night.

4.15 a.m. The All-together began at 5 minutes to 4. We crept out on to the duckboards and saw. It was more wonderful and stupendous than horrible. There was the glare before day-light of the searchlights, star-shells and gun-flashes, and the cracking, splitting and thundering of the guns of all calibres at once. The S.O.S. call has come for three of the Sisters, but I think no cases are here yet. No mines have gone up yet.

6.30 a.m. We have just begun taking in the first cases. An officer died soon after admission, between 4 and 5 a.m.

The Air people began streaming over at daylight adding their whir-ring and droning to the din. The mines have been going off since 5 like earthquakes. Lots of high explosive has been coming over, but nothing so far into this Camp. The uproar is almost stupefying. I'm going now to see how they are getting on in the Preparation and Resuscitation Hut.

Same day, 11 p.m. We have been working in the roar of battle every minute since I last wrote, and it has been rather too exciting. I've not had time to hear any details from any of our poor abdominals, but the news has been good till this evening: thousands of prisoners – and Ypres choked with captured guns and ammunition, and some few miles (?) of advance. This evening they tell of heavy counter-attacks and some of our advance lost. He is not retreating because he wants to, but is putting up a tremendous fight.[**] One Gunner Sergeant was pleased that he got his wound while dragging his guns over No Man's Land in broad daylight. We put up a terrific drumfire again this evening, and our monsters at our elbow are cracking away now at a frightful pace. You get tired of being violently jogged by the concussion every few seconds.

We have a lot of Germans in – all abdominals. Everything has been going at full pitch – with the 12 Teams in the Theatre only break-

---

[**] See Ludendorff's remarks in 1919.

ing off for hasty meals – the Dressing Hut, the Preparation Ward and Resuscitation and the four huge Acute Wards, which fill up from the Theatre; the Officers' Ward, the Moribund and the German Ward. That, and the Preparation and the Theatre are the worst places. Soon after 10 o'clock this morning he began putting over high explosive. Everyone had to put on tin-hats and carry on. He kept it up all the morning with vicious screams. They burst on two sides of us, not 50 yards away – no direct hits on to us but streams of shrapnel, which were quite hot when you picked them up. No one was hurt, which was lucky, and they came everywhere, even through our Canvas Huts in our quarters. Luckily we were so frantically busy that it was easier to pay less attention to it. The patients who were well enough to realise that they were not still on the field called it 'a dirty trick.' They were not gas shells, thank Heaven. Bursting shells are an ugly sight – black or yellow smoke and streams of jagged steel flying violently in all directions.

It doesn't look as if we should ever sleep again. Apparently gunners and soldiers never do: it is difficult to see who can in this area. Our monster shells cutting through the air are the dizzy limit. There was a moment in the morning when the C.O. and I thought he meant to do us in, but they stopped about one o'clock. And there was a moment about tea-time when I thought the work was going to heap up and get the upper hand of us, but the C.O. stopped admitting for an hour and sent them on lower down, which saved the situation. It is going to be a tight fit. Of course, a good many die, but a great many seem to be going to do. We get them one hour after injury, which is our *raison d'être* for being here.

General S., the Director of Medical Services 5th Army, came round about 2 p.m. I took him round and he signed chits for lots of things we want from the B.R.C.S. He was annoyed about the shelling.

It is pouring with rain, alas, and they are brought in sopping.

Wednesday, August 1st. Post just going. Soaking hopeless rain, holding up the advance; the worst luck that could happen. Poor Sir Douglas Haig. It has been so every time. Everything is a swamp and a pond, and tents leaking and dropping. Water in some of the Wards is half-way up the legs of the beds.

I got to bed between 2 and 7 and slept like blazes. This morning they really don't look so bad – for abdominals. Only 23 deaths. Some are sitting up smoking cigarettes and sorting their treasure bags. The noise has almost ceased, so those exhausted sopping gunners must be getting a sleep.

11.30 p.m. Just finished my last round. Soaking rain all day still going on, complete hold-up of British Army. Absolute silence of our guns and only an occasional reminder from Fritz. Pétain and his crack Corps have done very well. Our success has varied; one Corps went too far and got caught in the back. The abdominals coming in are very bad to-day – both Boche and British. The work thickens as the wards fill up and new wards have to be opened. We are to take Chests and Femurs too, as soon as No. 44 and the Austr. C.C.S.'s open, which are alongside getting ready. The staffing of the wards for Night Duty both of Sisters and Orderlies is the problem, even with my 33. Some of these are first-class. It is getting very ghastly; the men all look so appalling when they are brought in, and so many die. I don't see how the 'break-the-news' letters are going to be written, because the moment for sitting down literally never comes from 7 a.m. to midnight. It is a good thing we are all fresh and fit.

Wednesday, August 1st, 12.15 midnight. It has been a pretty frightful day – 44 funerals yesterday and about as many to-day. After 24 hours of peace the battle seems to have broken out again; the din is so terrific I can hardly sit in this chair. Our monsters are thundering over our heads from the giants behind us, and some of theirs are coming this way. Must go and look round.

Thursday, August 2nd, 11.45 p.m. The uproar went on all night – no one slept much. It made one realise how far up we are to have streams of shells crossing over our heads. The rain continues – all night and all day since the Push began on Monday. Can God be on our side, everyone is asking – when His (alleged!) Department always intervenes in favour of the enemy at all our best moments.

The men are brought in with mud over their eyes and mouths, and 126 have died in 3½ days. In spite of the awful conditions, a remarkable percentage, especially of the first ones who came in early and dry, are doing brilliantly.

The 5th Army Commander, Gen. Sir Hubert Gough, and some of his Staff paid us a long visit this morning. He was taken round everything by the Colonel and Capt. B. and me, and was very charming. The weather was doing its worst and he congratulated us on carrying on on such a scale in such difficult circumstances. The Advanced Abdominal Centre Scheme is on its trial and they were all agreed that the results fully justified the plan.* He was awfully nice to everybody, and most interested, and did a lot of the usual thanking for the Sisters' work. We stood in the rain and mud with streams trickling off our Brass Hats and Sou'westers down our backs, and he asked anxiously how we stuck it all, and I assured him we were all right. The Colonel told him about the shelling and said the Sisters enjoyed it! (Glad he thought so!) He sent a special message to me afterwards, through the Colonel.

Then the D.M.S. came all round (I didn't happen to see him) and was very pleased with the results. He has never been known to praise or thank anybody, but he had his appreciation and thanks to all ranks for 'very good work under trying conditions' put in Orders to-night. So we are all walking about with swelled heads. They were all immensely struck by the uncomplaining fortitude of the men. Gough talked like a father to them.

One boy of 18 said, 'Will you write to Mother? Give her my love. Say I'm all right; she's an invalid – mind you write her a comfortin' letter.' An oldish man wanted to be lifted up in the bed: when we'd done it, he murmured, 'What would we do without women in the world!' And they don't expect to find women up here.

Yesterday morning Capt. C., V.C. and Bar, D.S.O., M.C., R.A.M.C., was brought in – badly hit in the tummy and arm and had been going about for two days with a scalp wound till he got this. Half the Regiment have been to see him – he is loved by everybody. He was quickly X-rayed, operated on, shrapnel found, holes sewn up, salined and put to bed. He is just on the borderland still; better this afternoon and

---

* This opinion was somewhat modified later.

perhaps going to do, but not so well to-night. He tries hard to live; he was going to be married.

Sunday, August 5th, 11.30 p.m. Capt. C. died yesterday; four of us went to his funeral to-day; and a lot of the M.O.'s; two of them wheeled the stretcher and lowered him. His horse was led in front and then the pipers and masses of kilted officers followed. Our Padre with his one arm, Father E. H., C.R., looked like a Prophet towering over everybody and saying it all without book. After the Blessing one Piper came to the graveside (which was a large pit full of dead soldiers sewn up in canvas) and played a lament. Then his Colonel, who particularly loved him, stood and saluted him in his grave. It was fine, but horribly choky.

The weather has cleared and it has been hot and the ground is drying up a bit. They are going over the top to-morrow and we burst into a very 'useful' bombardment this evening to prepare their way. We are so much in the thick of War up here that no one talks or thinks of anything else on this earth. And how can you with 'Lizzie' splitting her jaws, shells screaming and bursting and bombs dropping. The last are much the worst. He dropped five at dinner-time about 70 yards away, and came over with some more about 10.30 to-night and some more later. There's no sort of cover anywhere and it is purely beastly. Shelling is nothing to it. The Sisters are extraordinarily good in it. Two new South African Sisters joined to-night – in the middle of the din.

The Medical Officers from up the Line who are attached here now are very horrified at our being up here, but I don't think any of the Sisters would go if they were asked to, now we've got the patients. No one sleeps much – either Night or Day Staff, and that will show before long. I'm finding it rather a job to think and remember things, and when you get to a certain stage of brain-fag you can't always see what matters and what doesn't.

We shall be busy to-morrow, so I'll have a shot at going to bed.

12 p.m., Monday, August 6th. Just got to bed after a topping hot bath and the Night Sister has brought me a cup of soup from the Night Staff meal. We have a man on in our cook-house all night. It has been a very quiet day after all – the quietest we've had: very few coming in and a nice lot of recoveries evacuated by Ambulance to the nearest Train 5 miles back, including one hero whose inside was dragged up by a bit of shell into his pericardium (the covering of his heart), into which organ the bit of shell disappeared. The surgeon followed it up three inches with his finger and then thought he'd better knock off and sew up. The man went on the Train to-day sitting up and smoking, with the hole and the shrapnel still reposing neatly in his heart!

We had some more bombs in the night and some shells this morning, and since then nothing – which is a great rest. Yesterday the D.M.S. was here and I put my case about the shortage of nursing orderlies. He said no reinforcements existed, but to-day 24 new ones arrived (lent to us) and I have posted 10 on Night and 14 on Day, and we are in clover. The posting of 10 Sisters from the Australians and 10 from No. 44 C.C.S. (both here and neither working yet nor likely to) for duty here, then came through, but I managed to get the 20 reduced to 10 Australians who have now arrived. It was a business putting up 10 more. We are now 44 – the official strength of a C.C.S. is 7. I got an empty five-marquee Ward divided into cubicles with tent walls and they think it's lovely, and have a batman to look after them. It makes a big Mess at meal times for the Home Sister. But it's splendid having two Sisters in each heavy ward, and enough orderlies.

Tuesday, August 7th. Had a much easier day and got to bed earlier. A big drumfire going on for the stunt that was to have been on yesterday and may be to-morrow. It is a very great relief to have the wards properly staffed for any business that may come along. The very nice Australian Sister in charge of the Australian C.C.S., which is not yet working, is getting my 209 break-the-news addresses into order for me to begin upon some day, and that since yesterday week. Does that give you some idea of what it has been like?

In its calmer moments this is an extraordinarily interesting Unit to belong to. The Senior Surgeons create a London sort of F.R.C.S. atmosphere and everyone is learning a lot. The keenness over the recoveries is intense and amounts to a deadly though friendly rivalry. They like to show one their pet cases in all the Wards and one sees a bit of every-thing. As to the Sisters, keen isn't the word, they never let one down and the feeling between Surgeons and Sisters is one of mutual co-operation and respect. The element of pettiness and gossip is practically absent, such is the influence of common interest, effort and danger. All this more than makes up for the output of work and anxiety.

The patients themselves, as always, establish their own intimate personal relation at once with us all – Sisters, Orderlies and Medical Officers – as soon as they are out of the anæsthetic. Nothing is spared to pull them through; eggs at any price, unlimited champagne, port, stout, fresh milk, chicken, porridge and everything you can't get at the Base. The Quartermaster scours the towns every day in a lorry.

I get car loads of Red Cross stuff nearly every day from the B.R.C.S. at Lillers, and Oxygen, drugs, instruments and Medical Stores pour in. In a venture like this, you've got to be thorough or not do it at all. And all this in an area where when a Sister and I went for a quarter of an hour's breather outside the Camp after dinner, down the one comparatively healthy road in a maze of camps, we had the evil screech of shells from Fritz over our heads all the time. All the officers and men you meet call out 'Good-night, Sister,' with a degree of warmth you never hear at the Base.

Friends of the Sisters come to tea every day, and brothers. I've broken out into an At Home to our Officers' Mess and any others every Sunday. In these Eve-less Edens such harmless socialities are of real value to the trench-worn officers and strung-up surgeons. So the Mess tables are taken down and the Tent drawing-room-ised with a muster of small tables and chairs and flowers and rugs and a party-tea and looks very nice.

A Jock boy lying next a young German introduced him to me with, 'This is Johnny Fritz. He'd like a fag if you've got one.' A boy called Reggie in the Moribund Ward was wailing, 'I do feel bad and no one takes no notice of me.' When I comforted him he said, 'You're the best Sister in the world – I know I'm a nuisance, but I can't help it – I've been out there so long and I'm so young – Will you give me a sleeping draught *and* a drop o' champagne to make me strong?' He had both and slept like a lamb, but he died to-day. A dear old dying soldier always would shake hands and say, 'How are you to-day?' He died last night. One boy in the Prep. Hut implored me to stay by him till he had his operation, which, for some reason, he dreaded (they seldom do mind), and he never came out of it. The ones who recover are tremendously proud of having done it, as they are always being told what marvels they are!

There is a fine broad duck-walk all down the middle of the Hospital with the Wards (huge tents) on each side, which in the evenings is a sort of Rotten Row for Surgeons and Sisters on their late round, where you compare notes and watch the barrage. The topics are exclusively abdomens, guns, Huns, shells and bombs!

'*Special Order of the Day.*'
3. 8. 17. 'The D.M.S. 5th Army wishes to place on record his high appreciation of the work done by – Casualty Clearing Station and thanks all Ranks for excellent work done under very trying circumstances.'

The simultaneous inundation of hundreds of abdominals, mud, floods, and bursting shells was what contributed to the 'trying circumstances.'

Wednesday, August 8th. The D.M.S. came to-day and told us to expect work to-morrow but the Satanic Power that presides over the weather in the War has decreed otherwise. Floods of rain dissolving the ground and a violent thunderstorm this evening must have put the lid on any sort of Attack for us.

Three men in the Dressing Hut were struck by lightning to-night, not severely fortunately. It was a cracking, spitting performance, but knowing it was lightning and not a bomb, there was no need even to jump. Officers from the line tell the grimmest tales. The conditions are appalling: the men are drowning in shell-holes and the enemy artillery are so 'active' that the dead are heaping up. It's no good worrying, nothing can be helped, and perhaps one day there will be Peace. And at least we don't only look on, but are privileged to do something to help – however little.

There is an adorable boy in the Officers' Ward getting better who rags us all and always keeps smiling. He insisted on marking me with a green ticket for Evacuation to-day. Two officers died this afternoon. I've got to bed very early to-night and Lizzie is pleased to hold her tongue, so there ought to be no noises till Fritz begins his Morning Hate in the form of gas shells over our heads – which he does every morning at day-light.

5 a.m. Just back to bed after one of our soothing incidents. Wakened at 4 by five devilish crashes on our left where they are always trying for a dump. I dashed out in my Jaeger dressing-gown and tin-hat and met the Night Family on the duckboards. The whistle had gone when his engines were heard, so they were all on the alert, and had put lights out. It was a pearly morning with a lovely sunrise over the battle line and stars and a brilliant half-moon. Had a cheery tea and no one any the worse. Our Archies banged and searchlights played and Lewis guns popped from one of ours who chased him off.

Thursday, August 9th. No. 44 C.C.S. alongside is to open to-morrow and has collected 35 Sisters and lots of Teams. The poor Australians are still working with us. They are a handsome crowd and very nice. Their Orderlies are different from ours – mostly gentleman boys in shorts and officers' ties and shirts.

It has been a fine day with lots of War in the sky. He brought down our nearest Sausage in flames this afternoon, and we've brought down a machine of his, but I didn't see that. The morning and evening H.Q. report is posted up every day outside our Orderly Room, which is very interesting. He has been shelling pretty close all day to-day; three men were brought in wounded this evening from over the way, but everything is very quiet now, 11-12 p.m., thank goodness. It really will be a rest to go to bed one day off the Alert and to sleep for many hours without a tin-hat on one side of you and a gas helmet the other. Of course one's great anxiety is anything happening in the Wards. Fortunately we are a very compact camp and everything is within reach.

There is a cheery little Military Decauville Railway for ammunition only, running immediately between our Compound and the main Duck Walk cutting our Hospital in two, and you are always having to wait to cross the rails while a series of baby trains puff through loaded to the teeth with shells, or coming back with empty cases. I've got a table made of a Red Cross box-lid nailed to the top of a 9.2 shell-case – and my letter-box is the brass case of a 4.5 Howitzer. Now No. 44 is coming in we are no longer the one and only: we are to take in alternate 50's of abdomens and compound fractured femurs.

The D.M.S. is ordering us six more Armstrong huts instead of bell-tents for our Compound, which will be an improvement in bad weather. The Engineer Officer risks his career by exceeding his instructions in trying to make us comfortable.

Friday, August 10th. He bombed about 3 a.m. and started his Morning Hate later, so it wasn't much of a night. To-day has been a dazzling day. All the Sausages hanging in the blue, and many Air flights. Archie barks alongside, and when the Gothas are overhead, Archie's bits come spattering down, but they don't do any harm.

The Attack began on the two corners of the Salient to-day – successful on one, and to be settled on the other to-night. A lot of abdominals and some femurs are still coming in. Some very dear boys have died to-day and are dying to-night (I've just finished a late round, 12 p.m.), but we've had an Evacuation by Train this afternoon – the first Train to come up past Poperinghe for over two years. They were much bucked. The officer babe went down with his puppy clasped in his arms under the blanket.

Sir Anthony Bowlby came round to-day and seemed pleased with it all. Thought they were doing well. A bashed-to-pieces Officer with both legs, both arms, face and back wounded, gassed, and nearly blind, saluted with one bandaged arm as I came up to his stretcher and said, 'I've been in the Wars.' He doesn't look as if he'd do. (Died at 8 a.m.) Good-night. Pray for Peace.

1.30 a.m. It really doesn't seem any particular use going to bed any night. He's just been over, flying impertinently low; in daylight we could have seen his moustache. I lay low till the first bomb and then dashed out in the usual tin-hat and coat, Sky ablaze with Searchlights and Archie roaring at him aiming low across us, Lewis guns popping and fearful uproar. He was chased away and some Howitzers of ours thumping near by are the only noises at present – and no harm done.

2 a.m. He came back, throwing his infernal bombs about . . . no one hit.
3.15 a.m. Back again, terrific uproar. Went to sleep about 4.30.

Saturday, August 11th, 10.15 and in bed. There is a thunderstorm on andit's pouring cats and dogs upon our Army, so possibly Fritz will stay at home to-night. He hasn't shelled to-day. We've had a very quiet day and have been able to get the wards and patients straight, quite like a Base Hospital – the Sisters say we have much nicer things for them than they are able to get at the Base. I tried to get a rest between lunch and tea but was routed out four times to settle various things. Our six new Armstrongs are being put up in place of the bell-tents.

Sunday, August 12th. It has been a fine day here. Sky fights going on all day. He brought down another of our Sausages, it burst into flames and the two observers came down in their parachutes – a nasty experience, I should think. Last night was the first peaceful night we've had. I slept like blazes all night.

Sunday is marked here, not by Church Parade, but by our At Home! It is being a great success. Visitors pour in and we entertain them in two shifts; one set of Sisters off till 5 and the other after. The tent looks awfully nice with rugs, chairs and little tables with pretty white worked cloths the Sisters produce, and party sandwiches and chocolate biscuits, etc. – I've sent an order to Wrights for cake and butter once a week.

Two long-legged Cavalry officers from Vlamertinghe come every time and burble over such possibilities so near the Line. They can't get over our being here at all and say it cheers them up just to know we're doing it '*and* in all these clean things and looking kind!' They were funny over it! The tea-tables and the party-tea, our uniforms, our work, our hospitality, our tin-hats, roaring guns and our other noises moved the biggest one to such soulful speeches I nearly laughed. 'And to think of all the beastly women at home selling flags,' he said in a pained voice.

We have a puppy and a kitten who are inseparable. They take each other for walks and rag each other all day. Some day they'll get run over by the ammunition train.

We have a lot of bad officers in – two died to-day – one was an R.A.M.C. Captain, and one a Gunner Major. A Flying boy has his right kidney smashed by a bullet first through his petrol tin and then into him. He brought his machine safely down and was operated on last night. He is doing well so far. He recognised me from No. 4 Field Ambulance at Béthune after Festubert in 1915. We are putting up a terrific barrage to-night. Good luck to it.

Monday, August 13th. Our 12 Australian Sisters and 10 Australian Orderlies rejoin their own Unit to-morrow, so I've had a lot of readjusting of the Staff to arrange. They open to-morrow and we three C.C.S.'s take in now in batches of 50 each, abdomens, chests, and femurs. Things will be happening before you get this unless the usual Weather Devil intervenes. It is a very fine night – just right for Fritz to come dancing over. We had a big Evacuation to-day – most of our pets gone down. He's doing a bit of shelling now, 10.30 p.m., not his usual time at all, but I don't think it's very close. We are doing more by a long way.

Tuesday, 14th. Lots of rain and thunderstorms again. Looks as if it was going to spoil the Show, as usual. Had a run of bad cases to-day, most of whom have died. He has been shelling a good deal all last night, and to-day. They drop about half a mile away and sometimes less.

An Irish Captain came to see me to-day to say that the 16th Divisional Boot Shop down the road would be delighted to repair our boots for nothing! He seemed anxious for the honour, and had all the usual things to say about our being up here. I invited him to tea on Sunday and also Col. W. of the H.Q. staff, who was a patient of mine at Lillers. Some Flying boys are coming too next Sunday. I've always been so unsociable everywhere else, but it is impossible here. There are no frills anywhere, and everybody is mutually friendly on the common background of mud, shells, and hard work. It is pouring cats and dogs.

Wednesday, August 15th, 11.30p.m. This has been a horrid day. He bombed a lot of men near by and all who weren't killed came to us. Some are still alive but about half died here. One of the saddest things I've ever seen is happening to-night. An officer boy is dying with his father (a Colonel) sitting holding his hand. The father happened to meet the Ambulance bringing him in, and the boy's servant stopped him and told him his son was inside. He's staying here to-night, and has just been pacing the duckboards with me, saying, 'The other boy is a darling, but this one is the apple of our eye. I knew it must happen.'

I was just going to have a hot bath when a shell screamed over and burst closer than is at all pleasant.

12 p.m. They are still canoodling over, but one learns not to take the smallest notice of them, as you can't stop them from going wherever they jolly well please, and it's going to be a lively night in any case, for to-morrow's Push.

2.45 a.m. Yes, it is.

I was having a nice funny dream when wakened by an uproar which I mistook at first for Gothas and changed out of my mosquito net into my tin-hat and tried to go to sleep again. After a bit it became clear that it was the British Army barking its way into the Thursday Attack on its most terrific scale, and what I thought was bombs cracking is Lizzie splitting her jaws and every lesser animal roaring full blast again. The stars are looking on and it is actually not raining. It deluged last night.

The Colonel's boy died at 12.30.

7 a.m., Thursday, August 16th. Bombardment still going on top-speed, bigger and longer than any in this world yet. The stream of little trains of H.E. shell passing through the last few days has not been for nothing. I couldn't tell you at the time but at the Canadian C.C.S. just before July 31st I saw a train pass through composed of 12 Tanks on special trucks with trucks behind carrying the crews, rollicking and cheering madly.

Thursday, 12.30 midnight and not sorry to be crawling to bed, as there was no sleep after the Blast began last night and we've had a mighty day to-day. The two Corps on the left of the Attack have gained their objective and done well. The Corps on the right was held up and it has got to be done again there. It's a big shove and for once it hasn't rained.

I feel dazed with going round the rows of silent or groaning wrecks and arranging for room for more in the night without opening new wards not yet equipped. Many die and their beds are filled instantly. One has got so used to their dying that it conveys no impression beyond a vague sense of medical failure. You forget entirely that they were once civilians, that they were alive and well yesterday, that they have wives and mothers and fathers and children at home; all you realise is that they are dead soldiers, and that there are thousands of others. It is all very like a battlefield. And between 10 and 11 to-night when I was writing to that boy's mother at his father's request, he dropped bombs on the Field Ambulance alongside of us, and killed an orderly and wounded others, and also on to the Officers' Mess of the Australian C.C.S. alongside of them – not three minutes from us, and killed a Medical Officer and a Corporal. Pretty beastly, isn't it? Shells are dropping about as usual – but farther off, I think.

Friday, 17th. More dying men all day. Brilliant dazzling day.

Capt. H. has gone to be O.C. Stretcher Bearers in the front line. He's already got an M.C. and will now get a funeral. The news is bad, parts of it like Gommécourt, July 1st 1916 over again. They let us through and then bobbed up behind and before us and cut us to pieces with machine-guns. Gas-shelling going on heavily too. Officers and men say it is the bloodiest of all the battles. Remnants of Divisions are coming out to-night and new ones going in. He's sure to come bombing to-night. I'm dog-tired, going to bed early.

Here he is.

Later. He came nosing round – just for fun, I suppose, as he didn't drop anything. We saw him and our shells bursting in flame points all round him – searchlights waggling, and tracer bullets from a Lewis gun near by leaving a flame track in the sky. All more pretty than sedative.

Saturday, August 18th. We had another beastly night. He played about all night till daylight. There were several of him. He went to C.C.S.'s behind us. At one he wounded three Sisters and blew their cook-boy to pieces. The Sisters went to the Base by Ambulance Train this morning. At the other he wounded six Medical Officers among other casualties. A dirty trick, because he has maps and knows which are hospitals back there.

Here we are in a continuous line of camps, batteries, dumps, etc., and he may not know. A big shell came over about 3 a.m. into the Gunners alongside of us and laid out 14 of them.

To-night we have darkened every glimmer of light everywhere. He is buzzing round already. The Sisters' quarters at the Australians and at No. 44 are sandbagged. I expect ours will be to-morrow. We have been taking in to-day but not so fast. The letters to relatives of died-of-wounds are just reaching 400 in less than three weeks. Entering them into one's book alone is more than one can make time for, but I do write to about a dozen every day or night; just going to begin now – 10 p.m. Miss McCarthy came up to-day. She was, as always, most helpful and kind. She was much distressed at the conditions and thinks we're too far up. I told her none of the Sisters want to go down. I don't think any of them would. This is the first day of no shelling, since that one in the night. Perhaps he is a bit farther off.

We've had two dazzling days, but as there is not a blade of grass or a leaf in the Camp, only duckboards, trenches and tents, you can only feel it's summer by the sky and the air.

Sunday morning. Lovely day. Early Service. A comparatively quiet night and an Evacuation.

Sunday, August 19th. It has been a peerless day, and we've had no take-in and have had time to look round a bit. I went with two Sisters to Evening Service at the Church Army Hut at the cross-roads, only standing room, all men soon going over the top. Very nice hymns. Then we went a bit up the road continuous with this, parallel to the line, all of it camps, Archies and all the various paraphernalia of War. There was an aeroplane caught in a tree and there was a model of the present offensive laid out in miniature in a field, with dolls' rails, trenches, cemeteries, farms and dug-outs – a fascinating toy.

We had a humming Pleasant Sunday Afternoon; they came early and stayed late. One Major hadn't spoken to an English woman since January! Our own Medical Officers turn up in force besides the outside Officers.

A Colonel of the Warwicks is arranging an Entertainment to-morrow in their lines, to cheer the boys up before going over the top! He asked the Brigadier if he might invite us, and was warmly supported; so the C.O. and I accepted and we go to their Camp to-morrow evening. There are to be refreshments and they are all agog to entertain us.

The mosquitoes are appalling to-night, so are the Gothas. There was a great battle on from 9-10.30. First, the wicked humming of his engines; then six bombs; then a blaze of searchlights. Our big searchlight picked him up and held him while the Lewis gun on one side of us and Archies on the other loosed off with a terrific uproar. Something got him; he was showing up like a golden butterfly; he wobbled, turned over, dropped a bit, righted himself and made feebly off in the direction of home. While this was going on, another dropped a bomb about 200 yards from our quarters – it made a red flare and heavy cloud of black smoke and knocked my photos off my shelf.

Colonel F. said to me just before they came, 'We're going to be bombed to-night.' I said, 'Yes, probably.' Then he said, 'I don't know how you women stick it – it's much worse here than in London, where you can go into your cellar.' I said, 'Well, we've got to stick it,' and he said, 'Well, I'm amazed at the level of calm of you Sisters.' I am too sometimes. They'd rather die than show any windiness, though everyone hates it. And to-day there has been shelling too – one just now. Personally, I wouldn't be anywhere else while the hospital is here, but it'll be a relief when the War's over!

Dreaming in those cornfields and woods at St. Pol in June, I used to think a lot about this Offensive, but I didn't think it would be as stiff as this. It is these fortified Pill-boxes and farms full of machine-guns that hold people up and then the Germans pour in behind and surround them. Two wounded Germans tell me their own dead are in thousands and speak bitterly of Der Kaiser Wilhelm.

A boy of ours with a fractured femur, army age 19, was really 17 and had been out 18 months!

Tuesday, August 21st. The Bombing on Sunday night was hardly over when one of our noisiest bombardments began, and lasted all night. Our

Gunners say they absolutely pulp the Germans from front line to far behind the lines.*Yesterday – another pearl of a day – they were trying to get one of our Sausages; shells whanging all day but they didn't get it. We brought an enemy aeroplane down after breakfast. Work was very quiet and we didn't take in till 6 p.m.

At 7.30 we were escorted to the Warwicks' Camp by one of their officers – about six minutes from here. We had a wonderful evening, and neither they nor we will forget it. There were about 36 officers in the Battalion and they were all ready for their job (St. Julien). The party was in their Mess Hut. A palatial supper at one end – lobster mayonnaise, fruit salad, jellies, sandwiches and champagne. Then a very good Concert with their own Band and their own star turns. The hut was decorated and lighted with candles in biscuit tin reflectors. They fell to entertaining us with unconcealed happiness and soon the room sounded like a huge dinner-party. The Sisters looked charming and enjoyed it all enormously. Some Canadian Sisters also came up in a car from Pop. A Major of another Battalion came up and told me what it means to them talking to and seeing people 'clean and fresh' after so many months cut off from their own womenkind, and 'just before we go over,' he said. There was no rollicking, but a sort of clutch of happiness that everyone could feel.

And at his usual time, about 9.30, Fritz came over. A Lewis gun 10 yards outside barked like a demon and the heavy Archies 100 yards on our other side cracked and roared and 7 bombs dropped on the Camps around. It was in a pause between songs (lights were darkened, of course, already) and the conversation never swerved, but the buzz got louder to be heard above the din.

The Hospital (Night Staff) meanwhile was coping with the killed and wounded from the 7 bombs. Some only just lived to get here, and some died here and some are in the wards. What a poisonous business it is. Most damage was done in a Labour Battalion Camp a little to the right of where we were. There's nothing in it where you are, really, as the man in the sky in the dark doesn't know where he's emptying his pockets; he's bound to get something in this area of adjacent camps.

---

* So does Ludendorff in his book in 1919.

I happened on a corpse-like child the other day being brought into the Moribund Ward to die and we got to work on resuscitation, with some success. He had been bleeding from his subclavian artery and heard them leave him for dead in his shell-hole. But he crawled out and was eventually tended in a dug-out by 'a lad what said prayers with me,' and later the hole in his chest was plugged and he reached us – what was left of him. When, after two days, he belonged to this world again, I got Capt. B. to see him, and he got Major C. to operate and tie the twisted artery which I had re-plugged – he couldn't be touched before – and cover with muscle the hole through which he was breathing, and he is now a great hero known as 'the Prince of Wales.' 'There's only me and Mother,' he says, so she will be pleased. But he is not out of the wood yet.

August 22nd, 6 p.m. This has been a very bad day. Big shells began coming over about 10 a.m. – one burst between one of our wards and the Sisters' Quarters of No. 44 C.C.S., and killed a Night Sister asleep in bed in her tent and knocked three others out with concussion and shell-shock. Another laid out the Q.M. Stores in the Australians and many more have had narrow shaves. The D.M.S. came up and was just saying he would close down No. 44 and the Australians and we would carry on with increased Staff from the other two, when two more came crashing down. The Q.M.G. (Army H.Q.) was there too and instantly said all must clear, patients and personnel. The patients have now gone and we are packing up for St. Omer to-night. I shall apply for leave when I get there.

Thursday, August 23rd. No. 10 Sta. St. Omer. I'm afraid you'll be very disappointed, but we are to re-open on the same spot so Leave is off. The Australians are not to go back, but we are to carry on the abdominal work alone as we did before they came up. I imagine that this week's Push has gone well and that we've shoved their line back a bit, or they wouldn't start the Hospital there again. Westhoek Ridge is ours. I don't know about St. Julien, but we've done well. The ground has been hard and Tanks have been able to get going, flattening out these Pill-boxes which held us up before.

I expected (for one rash day) to be telling you all about Tuesday at home to-morrow, but must write it now. The business began about 10 a.m. Two came pretty close after each other and both just cleared us and No. 44. The third crashed between Sister E.'s ward in our lines and the Sisters' Quarters of No. 44. Bits came over everywhere, pitching at one's feet as we rushed to the scene of action, and one just missed one of my Night Sisters getting into bed in our Compound. I knew by the crash where it must have gone and found Sister E. as white as paper but smiling happily and comforting the terrified patients.* Bits tore through her Ward but hurt no one. Having to be thoroughly jovial to the patients on these occasions helps us considerably ourselves. Then I came on to the shell-hole and the wrecked tents in the Sisters' Quarters at 44. A group of stricken M.O.'s were standing about and in one tent the Sister was dying. The piece went through her from back to front near her heart. She was only conscious a few minutes and only lived 20 minutes. She was in bed asleep. The Sister who shared her tent had been sent down the day before because she couldn't stand the noise and the day and night conditions. The Sister who should have been in the tent which was nearest was out for a walk or she would have been blown to bits; everything in her tent was; so it was in my empty Ward next to Sister E. It all made one feel sick.

Then we offered to put up their Night Sisters and they came over; three of them so badly shell-shocked that I got the C.O. to have them sent down to Boulogne there and then in an Ambulance. This went on all day. The Australians' Q.M. Stores, the Cemetery, the Field Ambulance alongside, the Church Army Hut, all got hit and the patients could hardly stay in their beds. Then the D.M.S. and the Q.M.G. 5th Army turned up, and there was a consultation on our middle duckboards, of them, C.O. of No. 44, our C.O. and me. 'No. 44 and the Australians will evacuate and close down,' said the General. 'You will carry on and increase your Staff from No. 44 and the Australians.' A discussion as to numbers of personnel followed and I reduced a proposal of 20 additional Sisters to 10. At that moment Fritz tactfully landed one of his best with a long-drawn

---

* She got a Military Medal.

crescendoing scream and crash, just on the railway. 'Oh,' said the General, 'that was rather close.' 'That settles it,' said the Q.M.G. firmly; 'all three will evacuate.' I made off to the Wards to tell the patients they were leaving, and you should have seen their looks of joy. 'But you Sisters don't stop here?' they asked everywhere with great anxiety, bless them.

In an hour all were packed into Ambulances whether fit or dying, and the Padre was burying the dead. It took us a few hours to get away ourselves and one shell came slick into the Wards of 44 (which was then cleared of patients and Sisters) and blew an Orderly's arm and leg off and tossed the Sergeant-Major, but he came down intact. By this time Ambulances were waiting for us and our kit, and the poor C.O. was frantic to get us away.

We reached St. Omer about 10 p.m., and it took till 1 a.m. before all were housed and fed and bedded (without any beds!) on the floors of an empty house. The personnel of our three C.C.S.'s came to over 100 and was divided between various Matrons here. We were dropping with fatigue by this time. Next day orders came to send 20 to No. 10 C.C.S near Poperinghe where our M.O.'s and men were. They were selected and sorted out after lunch into Ambulances. The other 17 evacuated the empty house and came to the familiar old Convent here, sleeping in the attic.

Of course there was a Raid that night – there would be! – and one had to tear upstairs and order them all down on to the next floor out of their beds; 10 civilians were killed and a lot wounded. We, however, looked on that as child's play; it seemed so far off, compared to our nightly entertainments. From 9 till 5 to-day I've been grappling with the Pay List, and finished in time to get a blow after tea. Then heard that we are to re-open, which we're proud to do. They are a game lot. They come up and say, 'Isn't it lovely to be going back!' They are bedding out in this corridor to-night instead of the attic.

It is only when you leave off that you realise how done you are, but fortunately having to begin again will correct that. I'm indulging in a pestilential cold, and a toothache. Otherwise I am very fit! The 36 Sisters to a man are loyal and good and vie with each other in attentiveness! The only real worry would be if they were tiresome.

The older Surgeons think it's dreadful having us there, but as the C.O. says, without us they couldn't carry on at all, so it's worth it.

Saturday, August 25th, 10.30 p.m. Brandhoek. Got back here at 8 p.m. Had a lovely run – found everything quiet, and all our quarters sandbagged to the teeth. The bell-tents are raised and lined inside waist-high with sandbags and our Armstrong huts outside. We have to sleep on mattresses on stretchers instead of on beds so as to be below the line of sandbags. It looks and feels most awfully safe and cosy. There is also a dug-out with a concrete roof, not quite finished. It will be sandbagged all over.

We are all very happy to be back and united again and in good fettle for work to-morrow, probably 12 Teams, as we shall be having no break in the Take-in now.

Sunday morning. Had a very quiet night. Fritz came over about 12, but got such a warm reception he soon went away.

Monday, August 27th. The rain began last evening and is still going on; an inch fell in 8 hours during the night. The ground is already absolutely waterlogged – every little trench inches deep, shell-holes and every attempt at bigger trenches feet deep. And thousands of men are waiting in the positions and will drown if they lie down to sleep. August 1-4 over again.

We have only 17 patients in and are all having a slack time and getting fit and rested. My cold is much better. I've been scouring the country to-day in an Ambulance with the family washing and succeeded in finding a place where they'll do it in Cassel, a beautiful town set on a hill some miles back. The Town Commandant said it was 'a village of a somnolent disposition,' but we thought it was lovely!

I am writing this in my extraordinarily cosy stretcher-and-mattress bed at 9.30 p.m., with the comfortable knowledge of two feet of sandbags between me and anything that may burst outside. Anything that may burst on top of you, whether armour-piercing 9.2's like Tuesday's, or bombs from above – you would know nothing about, as you'd merely wake to a better and more peaceful world.

Shells were singing over last night but not too close. We are bombarding rather sulkily to-night and may get anything in return.

I have only 4 Night Sisters on duty to-night instead of the usual 9. It is no good worrying about patients or Sisters on duty: as long as they put hospitals in such places they've got to be there, day or night, and can't take any cover, and you can't cover 300 beds. It is no good worrying over anything that you can't alter, so the whole subject settles itself into a sort of fatalistic philosophy.

Three of the men we have in will die to-night, and there's a brave Jock boy who's had a leg off and is to lose an arm and an eye to-morrow who said, 'If you write to Mother, make it as gentle as you can, as she lost my brother in April, died o' wounds, and it made her ill.' If he wants a drink when you're busy with somebody else, he says; 'Carry on, I can wait.' The 'Prince of Wales' with the subclavian artery died on the way to Poperinghe on Tuesday after that awful day.

Tuesday night, August 28th. Terrific gale all day, straining our Wards to their utmost limits. Each Ward is five big Marquees pitched as one, and containing 34 beds. The sky has been a brilliant blue since mid-day with dazzling Alpine banks of clouds, and it has been as peaceful as Peace Time till this evening, when the wind has died down and distant shells are travelling. This wind should help to dry the ground a bit.

Friday, August 31st. We are having an extraordinarily slack and quiet time, with a total Staff of 291 (including Labour Battalion) and 18 patients! 12 Theatre Teams seem rather superfluous, but events are waiting on the weather, which is, of course, hopelessly vile. And in bad weather we see and hear very little of Fritz and have had some peaceful nights and days; it is glorious to sleep from 12 to 6 without waking; we all feel quite different. It had been an awful strain on the Surgeons with their close and critical work with no decent sleep for several weeks. We couldn't have gone on indefinitely with it.

There's no appreciable geographical alteration since the events of last week and we are told that history may repeat itself any minute. If so, there will be another Evacuation and flitting, but that can wait till it happens before anyone worries about it.

Yesterday I went with P. for a walk and saw a great many Tanks in their lair; hideous frights they are – named Ethel, Effie, Ernest, etc.

Gen. Macpherson (Assistant Director General) and the D.M.S. came round to-day to see the Sisters' Quarters and their defences. They poked into our sandbaggy lairs and ordered electric light in the Elephant (the Dug-Out). You have to squirm into it, as the entrance is sandbagged across inside; corrugated iron and concrete outside. It is supposed to be bomb-proof and shell-proof except for a direct hit, and if any business is going on those not with patients can retire to the Funk Hole. Its technical name is an Elephant. They are seriously considering the much debated question of keeping patients here.

It is a gorgeous moonlight night. Fritz tried to come over but soon got chased away. He's been shelling towards Ethel, Effie and Ernest this afternoon, and a few pretty close this evening.

There's less than ever doing in the Hospital to-day – 3 died – the others who've been in some days are regular family pets and spoiled by everyone.

Saturday morning, September 1st. Same old nights again; Fritz overhead three times and High Explosive bursting just beyond us in the intervals.

Sunday, September 2nd. The weather has not cleared up enough yet for Active Operations, so we are still slack. General S. told me to-day the exact drop in the numbers of daily casualties, and it is a big one.

We have a piano in our Mess salved from 44. It brings the M.O.'s and their friends in every evening about 9 p.m., which is really bed-time, but one mustn't be too much of a Dragon in these hard times. And last night I let them keep it up till 10.30, as it was a good and cheery cover for some rather nasty shelling that was going on, and had been all day – on both sides and beyond us (behind us as we face the line). It went on all night too, and lots of casualties were brought in; 6 died here, besides the killed in the Camps. Of course in one interval he must needs turn up overhead too. I only slept about an hour all night.

Orders came to-day for the departure of six of the Sisters, which is a good thing. They went this afternoon. We have got a very nice Church rigged up, shared fraternally by the R.C. and C. of E. Early Service at 7 and 8 and Evening at 6.30.

Monday, September 3rd. The 6.30 Service was very nice; huge congregation rolled up. M.O.s, Sisters and Men, and we finished with 'Abide with me', which has much meaning under these conditions. It was a dazzling pearly evening with no wind and we reckoned on a lively night. All went to bed early after the bad night the night before. It soon began. He splashed his bombs about 9 at a time and then went home for more and came back 4 times till 5 a.m. Only one dropped near us and none in the Camp. Archie and Lewis guns and the searchlights and some of our planes were kept busy all night, and the uproar was practically continuous. Personally, as it was such a brilliant moonlight night and he was flying very low, I put him on his honour not to bomb the Hospital and went to sleep in the middle of it and slept again each time he woke me! – a thing I've never done before.

It is a brilliant day and everything has turned up again – battles in the sky, sausages up, and shelling beginning, but dropping some way behind us. As soon as Fritz knocked off for bed and breakfast our barrage began – always a cheering sound. Crowds of letters from mothers and wives who've only just heard from the W.O. and had no letter from me, are pouring in, and have to be answered, from my book of addresses and notes of cases; it takes up hours. I've managed to write 200 so far, but there are 466.

11.30 p.m. Still Monday. Haven't been to bed yet. About 9 p.m. some of our aeroplanes came over us on their way for a Reprisal Raid for last night. We wished them good luck. As soon as they were away he came over and stayed messing about for a couple of hours. Some of the Surgeons and the C.O. and I stayed up doing rounds, as it was pretty sickening. One of them got one in 44 (which is empty) with a horrid crash. There are very few patients in but they are rather scattered, in five wards, each with a Sister. And there is a boy dying peacefully in the Prep. Hut. The day-staff are all inside their sandbags. I hope asleep some of them. Capt. B. wanted me to go into the Elephant, but I don't feel like leaving the Hospital till the next burst is over. This is one of the lulls and he's just put two shells over, but not close, and now I can hear him in the sky again!

1 a.m. Another spell of hell let loose, and now brilliant moonlight, desultory banging of our heavies and occasional squeakers whining over from him. Peace for the minute overhead. Nearly all the patients are sleeping.

Later. Shells getting nearer had me back in the hospital. The last shell looked to be on the edge of 44; it was a big crash and spattered me with spent splinters. His damnable engines are now approaching in the sky – must be off.

2.30. I just got to a ward where the Sister is alone with one patient when the bomb fell and blew one of our Night Orderlies' sleeping tents out of existence: it is one of a group of Orderlies' and M.O.'s tents and one of the only empty ones at night. Wasn't it wonderful? They'd all have been wiped out if they'd been in bed, but they were all on Night Duty. No other tent was touched. Just left an excited group of M.O.'s in pyjamas, and men round the hole. It was in the compound adjoining ours.

I found poor Home Sister very worried and took her into my hut. She sleeps alone. She has flatly refused to go down to the Base. Some of us had moonlight tea on the parapet of our compound.

Tuesday morning, September 4th. Got to bed in my clothes, at 4 a.m., up at 7.30. Slept well. Brilliant morning; Archie racket in full blast. This acre of front so far bears a charmed life, but how long can it last? Shells and bombs shave us on all four sides. Mad, isn't it? Capt. B. and Capt. P. (the all-night-duty men) are topping people. We have huge jokes in the middle of it all – no one could stick it if everybody behaved with fitting solemnity and sang hymns. There is a bit of Thank God sometimes, but praying doesn't somehow come in, which seems funny! You can be doing that!

Later. Orders have come for the final evacuation of the Hospital – site considered too 'unhealthy.' We close down to-day, evacuate the patients still here, and disperse the personnel. I stay till the last patient is fit to be moved, probably to-morrow, or next day – then probably Leave for 14 days! But don't count on it, as you never know.

1 a.m. The 16 patients are on the floor: each one barricaded in with mattresses and iron bedsteads with two Sisters and two Orderlies, and we are summoned to the Elephant by a whistle every time Fritz comes. He's coming now, as usual.

Wednesday morning, September 5th. Dazzling and deafening. We scuttled in and out of the Elephant till 3 a.m. and every one is alive this morning.

Probably we shall all be off somewhere to-day. I'll wire from Folkestone if and when I get there.

On returning from leave the writer spent some months in charge of other Units at Godeswaersvelde and Estaires, and in February 1918 rejoined this C.C.S. in the 5th Army, which was now on the most southern sector of the Somme area about 7 weeks before the German advance.

6

THE GERMAN ADVANCE

ABBEVILLE AND NAMPES, FEBRUARY 6TH TO APRIL 6TH 1918 WITH THE 5TH ARMY (SIR HUBERT GOUGH)

LETTERS FROM MARCHELEPOT

Wednesday, February 6th 1918. Abbeville. Orders came the day before yesterday to report here, and I find it is for my own Unit, at a place behind St. Quentin – a line of country quite new to me.

None of my old Staff are coming but a new brood of chickens awaits me here, and I take three of them up with me to-morrow – the rest follow when the nest is ready. In a new Camp after a move there is nothing to eat out of and nothing to sit on, and it's the dickens starting a Mess and equipping the Wards at once, especially with a new crowd.

They sent me all the 60 miles in a car, which was lovely: bright sun over woods, hills and valleys. To-morrow morning we train to Amiens and thence by car. It is the part just taken over from the French.

This place, a Sisters' Rest House, is like a harem after Estaires!

Thursday, February 7th. Marchelepot, south of Péronne. 5th. Army. We left Abbeville at 9 p.m. by train to Amiens (the first time I've been by that enchanting bit of the Seine since No. 5 Ambulance Train) and got there at 12.30, to find two Ambulances waiting for us. I made them stop at the Cathedral, which I'd never seen. It is very much sandbagged, and rather empty, but more beautiful than anything else I've seen in France.

The rest of the run – about 50 Kilometres – was through open wide country all the way to our original front line, then over No Man's Land and all the horrors and desolation of the Somme ground, to this place – Marchelepot. There is a grotesque skeleton of a village just behind us, and you fall over barbed wire and into shell-holes at every step if you walk without a light after dark, even in the hospital. There is no civil population for miles and miles; it is open grass land – a three years' tangle of destruction and neglect.

All the C.C.S.'s are in miles of desolation behind the lines. There is everywhere here a spirit of expectation, of a healthy, optimistic and thoroughly Bull-dog nature which is quite pleasant to meet.

The Colonel and the Officers' Mess gave us a cheery welcome, and the Orderlies are all beaming and looking very fit.

I'm thankful only three Sisters came with me as we found no kitchen, no food, no fire and only some empty Nissen huts, but the Sisters of the C.C.S. alongside have fed and warmed us and we are sleeping comfortably on our camp beds in one of the Nissen huts and shall have the kitchen started to-morrow.

The Hospital has only been dug in since Sunday week and has done wonders in the time – shell-holes had to be filled in and grass cut before tents could be pitched or huts put up. There are no wounded anywhere; we shall be taking sick, dysenteries, etc., when we are ready. As you can see by the small Casualty Lists all the Armies are having a record small number of wounded.

That Article in yesterday's *Times*, 'Silence before Battle,' was very inspiring to read on the way up here.

Saturday, February 16th. I expect you're having about 20 degrees of frost as we are here. Everything in your hut at night, including your own cold body, freezes stiff as iron, but there is a grand sun by day and life is possible again. The patients seem to keep warm enough in the marquees with blankets, hot bottles and hot food, but it is a cold job looking after them.

The moon is gay now and Fritz has begun his familiar old games. Three whistles are blown by the guard when his engine is heard and all lights are lowered or covered till he is away. Yesterday evening he bombed all round, but nothing on us. We are wondering how long our record of no casualties will stand: we are a tempting target, and have no large Red Cross on the ground, and no dug-outs, elephants or sandbags.

Yesterday morning a very sad thing happened. A Flying man, Capt. S., flew over to wave to his Major, a patient in the other C.C.S., and played about for 10 minutes over our heads. With the last wave of his hand, his tail caught a broken tree on the edge of a wrecked wood in a hollow just over the road, and he crashed badly and was dead in an hour. His last ten minutes on earth, or rather in the air, were so gay and confident. He ought never to have flown so low, of course: luckily his observer wasn't with him as it was only a joy ride.

This afternoon I went to Péronne with the Padre and Capt. M. It was once a beautiful town with a particularly lovely Cathedral Church, white and spacious; only some walls and one row of pillars are left now. There are about two shops existing; one woman said she had been there a prisoner all through the German occupation. It is much more striking seeing a biggish town with its tall houses stripped open from the top floor downwards, and the skeleton of the town remaining tidy and cleaned up and empty, than even these poor villages, in rubbly heaps. Here comes Fritz!

Sunday, February 17th. Terrific frost still on. Early Service at 7.30 in a Marquee of the most arctic. Drumfire blazing merrily East.

I have been trying to draw these ruins. Nothing else of this 15th Century white stone church was visible from where I stood on a heap of bricks. It is quite like it, especially the thin tottery bit on the right. On the other side of my heap of bricks I then found an official War Office Artist* drawing it too, and we made friends over the ruins and the War. It is about 5 minutes from the Camp. The whole village is the same.

---

* Professor William Rothenstein.

Monday, February 25th. All is quiet here except the guns. I could tell you three different chapters of immediate future history: which will turn out to be the true one remains to be seen.

There is a cold rough gale on to-day, which is a test of our newly pitched Wards and of our tempers. Work is in full swing, exclusively medical: chiefly walking-cases of mild enteritis, who have to be cured and returned to duty, and lying-cases of 'trench fever,' and odds and ends. There is a good deal to be done in running the routine, but very little actual nursing. They all seem happy, however, which is a great thing.

General S. came along yesterday and was quite pleased with the progress of the place.

The Colonel knowing my passion for solitude has got me an Armstrong Hut as at Brandhoek and Warlencourt, instead of a quarter of a Nissen like the rest. It is lined with green canvas and has a wee coal stove and odds and ends of brown linoleum on the floor – all three luxuries I've never had before. It looks across the barbed wire and shell-holes straight on to the ruins and the Church, and from my bed I can see the Pear Tree where the blackbirds sing in the morning.

There is a Theatre Orderly who belongs to the Community of the Divine Compassion and nursed lepers before the War. He is an educated man with a sense of humour and a great capacity for work of any sort. He has fitted up an Altar with a red and white Reredos, a white panelled front and stained altar rails, and retable and everything. It makes a splendid little Church Tent, that really feels like a Church.

Captain B. and three of us went to see No. 5 C.C.S. this afternoon at a place the other side of Péronne about six miles from the line. It is a show C.C.S. that has been there since last June and everything is very up to date.

It is dazzlingly clear to-night.

There is a boy in the Wards who was at Passchendaele in the autumn and was one of a party of men who volunteered to go and dig some bodies out of the mud in case any should be alive. Some were, and some were dead: they had to wash their faces to identify them. One of the dead ones was his brother. Then he went home on leave to tell his mother.

A terrific bombardment began at 9.30 this evening, and the wind is in the East, so it is very loud.

It is going to be the most interesting and probably the most horrible year of the War – and possibly the last, with any luck. We have a beautiful old Boche in the Wards, with a head like St. Jerome. I should like an Italian conversation book if you've got one. We have a lot of Italians in, and all I can rise to is *Buon Giorno.*

We have seen a good deal of Professor Rothenstein. He brought his drawings over to our Mess for us to see.

February 28th. I suppose the newspaper men have long ago got the opening lines of their leaders ready with, 'The long expected Battle Wave has rolled up and broken at last, and the Clash of two mighty Armies has begun,' etc., etc. It may not be long before they can let it go. Yesterday the C.O.'s of C.C.S.'s of this Army were summoned to a Conference at the D.M.S.'s Office and given their parts to play – under 'Secret Orders.' My C.O. immediately told me his, and we have arranged accordingly and proceeded in all Departments to indent for Chloroform, Pyjamas, Blankets, Stretchers, Stoves, Hot Water Bottles and what not. The R.E. are working rapidly; Nissen Huts springing up like mushrooms, electric light and water laid on, bath-houses concreted, boilers going, duckboards down, and Reinforcements of all ranks – Officers, Sisters and Men – arriving. If events take a certain course, we take the walking wounded, operate and pass them on. If certain other events occur, which you can think out, the lying wounded come to us as well. Then one of two things may happen which you can also think out. A train is coming to clear the sick to-morrow.

This class of Battle-work is new to my lot of Sisters, but they are very keen and will fall in with what comes like veterans. The Orderlies are at the top of their form and working overtime (to out-do the other C.C.S., I believe!) in getting ready. We could take them on bald-headed now – and they got here a month before us. The new Sergeant-Major is a treasure. 'Very good, Matron, better get on with that at once,' is his invariable response to all suggestions. The Colonel says, 'All right, Sister; we are agreed on that, as always – *Ça sera fait!*' Captain B. says, 'Right o! I'll see the Old Man about it and put it through.' There's very little you can't wangle with that spirit in the place, and of course with each new Push you know better what is wanted and what to avoid.

Saturday, March 2nd. Nothing doing so far. No one will be surprised if the whole affair here turns out to be only 'wind-up' or German camouflage for something else. Everyone is posted to his right station for Zero and meanwhile the usual routine carries on. To-day there is *the* most poisonous blizzard whatever. The Camp is one vast shaking piercing draught and no place is humanly warm. It would be better to be buried at the bottom of one of these Boche dug-outs. I found one the other day roofed with actual trees two feet round. I have chosen this highly opportune moment to indulge in a vile cold and cough, but it is not surprising as this is a cold War. The thin canvas walls of my wee Hut are like brown paper in this weather, and this violent icy wind blows the roof and walls apart and layers of North Pole and snow come knifing in while you wash in the morning – but there is enough fuel for a tiny fire to go to bed by, which is a blessing beyond price. I expect you all have the same blizzard, but with layers of stout houses, carpets and fires between, instead of rocking marquees and tin huts. Thank heaven there are no wounded in yet. I shall never forget what they were like at Arras last spring.

Monday, March 4th. A mighty blizzard snowstorm has covered us and the Boche and there is nothing doing here. Three new Sisters turned up on Saturday, one sick, but we have warmed her up as far as can be and she is better.

Later. The D.M.S. has just been round again with more warnings; and consequently renewed preparations for Zero; more Sisters, etc., to come. He says we're in for 'A very hairy time.'

I've got some primroses growing in a blue pot, grubbed up out of a ruined garden in infancy before the snow, now blooming like the Spring. The only way of getting into my Armstrong Hut at first was across a plank over a shell-hole. The R.E. are fortifying our quarters against bombs.

The red spot on the enclosed cutting from the *Times* is where we are – about two miles from the blue waters of the Somme, which on a sunny day looks like a jewel in the brown landscape – where it widens like a lake.

To-day on another part of this vast ugly tangled battlefield, between a deep trench, some barbed wire and a winding road, we happened on some German graves under some apple trees. Among them was one with this inscription:

'Hier ruht ein tapferer Engländer*
Richard Rhodes, gefallen 5. 3. 17
L Coy. 2/5 Glosteres'

and his rusty rifle stuck in the ground at the foot. He is the only one enclosed in a rail.

We take in every other day and evacuate about every four days – almost entirely medical cases. An Italian is 108° this evening and another one 104°. We have a good many Italian Labour Corps men in. We also have some funny Chinese boys. They are always laughing and singing and are very inquisitive, and like to handle and examine every new thing. They love washing themselves and demand basins at all hours.

The Camp is beginning to look very smart. We have a white painted iron hand rail along both sides of the central duckwalk, made of Boche barbed wire props from the surrounding tangles. The theatre orderlies have produced a grand stove for our Mess out of a German officer's dug-out. We now have electric light in our Mess and in our own dug-outs, which you can switch off from your bed. And we are going to have a bath tent with real long zinc bath to lie down in. There are a few bell-tents in our compound for reinforcements if we have to have more Sisters. They are sunk three feet with the dug part lined with wire netting, tarred felt, and then canvas: wooden steps down to it and a wooden floor – most luxurious.

Friday, March 22nd. A ghastly uproar began yesterday, Thursday morning, March 21st. The guns bellowed and the earth shook. Fritz brought off his Zero like clockwork at 4.20 a.m. and in one second plunged our front line in a deluge of High Explosive, gas, and smoke, assisted by a thick

---

* Here rests a brave Englishman.

fog of white mist. Our gunners were temporarily knocked out by gas but soon recovered and gave them hell, which caught their first infantry rush, but they came on and advanced a mile and then their barrage slacked off a bit so as not to catch their own infantry. One of the three programmes that I told you about happened, and we suddenly became a front line C.C.S. and the arrival of the wreckage began, continued and has not ended. We began in the morning about 9.30 with our usual 14 Sisters and by midnight we numbered 40 as at Brandhoek. Only two Ambulance Trains have come to evacuate the wounded, and the filling up continues. The C.O. and I stayed up all night and to-day, and we have now got people into the 16-hours-on-and-8-off routine in the Theatre, etc. Some convalescent medical patients with a passion for helping their fellow men were found at all hours of the night working like galley slaves in the wards in the most inspiring way. The new Sisters fell to and stayed up all night and have gone to bed to-day. We had 102 gassed men in one ward, but only 4 died. There are about 50 wounded officers lying about or sleeping huddled up in corners. Ten girl chauffeurs drove up in the middle of the night with five Operating teams from the Base. They were frightfully thrilled at coming up here during a battle through the ruins in the moonlight.

On Wednesday I had applied for my leave for Good Friday, but was in time to tear up my application yesterday morning when the noise began and hell broke loose.

It's neck or nothing on both sides in this and there will be more dead men than ever.

Friday night, 11 p.m. Just off to bed after 40 hours full steam ahead. Everything and everybody is working at very high pressure and yet it seems to make little impression on the general ghastliness. This is very near the battle, and gets nearer; there are fires on the skyline and to-night bombs are dropping like apples on the country round. The artillery roar has been terrific to-day. Good-night.

Palm Sunday, March 24th, 9 a.m. Amiens. The night before last, after writing to you on my way to bed, things looked a bit hot, so I lay down in my clothes for a few hours rather than not go to bed at all, as history was making itself so rapidly, and the map was altering every hour for the worse. As you know by now, ours was the place where they broke through and came on with their guns at a great pace. We found the General of the 24th Division, one of the Divisions that took the brunt of the first onslaught here, sitting on the roadside outside our Orderly Room Tent with a few of his Staff, and the Divisional Flag stuck up in the field, using our telephone as his Divisional HQ. His Division was practically napoo for the moment – they did wonders afterwards – masses of his transport were spread out opposite and a steady stream of everything flowed past us all day the wrong way, like Mons. The Germans came straight through one of the other Divisions, the 16th, and another was the one you had for a year at Colchester – the 66th: it stuck it well. A Black Watch man on a stretcher was asked where the 9th Division were. 'They're in Germany now,' he said. They are all Scotch and South Africans. I've met them all through the War.

All the hot busy morning wind-up increased and faces looked graver every hour. The guns came nearer, and soon Field Ambulances were behind us and Archies cracking the sky with their noise. We stopped taking in because no Field Ambulances were working, and we stopped operating because it was obvious we must evacuate everybody living or dying, or all be made prisoners if anybody survived the shelling that was approaching. Telephone communication with the D.M.S. was more off than on, and roads were getting blocked for many miles, and the railway also. We had about 1,000 patients, all wounded except 130 gassed and 150 walking sick who were in before the battle, until a train came at 9 a.m. and took 300. Every ward was full and there were two lines of stretchers down the central duck-walk in the sun; we dressed them, fed them, propped them up, picked out the dying at intervals as the day went on, and waited for orders, trains, cars or lorries or anything that might turn up. At 10 a.m. the Colonel wanted me to get all my 40 Sisters away on the Ambulance train, but as we had these hundreds of badly wounded, we decided to stay and take our chance till definite orders came for us to run.

At mid-day the Matron-in-Chief turned up in her car from Abbeville. It was a stroke of genius on her part to pick out the one shaky place remaining on the whole front where Sisters were left and come to look out for her 80 Sisters – 40 with me and 40 at the other C.C.S. It was decided that Sisters must leave and transport be found for them. The Divisional General (24th) offered lorries if he could find them, but they were away in the blue looking for rations. The O.C. of the Motor Ambulance near by offered a despatch rider to get some of his cars from somewhere else. A made-up temporary train for wounded was expected, and we were to go on whichever Transport turned up first and scrap all our kit except hand-baggage. Miss McCarthy lunched with us, and saw the Sister-in-Charge of the other C.C.S. and the two refugee Sisters-in-Charge from farther up who were with us. She said nice things to us, and took two Sisters away in her car. They all behaved with the calmness of a garden party, and were all prepared to carry on with shelling, or Germans, or whatever might come; packing was done in reliefs from running the wounded, who were as quiet and uncomplaining and marvellous as ever. The Officers' Ward was a brave but unhappy place. The Resuscitation Ward was of course indescribable and the ward of penetrating-chests was packed and dreadful. Some of the others died peacefully in the sun and were taken away and buried immediately.

At about 5 p.m. the Railway Transport Officer of the ruined village produced a train with 50 trucks of the 8 *chevaux* or 40 *hommes* pattern, and ran it alongside the Camp; not enough of course for the wounded of both Hospitals but enough to make some impression. Never was a dirty old empty truck-train given a more eager welcome or greeted with more profound relief. The 150 walking-cases (all the rest were stretchers) were got into open trucks, and the stretchers were quickly handed into the others, with an Orderly, a pail of water, feeders and other necessaries in each. One truck was for us and our kit, so I got a supply of morphia and hypodermics to use at the stoppages all down the train Then orders came from the D M S that Ambulance Cars were coming for us. So the Medical Officers (one from us and one from the other) took the morphia and most of our kit to God knows where with the wounded, and we mustered on the roadside for the cars. There were 300 stretcher cases left, but another train was coming in for them. The Sister in charge of the other C.C.S. told me Rothenstein was helping in the Wards like an orderly.

The Boche was 4 miles this side of Ham, just into Péronne, and 3 miles from us – 13 miles nearer in 2½ days. We were trying to hold them at the Somme at St Christ, the little place we walked to the other day, 3 miles away, with the blue lake where the Yankee sappers were building a bridge. I am glad I've seen Péronne. The 8th Warwicks marched in on March 19th 1917. The Germans will take down our notice board on March 23rd 1918 and put up theirs.

We had a great send off and got off in 4 Ambulance Cars escorted by three Motor Ambulance Convoy Officers, one on a motor cycle and two in a Staff car. They had to take us some way round through Chaulnes, over battlefields with pill-boxes in them, and ghastly wrecked woods and villages, as he was shelling the usual road heavily between us and our destination, Amiens. We took five hours getting there, owing to the blocked state of the roads, with Divisions retreating and Divisions reinforcing, French refugees, and big guns being trundled into safety and other little affairs of that kind. He chose that evening to bomb Amiens for four hours, and we saw this going on, and waited under the trees a few miles out until he'd finished. He has been over bombing again twice this morning and is doing it this minute.

Sunday, March 24th. The Stationary Hospital people here (Amiens) were extraordinarily kind and gave us each a stretcher, a blanket and a stretcher-pillow in an empty hut. They had not the remotest idea they would be on the run themselves in a day or two.

We had tea and bread and butter and laid our tired heads and bones down at 1.30 a.m., and slept till early this morning when we woke shivering with the cold. After a hot wash in the Padre's room and a topping breakfast of fried eggs, 20 went off on a train to Abbeville and the rest go with me to-night, arriving there in the small hours. I went to High Mass at the Cathedral at 10.30 and had a good rest. 'That Cathedral has just rested my soul,' said my Scotch Sister, coming in hot and weary from the town. So it has mine. It has all been so critical that you don't have time to feel anything at the time. I think they'll soon be strafing this place like Paris.

Monday, March 25th. 10.30 p.m. Abbeville. It is in Orders that no one may write any details of these few days home yet, so I am keeping this to send home later, but writing it up when I can.

Yesterday afternoon I dug out Colonel Thurston, A.D.M.S. Lines of Communication, who was O.C. of 16 General when I was there, and asked him for road transport for my remaining 20 for this place. He was charming and arranged for us to go one on each car of a convoy of 25 cars, taking walking-cases from here to Abbeville and took one of mine himself in his car with a Consulting Surgeon. When the Convoy arrived it was loaded up too full to take us, so there was just time to wangle two of the cars to take our hand baggage to the Station to catch the only train, and get a warrant out of the R.T.O. without a Movement Order, which he gave me like a lamb – on only my authority, in a way unknown to history up to now.

On the Station (that vast place one comes to in the night on the way to Switzerland) was a seething mass of British soldiers and French refugees, some coming in from the invaded area and some leaving for safer regions still. There I found our Colonel at my elbow telling me all our kit was got away but he didn't know where to. He had brought the last 300 stretcher cases down the evening before in open trucks with all the M.O.'s and personnel. Our wounded were lying in rows along the platform with our Orderlies; they had been in the trucks all night and all day and only *one* Ambulance Car was found to take them to the Hospital in return journeys. One I saw was jerking with tetanus. Some had died, and were in a closed van lower down, but all were got away. The Padre was burying the others in the field with a sort of running funeral, up to the time they left. They were taken straight to their graves as they died.

What happened next to our patients I don't know as our train came in and we came here to find Sisters from 10 other C.C.S.'s of the 5th and 3rd Armies, also refugees, sleeping on the floors of every place. Everyone was very kind and did the best that could be done for us all. I was made to have a Night-Sister's bed with half her blankets and did well, and feel quite fresh and fit to-day. All my lot, except two, who are here with me, have been detailed for duty elsewhere, mostly in the three big Hospitals here, which are, of course, very busy. We Charge Sisters had to write reports for Miss McCarthy, our Chief. Now our C.C.S. has no equipment, we shall all, C.O., M.O.'s, Sisters and men, be used elsewhere. If this check on the Somme holds, some of them who have managed to save their equipment will carry on and form up on new sites, but I don't see how we and 34 can.

Miss McCarthy's Office Staff asked me to dinner to-night Our adventures have been a picnic compared to some of the others. The ones from Ham were waiting 5 hours on a shelled railway, dodging shells before they got away on ammunition lorries, sitting on the shells. But I believe in all cases wounded and personnel were got away in time – by a few hours. The last Communiqué says he has been stopped at the place on the river between Licourt and Brie, where we went to tea with the Irish Rifles on Sunday, and pushed back to the other side. We must have made a marvellous recovery there, to have got fresh guns and people up, as there were none there on Saturday evening. If their roads behind their lines are blocked in the same proportion of 10 to 1 as their Divisions are to ours, they must be at a standstill and a great target for our Air-work and Artillery.

Wednesday night, 27th. Yesterday I was sent up to No. 2 Stationary Hospital up the hill, to do Assistant Matron for Miss M., and we've had a busy day to-day, admitting and evacuating. They shelled Amiens last night and it has been badly bombed. Two of my Team Sisters who remained there were wounded last night, not very badly, and were taken to the Sick Sisters' Hospital here, to-day, by road.

I went to see the Railway Transport Officer for news of our lost kit, which may yet turn up, but it seems to matter so little now. There was a cheering French regiment in the Station full of buck.

A big W.A.A.C. Camp here has been evacuated to the coast, but as a corporal here said this morning, 'I'm not Pessy-eyed yet.' Isn't it a gorgeous word?

There are not many badly wounded coming down. In a Retreat, of course, they never do. The walking wounded are very cheery and not at all Pessy-eyed. There are many pleasant interpretations of the present situation and many unpleasant. I cling firmly to the first lot till the other comes off. If only one could see a week or a month ahead.

Even on the 23rd, on that hot morning, when it looked decidedly blackish and the Divisional Commander was sitting by our roadside, there were people who were not Pessy-eyed. A haggard-looking officer had come in to see if one of his friends was in our Officers' Ward (he was). I asked him – 'What's really happening?' 'Wind up,' he said, 'we're holding them all right', and it was true – there has nowhere been a complete rout.

Thursday, March 28th. As the communiqués are wired down the line, a copy finds its way to Matron's Office night and morning, so we see them before we see the papers. To-day's is better, especially the French accounts. I am quite sure even the Germans can't go on piling up their cannon fodder indefinitely. As far as our wounded go, there are no over-whelming numbers coming down. The Officers' Ward is just now the heaviest here. The number of deaths are negligible compared with what ours were up the Line. The Battle has just surged past Marchelepot.

I'm writing in my cosy corner in bed on 'biscuits'* and stretcher in the Home Sister's room, with a little coal stove going. The Matron has just been to ask me to look after an Officer's Father and Mother to-morrow who have arrived too late, and to take them to the Mortuary to-morrow morning early. She also said a C.C.S. was being got together to pick up the pieces, so to speak, behind our lines, and she thinks I'll be sent up for it.

Saturday, Easter Eve, March 30th 1918. Yesterday evening Miss McCarthy suddenly turned me into a Railway Transport Officer at the Railway Station, and it is *the* most absolutely godless job you could have. You must have command of (*a*) the French language, (*b*) your temper, (*c*) any number of Sisters and V.A.D.'s panicking over their heavy kit and losing their small, (*d*) every French porter you can threaten or bribe, (*e*) the distracted R.T.O. and his clerks. I got one lot of Sisters off at 8 p.m., another at 11 p.m. and another at 1.30 a.m. to different Base Hospitals, about 70 altogether, and then got home and slept a dog's sleep on my

---

* Square halves of a mattress, known as 'biscuits' in the Army.

stretcher. Began again this morning and got back to 5 minutes lunch at 3 p.m. and then back again. Another lot to go at 8 p.m. The trains are all 4 to 6 hours late and it is the dickens, but the Sisters are very good and don't grumble a bit. They have had to rough it all over France since this Battle began, as never before since 1914.

The news is better and it is raining cats and dogs which will hold up the German advance as it did ours in early August last year. I met some of my nursing orderlies from my C.C.S. on the railway to-day, homeless and wandering, gave them 20 francs and my blessing; how they got there I can't conceive. No mail has reached me since we cleared out this day week; do write soon to No. 2 Stationary Hospital.

I am quite fit.

Easter Monday, April 1st. It has been a dazzling spring day after the heavy rain – spent as usual on the Station – not as R.T.O. this time but as A.M.F.O. (Army Military Forwarding Officer), digging out masses of Refugee Sisters' kits with a Fatigue party of a corporal and six men, loading it on to trucks for the different Bases the Sisters had gone to. The day after I last wrote to you, I had a 24 hours' shift of R.T.O., i.e. all Saturday (having knocked off the last shift of the day before at 2 a.m. that morning), and all Saturday night. I didn't get finished with it till 6 a.m. on Easter Sunday and got to Early Service at 6.15 a.m., then breakfast and then blessed bed. It was rotten to spend Easter Sunday in bed, but what else could one do after puddling about the platforms at the Station in the cold and wet for 24 hours. There are no waiting-rooms, and the place was a seething mass of refugee families and French soldiers and my herds of Sisters and kits. But they all got safely landed in their right trains and no kit lost. All sorts of interesting things were going up and down the line.

A big Australian Flying Officer fresh from the Battle was full of buck about it all. He says every Division has its tail well up. We fly so low on to their herded masses and do such deadly havoc that the Boche morale is absolutely napoo, and not a man has the sense to put up his rifle and bring down the British flier, but they all go raving mad to get under cover, though there is none. It would have been better for us if we could have had more of this wet spell, to stick them in the mud while they're still in the rough country. It must be very uphill work advancing over that scarred ground. We used to find it hard to get to any given point in a straight line over the maze of deep trenches, dug-outs, shell-holes and wire, and practically impossible except on quite dry days: they can't now do much with guns and transport on those slithery sticky slopes.

I heard from Captain B. to-day. He is working with a sort of scratch C.C.S. in front of Amiens at Rosières, and says it is the most ghastly show he's struck in this War. I think it is getting better each day – that was the 26th, but of course things are always bad without equipment or Red Cross extras or Sisters. They can be appalling enough with all that, so one can imagine what it must be like without. I wish they'd find me another job with the Army in the Field; they probably will later.

I do wonder how it will work out with Foch as head. It is the right thing of course, but it will take a bit of handling.

Easter Tuesday. Had a very busy day at the Triage as A.M.F.O., with my fatigue party fetching and loading kit. Got finished at 5 and had a bath. R.T.O. jobs are for to-morrow with more A.M.F.O. in the intervals, if any. And a message came from Miss McCarthy this evening – was I ready and fit for another C.C.S.? The answer was in the Affirmative. That may be anywhere, and the sooner the better. I think our kit is on the truck to be sorted to-morrow. It would be expensive to have to get everything over again.

The Communiqué to-night is pretty good. How splendid the King hustling over like that.

Oh, I do want some home letters, and only get loving effusions from my late Staff.

Miss M. here is one of the best people I have struck in this war; we have great times in the Office and in her room at tea, etc., when R.T.O. merges into Matron's Ass, which is the polite name for Assistant Matron.

Wednesday, April 3rd. Letters at last, joy of joys. Just what I expected about the 1914 atmosphere at home and here, too. It is always when odds are greatest that the British Army and the British Public comes best up to the scratch. *The Times* man is right, the B.A. needs everything spiritual, intellectual and physical that England can give it, and it is all the things he has to leave out of his accounts, the little things officers and men from the Line tell us, that would show you why. And there are weeks of strain ahead; this is only the beginning.

But I'm glad the tanks are coming in with us now; it'll have a splendid moral effect.

There was a good story in the French paper to-night (related by the French) of a British General who came up to reinforce at a critical moment, after eight days' fighting. 'Your men are too fatigued,' said the French. '*Sans doute* we are fatigued,' said the British General – 'but is this quite the moment to repose ourselves?' – and in they went with the French.

I am fatigued to-night with a hectic morning of R.T.O., scratch lunch on the floor of a Y.M.C.A. hut and an afternoon of A.M.F.O. In one of the trucks I found my trunk and kitbag, but not my holdall with my new brogues, which I badly want, and daren't write home for as one's address is so uncertain.

Someone else out of a job went to that C.C.S. to-day. I am for the next. Wasn't it luck not being banished to the distant Bases, as every other Sister-in-Charge has been?

Saturday night, April 6th. All your letters of the first days of the Battle are coming in. I didn't quite realise you'd be really worrying. It came so suddenly, and running the wounded and the Sisters gave one no time at all to think, though I couldn't have let you know any sooner. We are plunged in work just now. Every available man has had to be put into the Wards, all the Clerks, Asst. Matron, Home Sister, everyone but the Cook and Mess V.A.D.'s. I am running two ramping Wards and everyone else is at full stretch. R.T.O. and A.M.F.O. are finished for the time being. All these three Hospitals are understaffed just now and are doing C.C.S. work. We get the men practically straight out of action, and hear all the news as it happens. We had 96 wounded officers yesterday. A young Australian Sergeant in my ward was blown up by a shell which burst on to five of them. 'Were they all killed?' I asked. 'They picked up the remains in sandbags,' he said grimly. They were all friends of his.

Captain B. and Captain M. turned up this afternoon and had tea with me. They'd got a car and looked me up as they were here, and finished the story from where we left them on the 23rd at Marchelepot at 6 p.m. Gerry was only three miles away, and shells were coming in when they left at 10 p.m. with the last of the wounded. Captain Lumley had an awful journey with the 300 on the trucks. 16 died. Our C.C.S. is now working with another which got its equipment away. All our Theatre stuff was saved, but nothing else. Heavy rain again – a good thing – though hard on the men.

There have been some Germans coming through in British officers' uniforms and panicking the French and English with breathless tales of imaginary German advances, besides the real one – to make the Allies run. The men seem in extraordinarily good spirits, and though fagged to the bone, look healthy enough. They sleep in heaps directly they get here, and go on indefinitely. When they talk it is exclusively about the ebb and flow and ins and outs, and narrow shaves and bits of bad luck and strokes of good luck in the extraordinary game they've been play-ing. To them, apparently, it is actually a game like football now, with the Hun-He-'Fritzy'-'Gerry' as their opponent, and it seems to rouse all their pride in brains, endurance and blind pluck and taking of risks, in a way that deadly old trench business never could.

A Night Orderly to-night, when I told him to look specially after an arm, said anxiously, 'Is there any 'ope of an 'oemorrhage?' which was a cheery way of putting it.

One could write indefinitely about things which may not be writ-ten down, it is tantalizing. This open fighting is so much more alive and individual than all the other great Battles. Tiny parties with one machine-gun find themselves counter-attacking one minute or holding back hundreds the next. We often go for him with rifles while he's going for us with Field Guns and Hows. The sporting instinct is tremendous both in officers and men, just as the Flying boys tell you they feel it in their most critical moments, when they're up against the 'Blighter' in another Plane, to the exclusion of any other feeling.

And any officer tells you how he hasn't slept ever, either because of the cold in the open with no blanket or because he's had to be walking up and down waking up the men, 'and they're priceless,' he generally ends up. 'And when I got hit that fed them up most,' said one in painful gasps, with a hole in his lung.

Friday, April 12th. Nampes. Orders came for me on Wednesday to take over the C.C.S. at Nampes. Two other Sisters came too, and we took the road by car after tea, arriving here at 11 p.m., after much losing the way in the dark and attempting lanes deep in unfathomable sloughs of mud. It is an absolutely divine spot, on the side of a lovely wooded valley, South of Amiens. The village is on a winding road, with a heavenly view of hills and woods, which are carpeted with blue violets and periwinkles and cowslips, and starry with anemones. Birds are carolling and leaves are greening, and there is the sun and sky of summer. The blue of the French troops in fields and roads adds to the dazzling picture, and inside the tents are rows of 'multiples' and abdominals, and heads and moribunds, and teams working day and night in the Theatre, to the sound of frequent terrific bombardments. It has never been quite so incongruously lovely all around.

This is the place where four derelict Casualty Clearing Stations amalgamated and got to work during the Retreat, without Sisters. Now it is run by one C.C.S. with a huge collection of Medical Officers and Orderlies and Chaplains from Units out of action, and with odds and ends of saved equipment.

It is still very primitive with no huts and no duckboards and only stretchers, with not many actual beds, but it is quite workable and a lot of work is being done. The asepsis is rather shaky, but it is all that is possible without the proper equipment.

The patients are evacuated as quickly as possible, and the worst ones remain to be nursed here. Of course, the rows of wooden crosses are growing rather appalling, but some lives are being saved. They are a good lot of Sisters. Captain B. and three others of ours are here, and about 12 of my Orderlies.

We live four in a marquee in a field below the road and have daisies growing under our beds, no tarpaulins or boards, but a few of us have iron beds and mattresses, the rest their own camp beds. I've acquired a tin basin and a foot of board on two petrol tins for a wash-stand and am quite comfortable. We unpack as little as we can. Our compound has five Marquees. French Gunners stray in and sleep on the grass all round us, and a constant stream of Poilus passes up and down the road. It is very noisy at night. A few Sisters of another C.C.S. work with mine and their Sister-in-Charge runs the Mess. The Cathedral has had two shells in it.

We are soon moving again, so don't send any parcels please till my address is more fixed. Isn't it divine weather? Leave is unlikely to happen ever – as far as I can see.

Do you see he's into Richebourg St. Vaaste, where Ralph R. K.'s grave is and in Laventie and fighting over Estaires? At Christmas, listening to the guns from my canopied bed there, I knew in my bones he'd be there this year. At Marchelepot, from the beginning, I planned my kit to escape with, and my kit to leave to him.

Isn't it funny to be a soldier of General Foch's now?

We live on boiled mutton every day twice a day, but with Plum and Apple jam as a substitute for red currant jelly, you can eat it and be thankful: tea, bacon, bread and margarine in ample quantities does the rest.

Like the men, it is only when things are soft and prosperous that Sisters grumble. Here the colder, wetter and tireder you are the less grumbling there is.

I should like to stay with this Unit; there are some quite good people in it and it is very keen.

I am hoping to get a mail to-day, sent on from Abbeville. It is a bore not seeing any newspapers; a three days' old Continental *Daily Mail* is fairly scrapped for when one turns up.

Write lots and often. I am very fit.

Rumours of big German bags up North. I wonder? That ground is so familiar to me personally, these four years, that it feels almost as if they were overrunning Essex.

My poor Germaine is now a refugee from Estaires and so are all my French pals at Lillers.

Our Mess Cookhouse is four props and some strips of canvas; three dixies, boiling over a heap of slack between empty petrol tins, is the Kitchen Range, in the open. We get a grand supply of hot water from two Sawyer boilers under the tree, but just now it's too cold to have a bath at night on grass in a single-fly tent, and there's not hot water in the morning. The French village does our laundry.

Sunday, April 14th. He is at Merville, and what next I wonder? Here we are holding him all right, but each night of uproar one wonders when we'll next be on the road again. The French troops are splendid, older and more set than ours. I've never seen such thousands of them.

The weather has changed and the dry, sunny valley has become a chilly, windy quagmire. There are no fires anywhere and very little oil for the lamps; it is very difficult to keep the men warm, many of them are better dead, and the crop of wooden crosses grows daily.

An Officer (among many) atrociously wounded and dying by inches, has been passionately asking to be allowed to die, and he got his wish this morning. Another, Captain C. E. with a wonderful face, and his brain showing, has his pocket-book full of Rupert Brooke. He died rather suddenly, just after showing possibilities of recovery.

April 22nd. We are on the move again, but you had better go on address-ing as before as we may soon join up again. The patients left to-day, and the tents are down this evening. I expect we shall go to Abbeville, while they dig themselves in at the new site about 7 miles North of Amiens. Everything is very quiet here, except occasional violent artil-lery duels and bomb-dropping at night. Yesterday the Colonel gave us a car and four of us went a splendid run through sunny, wooded, hilly France down to Beauvais and saw the Cathedral, and had tea at a Café, and had a grand run home, about 30 miles each way. No sign or sound of War except French troops on the roads. Their horizon blue when it gets dusty is a very clever camouflage at a distance of half a mile.

This village is full of a red-turbaned Algerian Regiment, 'Shock' troops, some French, some Moors, who have been out since 1914. Their band played to us on Saturday.

Tuesday, 23rd. A month since we up and ran away from Jerry. It is Abbeville, and we are sitting on our kit waiting for transport. The news from the North seems a bit better. There is an inborn feeling in every British bosom that has been out any time that he shan't get Béthune, and he's finding it a tough nut to crack. He evidently can't run two shows simultaneously as he's been sitting quietly here ever since he began business in the North.

I wonder how black it looked in England on Saturday week, when Haig said, 'We have our backs to the wall' – worse than close to, probably. Doesn't it give you a good safe feeling that Foch has us all in his clever grasp now? It does on this side, and what a Heaven-sent breather it must be for Haig.

7

THE ALLIED ADVANCE

MAY 13TH TO AUGUST 10TH 1918
WITH THE 4TH ARMY (SIR HENRY RAWLINSON)

LETTERS FROM PERNOIS

Monday, May 13th. Pernois (between Amiens and Doullens). There is so much to see to in starting a new site with a new Mess consisting of Nothing, and with patients already in the Wards when we arrived, that there has not been a moment yet to unpack my kit, barely to read my mails, let alone to write letters, other than official and Break-the-News, till now, 10.30 p.m.

We had our first rain to-day with the new moon, and the place has been a swamp all day.

The great Boche effort is supposed to be imminent and this wet will delay and disgust him. He had 24 Sausages up yesterday over one place, spying out everything he could see, and it was a day of divine visibility luckily for him.

I had a letter from a mother yesterday whose 5th son has just been killed – or rather died here.

There is a negro Labour Company boy from Jamaica, black as ink, in one of the Wards with pneumonia. When Sister wanted to feed him he said indignantly, 'Me not piccaninny, me Man!' We have had some Indians, too. There are some extraordinarily nice woundeds in the Wards.

The C.O. of this Unit is very keen and full of brains, discipline and ideas. Everyone is out for efficiency and we are all working together like honey bees, and hastening to fall in with each other's brilliant suggestions! Let us hope such a Utopia is not too good to last. There is really a very fine spirit in the place and the N.C.O.'s and men have got it, too. The Sisters are all so pleased with our unique Quarters that they're ready for anything. The C.O. has gone this time to the opposite extreme from daisies under our beds and we are sleeping in the most thrilling dug-outs I've ever seen. They are bell-tents; but instead of the usual damp floppy, windy, squashy affair, you enter through two little green canvas doors into a porch and then descend by lovely steps made of ammunition boxes down into a little round dug-out room, with a boarded floor and lined walls for 3½ feet up to the ground level. Then come two feet of sandbags and then the bell-tent begins! The tent pole is done away with and the top supported by a stout wooden tripod from the walls – at ground level. Large portholes are made in the sandbags, lined with wood or tin – as windows – and ledges are fitted in as shelves. We have 5 solid feet between us and bomb splinters* and are warm and cosy and dry and as airy as we like with door and windows, and we can loop the tent up anywhere above the sandbags. I have one to myself and the others are two in one, with ample room. It even has a tiny window of oiled linen let into the roof of the porch.

The Camp itself is very well laid out with roads to the entrances to the wards for Ambulances, to save carrying stretchers a long way. We evacuate by car to the train at the bottom of the valley. We are on the hill-top and look over the tops of the trees in the valley to the opposite side. It is very open and there are lovely views. Our Compound has a large bit of clover field railed off as our garden and overlooks the best bit of the view.

Major S. has been with a Brigade up the Line a long time and loved it. He says it's 'a grand life: there's such a wonderful spirit of self-sacrifice

---

* Later on in the year when the Army was on the move, and Casualty Clearing Stations had to be mobile, and there was no time for sandbags, 'graves' were dug inside the Sisters' Tents, large enough to contain a stretcher-bed.

among those chaps and never any petty jealousies or spite.' I've never met a decent M.O. from up the Line who didn't say the same.

We haven't got a Church Tent yet and the Padres have asked me to try and jog the O.C. about it. He shall have no peace till we do.

May 22nd, and hottest day this year. This full moon is, of course, bringing an epidemic of night bombing at Abbeville, Étaples and all about up here. People here, not the seasoned experts, call it 'very near' when he drops things 2 kilos away: let them wait till he really does come near. Nowadays he doesn't cause me a single flutter: he might be nightingales for all the difference he makes, except that one gets to bed later every night.

A charming Australian Bishop came to-day. We have had some very nice officers in Officers' Ward and lots of wounded 18-years-old boys about the Wards – called the War Babies. I had a lovely motor run to the Southern Area B.R.C.S. Depôt yesterday, through shady roads with orchards blazing with buttercups – country like Oxfordshire.

May 25th. Nothing to report here: people seem to think he has his tail down too badly to come on, and it looks like it. The Yanks are much liked about here and are said to be a stout-hearted lot.

Surgeons are getting very skilful at opening up chests and dealing with lungs – a thing not dared till recently. It is a very critical business, but the results are astonishingly good.

I was invited by my three Australian Sisters the other day to a picnic with seven Australian officers. It was charming. There is a naturalness and utter absence of self-consciousness about the Australian girl or boy which is most refreshing. And they're so amusing.

The Yanks are affording huge amusement to the British Army generally by their Bret Harte phraseology and freedom in addressing British Colonels. Our black boy is still very ill. He sings hymns and says 'Nursie, stroke my face' just like Uncle Tom's Cabin.

An inimitable Jock told me to-day that you only had to fill a Scot up wi' rum and he could do for as many machine-gun nests as any Tank, and 'No teetotaller ever got a V.C.'!! A Tank boy said that when a Tank he knew once went into action without a horseshoe it always carried for luck, a shell knocked it out and killed the Commander and the 8 men – but another Jock said no, it wasn't the horseshoe but 'its time had come, same as for everybody else: it's only when your time comes you get hit.'

May 28th. I went to Abbeville yesterday for shopping. They've had bombs in the Town for the first time. I hear he has attacked on the Chemin des Dames and advanced 10 kilos, but the French won't let him sit there. He naturally needs to divert them from our parts. There's been a lot of shelling this week.

There's nothing to say that one may write about, but a good deal to do. An R.F.C. boy is in Officers' Ward with a wound in his thigh. He has a hole in his forehead through which you can see pulsation – he got it at Loos in 1915. When this was healed he bluffed them at Astral House and wangled himself into the Flying Corps without a Board, and has been flying ever since. Isn't it mad? – a Pilot, too. He giggles over his present wound: 'Oh, I ran into 8 Huns and they went for me' – as if they'd been grazing cows.

Whit Sunday. We've had a divine day here and it's a translucent night of sunset, stars and moon and aeroplanes, and spoilt by the thunder of the guns, which as you know are very busy just now on both sides. We fitted up a Marquee as a Church for Early Service, and it looked lovely in red and white, with lots of green branches in shell-cases. We had a United Service this evening, conducted by the two Padres together, C. of E. and Presbyterian. Incidentally, in moments snatched in turns from the wards, where we are rather busy, we gave a House Warming in our Mess and had a great many officers, finishing up with a Corps Commander and all his Staff, and one of the Australian Bands playing in the Hospital. Our sensational Dug-Outs were on view and were much admired.

This is a Sky Thoroughfare between many Aerodromes and the Line, and from sunset onwards the sky is thick with planes, and the humming and droning is incessant and very disturbing for sleep. Fritz comes over pretty regularly but has not wasted any of his eggs on us so far.

There are a hundred interesting things one would like to tell you, but everything comes under forbidden headings – some very amusing and some splendid and some tragic. I haven't seen so much of the men personally for a long time, and it is marvellous to find practically the same spirit, the same detached acceptance of their injuries, and the same blind unquestioning obedience to every order, and the same alacrity to give up their pillows, their time, or their pudding to each other, as in the beginning of this War, when all the men were the old Regular Army. And they are all like that – the Londoners, the Scots, the Counties, the Irish, the Canadians and the Aussies and the New Zealanders.

The Jock can 'see red' and get home with the bayonet and smash up a nest of Machine Gunners, or throw his Mills bombs into a dug-out full of Fritzies, perhaps better than a Canadian or an Aussy, but when that is all past and he is helping in a Ward he bends over a pneumonia man helping him to cough, or cajoling him to take his feeds, with an almost more than maternal tenderness. Or he picks up a compound-fractured limb off its splint while helping with a dressing with a gentleness and delicacy that no nurse could hope to beat.

Their obedience is another unfailing quality. You say, 'I'd like to have all the tables taken out and scrubbed to-morrow morning, boys,' and when you come on next day every one is shining. Or you say, 'Paddy is only to have milk to-day, Smith,' and you needn't give it another thought. At dinner-time someone will call out, ''Ere – that bloke ain't got to 'ave nothin' only milk. Fetch back that puddin'.'

When a Convoy comes in at night they're out of bed in a second, filling hot bottles, and undressing the new patients and careering round with drinks. 'Is there another so and so?' you ask. 'He can have mine,' is the instantaneous answer, whether it's a custard pudding or a blanket or a safety-pin. If a boy asks for a fag after a bad dressing they literally rush to be first to get him one of theirs.

A rather loutish Gunner, of no apparent parts, asked me yesterday to get him marked out. 'I'd rather be up the Line doin' a bit,' he said. 'Been up there 3½ years and I got kind o' used to a dug-out and that.' This particular man would go on contentedly in a dug-out where he is socially at his ease, any number of years!

A Jock was saying how many shells we put over to their one. 'Why, every one of our guns gets barkin' at him when he puts one over. You can't help feelin' sorry for puir old Gerry,' he said sadly.

There are some fascinating wooded valleys not ten minutes off, but I haven't had time to explore yet. Major R. and Major S. have a lark's nest they're very proud of with four eggs.

The noise and vibration at this minute is like being inside a gramophone. We have a wounded Yank who says he feels 'elegant' to-night.

I could do with some more Sisters.

Must do a round now and see what's likely to be wanted during the night.

Tuesday, June 4th, 10.30 p.m. He is at this moment making the dickens of an angry noise about 100 feet directly overhead: whether he means to unload here or not remains to be seen.

We've had rather a busy week. One boy was kicked in the chest by a mule and his right lung crushed. He died practically of suffocation, and 10 minutes before he died, when I asked him if he had a message for his mother, he gasped out (one word at a time): 'I'm trying to control myself. Tell her I'm getting on fine. Tell her the Sisters and Orderlies are all very kind to me – that'll please her.' He was a wonderful boy. There's a little pneumonia boy who wails to have his hand held: a boy who is up instantly goes and sits on his bed, strokes his hand and says gravely, 'He wants me to tell him a tale, I think.' The black child died, alternately cursing and singing hymns.

The weather continues unnaturally radiant. I have never worked in a more lovely spot in this war. There is always a breeze waving over the cornfields and the hills are covered with woods near the valleys, with open downs at the top. Below are streams through shady orchards and rustling poplars – and you can see for miles from the downs. Sir Anthony Bowlby went away saying, 'Well, I can wish you nothing better than to stay here all the summer, and I hope you won't have shells spoiling this nice compound.' We have cinder paths outlined in white stones and white posts and ropes and clover, and no dirty linen, slops or refuse visible anywhere at any hour: owing to the much abused Army clockwork standard. A C.O. late of a Field Ambulance like our C.O. has a much higher standard in these things than the Civilians who come up from the Base.

We had two French girls, sisters of 19 and 16, in, badly gassed and one wounded. I took them to the French Civilian hospital at Abbeville the next day. It is a filthy place. They were such angels of goodness, blistered by mustard gas literally from head to foot, and breathing badly. They came from near Albert.

Fritz has made a horrid mess of Abbeville since we were there a month ago: 10 W.A.C.'s were killed at once one day.

This is going to be a year of movement all the time, but he won't get to Paris or Calais.

Sunday, June 16th. I suppose you've had the same heavenly mornings we've had. We emerge about 7.30 (6.30 in real life) from our dug-outs, to a loud continuous chorus of larks singing their Te Deum, and also to the hum and buzz of whole squadrons of aeroplanes, keeping marvellous V formations against the dazzling blue and white of the sky. The hills are covered with waving corn, like watered silk in the wind, with deep crimson clover, and with fields of huge oxeye daisies, like moving sheets: they are of enormous size, very tall and as many as six on one stalk. To-day there is no sound of guns and it is all Peace and loveliness. All the worst patients are improving and the Colonel has come back from his leave. One of my Sisters goes on leave to-day and the rest go in turn: mine is timed for the last week in July or the first in August with any luck.

We are able to get fresh butter, milk from the cow, and eggs, from the farms about and generally fresh vegetables.

Monday, June 17th. Yesterday afternoon Sister C. and I escorted the Leave Sister to the city of Abbeville and came home by a long roundabout way. It was a glorious 50-mile run through sunny France and it took us up near the Sausage Balloons, 9 kilos from Amiens, whose lovely spire we saw reigning over the unhappy town. It seems funny to think how we drove 40 kilos beyond that spot in February and 40 kilos back on March 23rd!

Last night he was over again working up to his old form: he passed overhead flying very low a good deal, from 11 p.m. I had just got to bed and to sleep when 5 loud cracks at 1.30 made us sit up: he smacked them into the village but there were no casualties. To-night it is thunderstormy and may keep him off. The sky illuminations in this wide expanse on these occasions are lovely: searchlights, signals, flares and flashes. We had a busyish night with operations.

June 29th. We are still very busy with influenza and also some badly wounded. An extra Sister is on her way, and we have a Relief Sister for the leave. I've had a mild go of 'flu myself, but haven't knocked off for it and am now better.

Jerry comes every night again and drops below the barrage, seeking whom he may devour: I think he gets low enough to see our huge Red Cross, as even when some of our lads butt in and engage him with their machine-guns, he hasn't dropped anything on us, though there is lively scrapping overhead. It is very interesting but too critical to be amusing.

Nearly all the wards are dug in about 5 feet and were much approved by the D.M.S. yesterday. He said the Army Commander (Rawlinson) has said that he will pull down any C.C.S. he finds not camouflaged.

A man has had his left arm and left leg off to-day – they seldom recover. A boy the other day had to have his second leg off and died the same night. He had been craving for strawberries and by great luck we got some for him the day before. I wish we had a lot for them.

There are four badly wounded officers who need a lot of looking after, besides a crowd of sick ones.

The problem is to get the influenzas well enough to go back to the Line and yet have room for the new ones.

Tuesday, August 6th. For a week past the air has been thick with rumours of a Giant Push, of Divisions going back into the Line after only 24 hours out, of 1,000 Tanks massing in front of us, Cavalry pushing up, and for 5 nights running we heard troops passing through our village in the valley below to the number of 40,000.

To-day two trains cleared us of all but the few unfit to travel, and to-night we have got the Hospital mobilized for Zero and every man to his station – decks cleared for action. This will not be posted until it is History.

There happened to be for the first time an Expeditionary Force Canteen Mobile Cinema visiting us, and at 7.30 p.m. we had a very fine show of The Better 'Ole in our big Reception Tent close to the road, between No. 4 and us. It ended on the note of 'Keep on Carrying On,' and as we streamed out the 1st Cavalry Division was trotting by in the dark, the men calling cheerily, 'Keep an empty bed for me.' 'See us again to-morrow, Sister,' or 'We're going to Berlin this time.' It was extraordinarily vivid after the realism of the Bairnsfather pictures to come in touch with it like that in five seconds. The sky was lit with gun flashes, searchlights and trails of Tracer bullets, and Gerry is at this moment scouting overhead. We have only a dozen patients in, and only two Sisters on.

I am praying that my leave doesn't come through. I think it won't. Why didn't I either put in for it last month or wait till next?

Wednesday, August 7th, 11.15 p.m. Brilliant sun to-day for a welcome change, after the heavy rains for weeks past. We've had a long day of renewed preparations, arrivals of Teams and a cheery visit from Sir Anthony Bowlby. Only the usual Take-in, which passed straight on to one of the trains waiting below in the village. One Team was from my old C.C.S. and brought 6 of my own Nursing Orderlies, bless them.

All is ready for Berlin. I'm hoping breathlessly that they hold back my leave to see this through.

Thursday, August 8th, or rather 4 a.m. August 9th. 20,000 prisoners, 20 kilometres, 200 guns, transport captured, bombs continually on the congested fleeing armies – and here on our side the men who've made this happen, and given their eyes, limbs, jaws and lives in doing so. It is an extraordinary jumble of a bigger feeling of Victory and the wicked piteous sacrifice of all these men. And they are marvellous as always.

I have 34 Sisters and the place is crawling with Surgeons (one is a V.C.) but we want more stretcher-bearers. The Orderlies are coming up to the scratch like Britons and I think the Colonel is rather pleased with everything. We have a baby Lt.-Colonel of 24 covered with crosses and bars.

Saturday, August 10th, 10 p.m. There are wonderful things happening. By now we ought to be in Marchelepot again. It is fine to hear of our bridges at Péronne and Brie, that we knew and saw being built by Sappers, being bombed before he can get back over them. (The sky at this moment is like Piccadilly Circus, with our squadrons going over for their night's work.)

The wounded, nearly all machine-gun bullets – very few shell wounds, as his guns are busy running away – are very happy: very few walking wounded have come down compared to last Battle, because they won't miss the chase – that is to say they are in fifties rather than hundreds at a time, but we have a lot of stretcher-cases. Of course we are all up to our necks in dealing with them, with ten Teams.

There are great stories of a 15-inch gun mounted on a Railway, with two trains full of ammunition being taken; of an Australian Division that caught a complete Battery of 5.9's; of a Boche Hospital Train with patients, orderlies, M.O. *and Sisters*, who were taken to 61 C.C.S., two miles from us, and are now at the Base! They'll be thoroughly fêted, I hope: a Sister can't do more in a Battle than be captured with her wounded, can she? We have a great many German wounded: one Baby Jerry is the pet of the place – a fair smiling clean boy who was, he said proudly, 'nur ein Tag' in the Line. For some never-failing reason the Orderlies and the men fall over each other trying to make the Jerries comfortable. Their instinct is purely for hospitality, I think.

We have an officer with his right arm and right leg off. I think he is going to recover. By the by, they caught a Divisional General and all his Staff. There's a funny story of Americans being sent up to relieve the Australians and they haven't caught them up yet!

A German prisoner continued to chuckle while his wound was being dressed. I asked him what the joke was. 'You've won the War,' he said. 'We shall all go home now!' And this on August 10th!

Must go round the Hospital now and then to bed. The Colonel tells me nothing has come through yet, thank goodness, about my leave. He says he has written a letter to our H.Q. that would melt a heart of stone.

August 11th. Orders have come for me to 'proceed forthwith' to Boulogne for leave. That probably means that I shall not rejoin this Unit.

The letters after this date until the Armistice are written from a Base Hospital and are of no special interest beyond the ordinary routine of a Military General Hospital in War-time.

POSTSCRIPT

Kate Luard left France on 28 November 1918, resigning from the nursing service so that she could return home to look after her ailing father. Following his death, she resumed her role as Matron of the Berks and Bucks County Sanatorium, but was clearly restless. On 20 March 1919 she wrote to Maud McCarthy, her former Matron-in-Chief, requesting a reference. It seemed that her age was making it difficult to secure a senior hospital position (she was, by now, almost 50). McCarthy responded with glowing testimonials and Kate was appointed to the South London Hospital for Women.

Her last position as a nurse was as Matron at Bradfield College, a private boys' school in Berkshire. She inspired complete confidence in masters and parents alike who learnt too the full benefit of her great experience and skill. An Old Boy wrote that, although would-be malingerers received short shrift, she displayed 'devotion, gentleness and efficiency' to those who were truly ill or injured.

She retired from Bradfield in December 1932 due to a back injury which caused her much discomfort and often considerable pain. On leaving she returned to Essex sharing a village house in Wickham Bishops with her two sisters 'G'* and Rose. She continued to travel

---

* Kate's sister Georgina known to her family as 'G' and often called 'Gkins' by Kate.

whenever she could, generally with one or other of her sisters, and never without her sketchbook. With her brother Percy she toured the battle-fields on the Western and Eastern Fronts

Gradually her back became more troublesome and she had to abandon the local activities which were her interest and the garden which was her joy. She retired from being commandant of the Essex 24 Women's Detachment of the British Red Cross Society in 1940 and was made a life vice-president.

As time passed she became increasingly incapacitated and finally bedridden. However, to the end she retained a close interest in Bradfield, and nothing gave her more pleasure than a letter or a visit from someone connected with and informed about the school. She also enjoyed the visits and the support of her surviving siblings and her nieces, nephews and friends.

She died, aged 90, on 16 August 1962. Her grave and headstone are in St Bartholomew's churchyard, Wickham Bishops, alongside those of her sisters G and Rose.

Family Letters

Hundreds of additional letters exchanged between Kate Luard and her family over the course of the First World War are preserved with other papers and journals in the archives of Essex Record Office; together with those written during the Boer War. Whether some of these additional letters were omitted from her two books because they were considered at the time too personal, or in some cases too controversial, is not known. But they contain examples of her writing that are as powerful and moving, poignant and humorous, as anything of hers that has yet been published. As well as shedding new light on Kate's own character and background, the letters from her family help bring to life those to whom she was actually writing – those closest to her – and at the same time present a vivid picture of wartime rural Britain and an almost Victorian way of life that was to vanish for ever.

Many of Kate's letters were written for the whole family and were intended to be sent on as round robins. Others were addressed to individual members of the family or to the 'inner circle' which comprised only her closest sisters, but sometimes included her brother Percy and occasionally her father. Kate was known to most of her family as Evelyn or Evie. Her ten surviving siblings, in order of age, were Fred (born 1861), Hugh (an army surgeon in the IMS on the North West Frontier 1890-1901), Frank (Royal Marines), Georgina (G), Nettie, Percy (who took over from his father as Rector of Birch), Lucy, Trant (Royal Marines), Rose and the youngest Daisy (born 1880). Some letters appear here in the form of extracts:

From Daisy – August 22nd 1914
Dear Kate

Great excitement at getting your 1st censored p.c. with news of your arrival 'there'. It was glorious to hear of the landing of our troops, but of course we are all dying to know where they are now … We are still madly Red Crossing. The Colchester Red X have been mobilised and have 5 patients – sick Territorials. 3000 Territorials marched past here on Wed. … We had a bedmaking practice on Thur and were distinctly improved. We had Sissy as a patient and found her distinctly weighty!

From Kate – Friday September 25th 1914 – Hospital Ship Carisbrook Castle, St Nazaire
Dear Girls & Percy & Nobody Else

At last a chance to write uncensored. I brought down 450 wounded & sick yesterday from Le Mans. Came on here this morning to get my last instalment of up to date diary posted. There are a lot of wounded officers on board – limping haggard wrecks. I read French's despatch of the 11th about the Great Retreat, the most heroic and brilliant thing in History. Surely no one grudges their best of sons & brothers & husbands who gave their lives in that. And this Battle of the Marne is doing the same – when you stand off for a few hours from the gruesome details, & pathetic streams of broken, dirty ragged bandaged cripples that one is occupied with all day, it gets more and more unfathomable & heartbreaking. ... Everyone is struck all of a heap by the pluck and cheeriness of the wounded. ...

(PS) You all say you are aching to hear from me, but you've no idea what it's like to bottle it all up and not be able to tell you all about it, all day long. That is why my diary oozes out of me, like a vent, on the chance it reaches you.

From Percy – Michaelmas (September 29th) 1914
... It's awful to think that there are thousands of wounded in England now from the Battle of the Aisne & that the battle is still going on! From all over England officers of most of the local families are dead, Second Lieuts by the score. As to the Tommies I wonder when we shall ever know how many: practically no lists have been published yet tho' the W.O. lets their people know at once if they're reported missing or dead.

From Kate – Monday October 5th (1914)
... It's glorious to get your letters so soon after you write them and not feeling miles away at the end of a different bit of string. I'm almost hourly expecting the summons to Ambulance Train No.1. ...

From Daisy – October 1914
... You are a lucky devil waltzing to the Front like that. The family is much amused because you're the 1st to get to the Front, 1st to go up in an airyoplane (*sic*) & only one to get to the last war. Always so dashing ... Give our love to the fighting line and tell them what we think of them. By the way you libel me blackly – I've written every blooming week, so there. Not my fault if yr silly old post office don't give them to you. I suppose in spite of the horrors you are having the time of your life – can't I come as a female orderly on yr train? Your exploits cause a great sensation here – Florence Nightingale is nothing to it. Dr Cooke was spluttering with excitement over you last night. Everyone is screaming to

see your letters ... N and I spend hours reading and sending or copying your cards. ... It's what we live for nowadays.

From Kate – October 18th 1914 – Ambulance Train, Rouen
My dear Family, Friends & Acquaintances
    Will you start a fund with £1 of my money and send me a case of comforts for the Tommies on my train: it is hateful to have nothing they want – as follows:
    Packets of cigarettes
    Packets of shag
    Slabs of hard tobacco
    Packs of cards
    Pipes (not expensive ones)
    A few cheap sets of draughts
    Cheap coloured handkerchiefs
    Envelopes containing writing paper, envelopes & indelible pencils & thin postcards
    Some cheap sweets of sorts
    Chocolate. Matches
    Separately from the above list, Nursing Sister K would be glad if her father would send her a tin of Birch Bullseyes, another tin of biscuits (oatmeal) in a high narrow tin. ...

From Nettie – November 19th 1914
Dear E, Your first censored diary arrived yesterday. The names of places and about 3 sentences were heavily scored out in purplish ink. ...
    I'm afraid you will really feel the cold in your train – and it's becoming unusually cold for Nov here ... raw sleet storms. Those poor dears in the trenches.
    Old Fred has got a job at last – E. Surrey Regt ... it ought to bustle him up a bit. They must be awfully short of officers everywhere.
    Our recruits are trickling away from Birch ... They'll v soon be in France ... then we'll only have 3 choir men left. We look with pride on

our empty places in the choir. There are rumours German submarines were seen off Mersea. They are digging trenches near the coast, and near Witham which is the 2nd line of defence. Frank doesn't believe an invasion can come off – they would be cut down before they landed.

From Percy – December 19th 1914
My most loving Christmas wishes – may it be your last on Active Service … My present to you is the electric torch (I hope they sent 2 extra batteries). You must want it in your wet and sloppy sidings at night …

From Hugh – December 20th 1914 – Ruebury House, Yorkshire
My dear Evelyn

I'm afraid this will hardly reach you by Christmas … I dare say you will spend this one within the sound of guns and with arduous and trying duties. Your journals are splendid reading and you have the satisfaction of doing grand work.

On Wed we did actually hear the sound of guns which proved to be the Huns bombarding Whitby (about 25 miles away) and other defenceless towns. They did a lot of damage, and killed over 100 and wounded 500, mostly civilians. This particular raid has been taken with astonishing calm …

From Percy – January 19th 1915
… Your letters continue to be thrilling … G & I & Frank – and the others too – think that your diary, duly edited, would make a most exciting and readable book after the War!

From Nettie – January 29th 1915
Dear E, a long diary came yesterday with account of your going to Versailles. We had to tear out 2 pages about the horrors in Oct before we could show it to father … do put such things on a separate bit of paper

for us and don't mix it up in the diary – it's such a bore to cut off pieces, paste pieces on, etc.

Rose says Cambridge is in total darkness at night. Bells & clocks are stopped, sentries with fixed bayonets meet you at every turn and no motors are allowed to enter or leave the town after dark!

From Kate – February 2nd 1915
... So G has had a visit from a JJ!!! But yours G was a Bug, a comparatively aristocratic animal compared to ours which are Body Lice! Ours lays eggs in clothes & breeds large families, which come out every three hours for a meal, & they go to sleep in the seams of your clothes till hungry again! They are small, grey, pointed flat creatures, rather like torpedo boats, with many legs.

From Nettie – February 6th 1915
So sorry you're such a seedy worm ... my good girl of course you must take ten days leave at once ... it's a good time for a holiday before the advance – so come along. What a lark it will be ... you shall have every luxury & comfort yr family can provide – chairs to sit on, warm fires, cups of coffee, cushions on your lap ... admiring crowds to look at you and hang on your words!

From Father (Rev BGL) – March 15th 1915 – Birch Rectory, Colchester
Isn't it thrilling Frank being in the Dardanelles. ... Isn't it sickening for poor old Trant to be kicking his heels in Columbo when every one of his friends and relations is in the thick of things in Europe & the North Sea.

From Daisy – April 5th 1915
Your letters thrilled us to our marrows. ... Here sitting around the fire, of your deeds we never tire. I have been busy saving England all week by toiling at the potato patch and coping with a war savings audit. ...

From Kate – April 8th 1915 – Officers Dressing Station – No. 4 Field Ambulance
… One goes about with a grin of inward joy, varied by thrills of heaving patriotic pride when the lines of upcoming troops of the New Divisions march past, and by sobs of choking pride when the men with the Trench-Look tramp back – such as are alive each day …

From Kate – April 10th 1915
I've taken half an hour now for a cigarette which always pulls me together & is worth it or one might bust up. … Four of the new sisters are top-hole. Cigarette finished – must stop.

From Nettie – April 22nd 1915
As for those No. 4 FA* letters – what a thrilling place … Seeing the everyday life of the army at the front & meeting soldiers tramping back, war worn from the trenches … We're sending some more cigs and chocs for them. We're all knitting socks now …

From Kate – May 2nd 1915 – Sunday 1am
… I'm writing in the ward … Opposite me is a boy of 22 with his shoulder, left arm and left leg all in shell holes – he has curly hair, blue eyes and a serene face. His temp is 103 & his pulse 136 … His dressing this morning was half an hour of agony … I treat you to all these medical details now as a medical professional. I look on it as a great privilege to be mother to these young heroes, wouldn't you?

You don't seem to have got my Trenches letter yet – wonder where it's got to. This Ypres battle has been another gory gassy mess – u.b.c.** all over again.

---

* Field Ambulance.
** An acronym frequently used by Kate to describe anything horrific. It apparently stood for 'utter bloody chaos'.

From Percy – Ascension Day (May 17th) 1915

... A lot has happened since I last wrote. The Spring Offensive has broken out; the Gallipoli landing has been gloriously accomplished (and Frank has been wounded, last Monday – but very slightly we hear today ... tho' his battalion has been terribly knocked about, 14 officers killed and wounded).

From Frank (to family) – July 11th 1915
(Back in Gallipoli, after being treated in Alexandria for the wound he received two months earlier, when he was shot through the knee.)

We did not go back to the trenches as expected ... The men however don't get much rest as we are digging new communication trenches ... We lose a man or two each day as the enemy are shelling where they think we are working ... The middle of the day is very hot – too hot for sleep – and pervaded with myriads of flies which cover your food, face and hands. We are all a good deal troubled with diarrhoea – one part of the treatment is brandy and port. ...

(Two days after writing this letter Frank was killed in action. According to the official records he 'died most gallantly at the head of his battalion, whilst leading his men'. His grave remains in Gallipoli, his widow Ellie saying, 'I wouldn't take Frank's body from the field of glory for anything – what could be finer than to lie there where his work was done that day'.)

From Trant – October 31st 1915 – Shepherd's Hotel, Cairo
Dear Evelyn, Heartiest congratulations on becoming both an authoress and a Matron. I AM glad you've got such a good show to run on your own. ... And to be right in the thick of it again – you really are a lucky beggar.

From G – November 26th 1915
I was constrained to speak at a CS Union conference this week about the war and women's work. There is a tendency now to say education

doesn't matter ... and the schools are being closed because there is no one to teach in them – an awful crisis is coming on which I can't get people to see. But it's the children of today who are to pick up the pieces and make the new – and better – world after the war ... teaching is war work as much as munitions.

From Kate – January 18th 1916 – to her father
... Miss McCarthy sent me my new ribbon yesterday in a registered letter with her congratulations. It was the first I got with the magic letters after one's name, which nothing but a courtmartial sentence can now take away. (RRC).

From Nettie – April 5th 1916
... In the evening we had a Zeppelin to liven us up. It was exciting seeing the monster for the 1st time (even **you** haven't seen a Zepp have you!) ... we heard lots of distant bombs and guns that night and the Zepps were evidently having a good strafing from our anti-aircraft guns – wasn't it splendid bringing one down? ... Friday was the worst raid – 4 people killed at Braintree. Ipswich had Zepps 3 nights running, 5 people killed, and it dropped bombs at Chelmsford.

From G – May 29th 1916 – Whitelands College, Chelsea
Dearest Evelyn,
   Your last U.B.C. letter thrilled me to the marrow and I count the hours till I get your next and fear being away from here will delay it. The Vimy Ridge affair sounds quite horrible. Your letter reminded me more of the Béthune one than any since. How splendid to have got your C.C.St. so ready and perfect to receive the wounded. It really is a 'spot' hospital – now – isn't it?

From Kate – Undated

It is ages since I heard from home, not a word since the Naval Battle of Glorious & Immortal memory. And now old K of K has won his place in the Roll of Honour too. It's grand that he didn't die in his bed of an apoplectic stroke but at the hand of the enemy ... They are trying to break through at Ypres but they won't do it, though it is u.b.c. for us while they try.

The French don't seem nervous about Verdun, but they ought to be. It's cheering of old Russia to buck up and have a dab on the right side just now. I wonder what the Greeks of Saloneek are going to do. Poor old Italy may have very fine Botticelli pictures of squirming naked ladies paddling in seashells but it can't fight Austria very brilliantly.

(*This letter was written in late June 1916, judging from the events referred to. The Naval Battle of Jutland ended on June 1; Lord Kitchener [of Khartoum] died on June 5 when the cruiser on which he was travelling to Russia on a diplomatic mission hit a German mine; Fort Vaux was stormed by the Germans on June 2 as they advanced towards Verdun; Italy's premier resigned on June 11, amid continuing stalemate in the country's war against Austria ; on June 21 Russian forces took Bukovina from the Austro-Hungarians; and on the same day the Greek cabinet resigned under pressure from the Allied powers, who had turned the Greek port of Salonika into a military base.*)

From Nettie – June 18th 1916

My poor girl, I got back from Colchester to find a note saying you were down with Trench fever ... I hope you get nice beef teas and bread & milk & eggs etc. It would be a howling nuisance to be sent back to the base hospital.

From Nettie – June 27th 1916

Glad you've risen from yr bed of sickness ... hope it hasn't left you feeling as weak as a cat. ... I wonder if the big bombardment is the start of the great advance – we've heard the distant thuds hammering the last few days – they never seem to stop.

From Nettie – July 26th 1916
Last week we haymaked madly – P (Percy), D (Daisy), I and the maids –
hot and hard work but satisfying.

From Nettie – August 5th 1916
... It is an amazing thing that you should be knocking up against & talking to all those Marines – the men who knew Frank so intimately in his
working life as well as social – and the privates who were with him on
his last day ...

And what a roaring – not to say gay time you seem to have! Careering
round with Naval surgeons and tea-ing with Generals! You're a lucky
dog and no mistake. I couldn't write last week as working at the Hosp
... and when I got back at about 3.30 I only felt like a deck chair in
the garden ...

From Kate – Sat September 2nd 1916
... Our emergency cases come steadily dribbling in, night and day, & for
many of them it is only a halting place for the little cemetery. Two boys
of the Hawke Battalion came in together and both died. One told me
to tell his mother it was 'only slight', & he was then pulseless. And when
some more came in he said 'Never mind me, there's them others to see
to'.

A Plymouth Marine is having a very uphill fight with two infected
legs. I asked him if he knew the Col. of the Portsmouths in Gallipoli &
he said 'Colonel Luard?'. I told him he was my brother & his face lighted
up. Then he said 'Hard luck'.

The German officer is getting slowly better but is still paralysed down
one side. ... He talks perfect French & a little English but I converse
with him in German. ... The men who are up light his cigarettes for
him and the orderlies feed him in a loving manner.

If Daisy could do a little shopping for me in Colchester I should be
greatly transported, for le petit Charles & Clothilde et la mère. They are
so absurdly good to me. ...

Long & exciting interruption on the part of a Boche Airplane who toured around exactly overhead for half an hour. Bursting shells from an Archibald on each side of us made a ceiling for us and a floor for him as he frisked merrily round 1000 feet above their highest range. ...

From Trant – December 17th 1916 – Sultan Hussein Club, Alexandria
Dear Evelyn

... They all say at home you look younger and more blooming & cheerier every time you come home. How you do it beats me with all you are seeing and hearing and dealing with ... Do try and meet Maurice Festing, who's a brigade major and the best pal I've got in the corps. ...

From Kate – March 5th 1917 – 32 CCS, 3rd Army, BEH
Beloved Gkins

We suddenly got orders to rejoin and moved here ... This is a topping place – just what I've been out here for from the beginning of the War ... On a big field on high open ground ...

Our Compound is absolutely pet walled in by canvas screen all round – & containing Armstrong Huts for sleeping, a Nissen Hut for Mess Room, a tin shanty kitchen, & another for Aunt.*

... I have a hut to myself with my own camp furniture kit. It is absolutely IT. The Colonel and I trot round the camp & plan things out & indent for equipment.

I have an awful lot to do, creating a new mess, finding laundry, arranging my new office, organising dressing equipment, stationing orderlies & Sisters, fitting out a huge theatre with equipment for 4 (operating) tables at once, getting dark blinds made for all windows, fixing up Red X stores etc. ... The nearest town is 10 miles away & there is no village even here – so it is not easy to find fresh butter eggs milk & laundry women.

---

* Lavatory.

... The quagmire of melting snow & trodden field is beyond words; we have hobnailed Army boots of Bantam size – topping. As usual when we move to a new place we get shells or bombs. This time it was shelling ... they came screaming overhead ...

From G – May 14th 1917
Darling Evelyn ... My chief feeling always is to thank God you – with your particular parts & experience & character – are there to cope with these hideous crises. ... If you could know what it feels like to care as much as you do and yet be quite impotent to help, you'd know how the Good God had especially blessed you. ...

From Percy – August 12th 1917
Your letters are absolutely IT ... and they fill me with awe & wonder & admiration & joy. ... It is good to know the great Advanced CCS is such a success & that you are in charge of it ... Life here is mostly made up of cabbage seeds, wheatfields, bereaved parents, War anniversaries & showers of rain; yours is made up of abdomens, bombs, floods, shells and funerals.

From Kate – June 4th 1917
Today I took a book, a cigarette, the last Birch bullseyes and a sun umbrella to a green valley with a running stream where I paddled and dried my feet in the sun while Bristol fighters and tri-planes came and took photographs of the German positions to send to HQ. Whatever lovely peace is about you there is always War in the sky. Now it's blue, with larks singing in it.

From Kate – Sat August 4th 1917
Dearest G, Yes, it is chiefly ubc of the ghastliest and in the most midwinter conditions of night and day pouring rain and sloughs of despond underfoot – inside the wards as well as out. And all the Push a washout,

literally. I think I am getting rather tired and have got to the stage of
not knowing when to stop. When I do I immediately begin to cry of all
the tomfool things to do! But outside my Armstrong hut one can keep
smiling. It is the dirtiness & wasted effort of War that clouds one's vision
– late – 1am, just into bed & quite cheery again – but we had 56 funerals
today so can you wonder? … Can't I ever have a copy of Trant's letters.
He's my brother too!

From Kate – Christmas 1917
My darling father,
   The Division is busy giving concerts in our big theatre this week.
Each Battalion has its own troupe and the rivalry is keen. We three sisters are the solitary and distinguished females in a pack of 600 men and
inspire occasional witty & polite sallies from the Performers. We sit in
the front row between Colonels of the 3 DG's* and 2nd Black Watch
& others. Each concert party has its 'Star Girl' marvellously got up as in
a London Music Hall. Some sing falsetto & some roar their songs in a
deep bass coming from a low neck & chiffon dress, lovely stockings &
high heels!

From Kate – February 8th 1918
… There is a large Labour Battalion of Italian soldiers working here, also
Chinese and Indians … The Italian officer was horrified because I go
about in a Trench Coat & Sou'Wester instead of white robes with large
Croix Rouges on them as ladies of the Red Cross do in Italy …

From Kate – April 18th 1918
… The enemy made a great bid for Villers Bretonneux early yesterday
morning, beginning with a terrific drenching with gas shells.
   We had over 500 gassed men in and every spot of every floor was
covered with them, coughing, spitting & crying with the pain in their

---

* Dragoon Guards.

eyes. All hands were piped to cope ... They have to be stripped as their clothes are soaked with gas and their bodies washed down with chloride of lime, their eyes & mouths swabbed with Bicarb of Soda & drinks & clothing given. ... You give them jam tins to be sick in and go round with Soda Bicarb in large pails. The worst are in a special ward having continuous oxygen, but some are drowning in their own secretions in spite of it. Two trains are now evacuating all fit to be put on them.

It is pouring with rain, and the ground is a slithering quagmire.

During her time at the front, as sister in charge of a CCS, Kate must have written hundreds of 'break-the-news' letters, which were sent almost daily to mothers or next of kin of the soldiers under her care. These were usually sensitive messages of condolence and reassurance but sometimes contained the good news of recovery. There were many occasions when Kate had so many to write that she despaired of ever getting through them all and they were written in spare moments, often late at night. The following is typical of a letter she received in return:

Victoria League, Millbank House, Westminster – July 28th 1916
I think you would like to know what very great comfort & pleasure has been given by a letter from you. One of the girls ... came a long way a few nights ago to tell me of the death of her only brother, shot through the throat. The one thing that relieved their overwhelming trouble was the letter you had written about him, and the little bit of paper you sent home on which he had written answers to your questions, & his address. They knew it all by heart and repeated it over to me several times – and just made all the difference.

You must have many such cases but perhaps it may help a little to lighten the strain of your work to know of one case in which the letter you found time to write has meant more than words can say to the mother and sisters. They were quite delighted that I knew your name and could tell them a little about you ...

Yours very truly,

Gertrude Drayton, Acting Sec.

ABBREVIATIONS

ADC	Aide-de-Camp
ADMS	Acting Director of Medical Services
AMFO	Assistant Military Forwarding Officer
ASC	Army Service Corps
BA	British Army
BEF	British Expeditionary Force
BRCS	British Red Cross Society
CCS	Casualty Clearing Station
C-in-C	Commander-in-Chief
Coy	Company
DFC	Distinguished Flying Cross
Div	Division
DMS	Director of Medical Services
DSO	Distinguished Service Order
FA	Field Ambulance
FRCS	Fellow of the Royal College of Surgeons
FRS	Fellow of the Royal Society
GHQ	General Headquarters

GOC	General Officer Commanding
HAC	Honourable Artillery Company
HE	High Explosive
HQ	Headquarters
MC	Military Cross
MM	Military Medal
MO	Medical Officer
NCO	Non-Commissioned Officer
OC/CO	Officer Commanding
OH	Officers' Hospital
QAIMNSR	Queen Alexandra's Imperial Military Nursing Service Reserve
QM	Quartermaster
QMG	Quartermaster General
RAMC	Royal Army Medical Corps
RE	Royal Engineers
RFA	Royal Field Artillery
RFC	Royal Flying Corps
RMA	Royal Marine Artillery
RMLI	Royal Marine Light Infantry
RNVR	Royal Navy Volunteer Reserve
RRC	Royal Red Cross
RTA	Required Time of Arrival
RTO	Railway Transport Officer
VAD	Voluntary Aid Detachment
VC	Victoria Cross
WAAC	Women's Auxiliary Army Corps
YMCA	Young Men's Christian Association

GLOSSARY

Advanced dressing station: a basic care point. The wounded were brought here by stretcher or other means from the regimental aid post which was only a few metres behind the front line. They were set up and supplied by the field ambulances but provided only limited medical treatment and did not have any holding capacity.

Aerial torpedo: a light torpedo dropped from an aircraft.

Ambulance trains: these trains transported the wounded from casualty clearing stations to Base Hospitals at one of the Channel ports. In 1914 the wounded men were lying on straw and conditions were primitive. Later the trains were fitted out as mobile hospitals with operating theatres, bunk beds, kitchen etc. and a full complement of QAIMNS nurses, RAMC doctors and surgeons, and orderlies.

Ammunition boots: or boots general service; black or brown leather ankle boots in dimpled leather with metal-studded soles. Hard-wearing and uncomfortable.

'Archie': anti-aircraft fire/anti-aircraft gun.

Argylls: Argyll and Sutherland Highlanders.

Armada Belfry: this fifteenth-century sandstone bell tower remained standing amid the ruins of Béthune after German bombardment in 1918.

Armstrong hut: a canvas and wood collapsible hut used by the British. It was designed by Colonel Armstrong of the Royal Engineers and used in CCSs, which often had to move at short notice.

Army formations: the British Expeditionary Force comprised several Field Armies, each commanded by a general, and each one made up of:

Nineteen corps plus a cavalry corps commanded by a lieutenant general.

Seventy-five divisions plus three cavalry divisions and one cyclist division. A division was a complete fighting unit commanded by a major general and comprised infantry, cavalry, artillery, engineers, signals, transport, veterinary units and stores.

Three brigades made up a division, each one commanded by a brigadier.

Four battalions comprised a brigade, each one commanded by a lieutenant colonel.

The regiment, the basic unit of the British Army, was made up of two or three battalions, and in the First World War often many more.

Asepsis: the complete absence of bacteria, fungi, viruses and other microorganisms that can cause disease; the ideal state for the performance of surgical operation and achieved by sterilisation techniques.

Atropine: a drug extracted from deadly nightshade (belladonna), which inhibits the action of certain nerves of the autonomic nervous system. It was used to treat wound shock in the First World War.

Barge: many wounded were transported by water in hospital barges. Although slow, the journey was smooth and the time allowed the wounded to recuperate.

Base hospital: usually situated in requisitioned buildings at or near a channel port such as Boulogne or Le Havre and acted much like a fully equipped hospital in the UK.

Battalion: an independent fighting unit and part of a regiment. Several battalions make up a regiment and consist of up to 1,200 men divided into up to five companies and subdivided into platoons.

Battery: an independent fighting unit in an artillery regiment usually consisting of eight guns.

Bell tent: a circular tent with a central pole.

'Biscuits': Army slang for the square halves of a mattress.

Black Watch: Royal Highlanders, (named 'Ladies from hell' by the Germans).

Blighty: a slang term for Britain/England, first used in the Boer War and then widely in the First World War. Often used sentimentally.

Boche: German/s; a term used in the First World War (from the French *alboche*).

Brass hat: high-ranking staff officer.

Bret Harte, Francis: (1836–1902), American author and poet who became US Consul in Glasgow in 1880, after which he lived in England. Known for using Californian miners' dialect in his writing.

Bright's disease: nephritis – inflammation of the kidney. (R. Bright 1789–1858, British physician.)

Buffs: (Royal) East Kent Regiment.

Camerons: Queen's Own Cameron Highlanders.

Casualty Clearing Station: part of the casualty evacuation chain after the regimental aid posts and field dressing stations/field ambulances. They were generally located near rail lines and waterways so that the wounded could be evacuated easily to base hospitals. A CCS often had to move at short notice as the front line changed. Although some were situated in permanent buildings, many consisted of large areas of separate tents and marquees, often covering ½ sq mile. Facilities included medical and surgical wards, operating theatres, dispensary, kitchens, sanitation, medical stores, incineration plant, mortuary, ablution and sleeping accommodation. A CCS would normally accommodate a minimum of 50 beds and 150 stretchers and cater for 200 or more wounded. Later in the war a CCS would be able to provide accommodation for more than 500, and up to 1,000 when busy. Several CCSs were usually located near each other to enable flexibility.

Censoring: all letters from the military/nurses were heavily censored to eliminate names of people, army units, troop movements and anything that might affect morale.

Chlorine: a toxic, pungent greenish-yellow gas.

Colotomy: a surgical incision into the colon.

'Contemptible Little Army' of Sir John French: supposedly a quote from the Kaiser after hearing that German Forces were being held up on their way to the French capital. The British Army veterans used the quotation to call themselves the 'Old Contemptibles'.

Crocodile: a long open rail wagon used as a mount for large guns.

Decauville military railway: French narrow-gauge system easily assembled and used extensively in the First World War by the French and British Armies to transport munitions and artillery.

Devons: Devonshire Regiment.

Digitalis: an extract from dried foxglove leaves, which is used medicinally as a heart stimulant.

'Done': slang for recover.

Drake Battalion: a battalion of the Royal Naval Division. Saw service in Gallipoli and in 1915 served in France.

Drip splint: a splint for immobilising the arm whilst fluid is infused into the vein.

Elephant: a small dugout reinforced with corrugated iron. Sometimes known as a 'funk hole'.

Empyema: pus in the pleural cavity, usually secondary to lung infection and relieved by aspiration or drainage. Life threatening.

Eserin: or serine; a drug used in eye treatments to constrict the pupil of the eye and to reduce pressure inside the eye.

Field ambulance: a mobile front-line medical unit for treating the wounded before they were moved to a casualty clearing station. Each division would have three field ambulances, which were made up of ten officers and 244 men. A field ambulance would include stretcher-bearers, tented wards, nursing orderlies, cookhouse, washrooms and a horsed or motor ambulance.

Flavine: used as an antiseptic and to disinfect contaminated wounds.

Fosse: slag heap of mining spoil or a moat or defensive ditch in fortifications. From the Old French *fosse* – dug earth.

Fosse 7: Military cemetery in Mazingarbe, Pas de Calais.

Fritz: a name given to German troops by the British and others in the First and Second World Wars. Sometimes used as a nickname and originated as a German nickname for Friedrich or Frederick.

Gas gangrene: death and decay of wound tissue infected by soil bacterium producing destruction of connective tissue with the generation of gas. Treatment is usually by surgery/amputation. One of the most common conditions of the First World War.

Gas-shelling: the most feared weapon in the First World War was the gas shell. Since gas is heavier than air, diving into a hole for safety would be fatal.

Glosters: Gloucestershire Regiment.

Gordons: Gordon Highlanders.

Gothas: German heavy bi-plane bomber. The improved GV entered service in 1917.

'Grandmother': British 15-inch gun.

Gunners: Royal Artillery.

'Hate': bombardment.

Hill 70: the Canadian corps occupied Hill 70 near the city of Lens as a diversionary tactic to draw German forces away from the 3rd Battle of Ypres. Six VCs were awarded to the Canadian forces. The 44th Brigade of the 15th Scottish Division was also involved.

Hohenzollern Redoubt: a heavily defended German fortification at Auchy-les-Mines, a pre-war mining complex called Fosse 8. As part of the Battle of Loos during September to October 1915, the British failed to take this stronghold with horrendous loss of life. Involved were the 9th Scottish Division and the 46th Northern Division. Several VCs were awarded for conspicuous acts of bravery during the actions.

Howitzer: German heavy gun, the most famous being the 16.5-inch 'Big Bertha'. Generally a large-calibre gun with a high trajectory and short barrel. Term also used in the British Army.

Huguenots: Members of the Protestant Reformed Church of France during the sixteenth and seventeenth centuries. Many fled from France during a series of persecutions, including Kate's ancestor Abraham Luard, who was reputedly smuggled over to England in a barrel in 1685.

Hun: a term used for German soldiers in the First World War.

Identity disc or 'dog tag': a new 35mm disc was introduced in 1914 made of red/brown vulcanised asbestos fibre. This would carry the army number, rank, regiment and religious denomination of the soldier.

Jerry/Gerry: nickname for Germans, originating in First World War but more commonly used in the Second World War.

'JJs': slang for lice, of which there were often infestations. They would attach themselves to hair and clothing and could also transmit diseases.

Kaffir: from an Arabic word used by the white South Africans to describe black people.

Lewis gun: a light air-cooled gas-operated machine gun used chiefly in the First and Second World War. It was named after I.N. Lewis (1858–1931), a US soldier. Also used in aircraft.

Limber: an attachment for a gun carriage, consisting of an axle, pole and two wheels, for carrying ammunition.

'Lizzie': 15-inch naval gun with shells weighing 1 ton used on battleships of the Queen Elizabeth class. During the First World War 15-inch guns were also deployed ashore with the Royal Marine Artillery.

Machine gun: a feared weapon in the First World War, which could fire up to 500 rounds per minute. The Vickers water cooled .303 became the standard machine gun of the British Army and was so reliable that it remained in service until the 1960s. Air-cooled versions were used in aircraft. The other machine gun in common use in the First World War was the Lewis gun.

Mentioned in Despatches: official report by a senior officer and sent to High Command describing gallant or meritorious service. Published in the *London Gazette*. Indicated by a bronze oak leaf attached to a medal ribbon. Kate Luard was mentioned in despatches in the *London Gazette* of 31 December 1915.

Middlesex: Middlesex Regiment.

Millbank: Queen Alexandra's Military Hospital, London, opened in 1905. It was used as a general army hospital during the First World War, specialising in the treatment of trench fever, frostbite, shell shock and gas gangrene.

Mills bomb: a type of high-explosive hand grenade named after British inventor Sir William Mills 1856–1932. Introduced in 1915.

Minnenwerfers: First World War short-range mortar used by the German Army.

Moribund ward: a ward where the dying and critically wounded were placed. Later in the war the very severely injured would be cared for in a resuscitation ward and the term moribund was discontinued.

Morphine: the main method of pain relief during the First World War. All medics carried morphine and syringes.

'Napoo': army slang from the French *il n'y a plus* (there is no more) meaning finished/gone/dead/wiped out.

Naval Division: The Royal Naval Division was formed at the outbreak of war comprising eight battalions (named after famous naval commanders) and four marine battalions.

Nephritis: inflammation of the kidneys

New Army: 'Kitchener's' army of men recruited into the army at the start of the war as a result of Lord Kitchener's appeal for volunteers.

Nissen huts: a military shelter of semi-circular cross section made of corrugated-steel sheet, designed by Lt Col Peter Nissen 1871–1930, a British mining engineer.

Observation balloons: large balloons (nicknamed 'sausages' because of their shape) filled with hydrogen, which is highly flammable. They were tethered with a cable to a height of around 3,000ft and were used for intelligence gathering and artillery spotting.

Oedema: accumulation of fluid in the body tissues.

Orphelin: French orphan.

Over-the-top: make an attack, to go over the top of the trench parapet.

Padre: a military or naval chaplain.

Perfection lamp: a basic lamp/stove with a patented wick and run on kerosene. Invented in Cleveland, Ohio, and initially manufactured by the Perfection Stove Company.

Phosgene: a colourless poisonous gas used in chemical warfare.

Pill-box: or pillbox; a concrete guard post, circular or hexagonal (named after medical pillboxes), with slits for firing weapons.

Pilocarpin: or pilocarpine; a drug with actions and uses similar to eserine, administered as eye drops.

Poilus: a French First World War infantryman.

Poison gas: extensively used in the First World War. Types include phosgene, chlorine and mustard gas.

Push: a large-scale attack on enemy positions.

QAIMNS: Queen Alexandra's Imperial Military Nursing Service. It was founded in 1902, replacing the Army Nursing Service, and named after its first president, Queen Alexandra. Its uniform was grey with a scarlet cape. There were no military ranks until the Queen Alexandra's Royal Army Nursing Corps was formed in 1949, although all sisters and matrons had officer status. By the end of the First World War there were over 10,000 QAIMNS and Reserve.

QAIMNSR: The Reserve of the QAIMNS was formed in 1908. All members had to complete at least three years approved hospital training. Its uniform was as QAIMNS, but with a grey cape edged in scarlet.

Rifle grenade: a grenade fired from a rifle-based launcher that can project a larger grenade a much greater distance than a hand grenade. Widely used in the First World War.

RRC: a decoration originally only awarded to qualified female military nurses (now also awarded to male nurses) who have shown exceptional bravery or devotion to duty. It was instituted by Queen Victoria in 1883, and one of the first recipients was Florence Nightingale. There are two classes: First: RRC and Associate: ARRC. RRC is a class 2A decoration and comes above the George Medal and Military Cross in order of precedence. A Bar can be added to the decoration. By the end of the First World War, Kate Luard was the only nurse below the rank of Acting Matron to be awarded the Bar.

Sam Browne: brown or black polished leather belt with a strap over the right shoulder, worn by officers of many armies.

Sappers: Royal Engineers.

Sawyer boiler: a cylindrical metal stove with attached flue and chimney. The lower half is the firebox and under the flat lid (used for cooking on) is a separate water boiler. It was invented by Alexis Soyer (1810–58), a French celebrity chef working in London. He designed the Soyer stove to provide cooking facilities for the troops in the Crimea. The Army Catering HQ is known as Soyer's House.

Seaforths: Seaforth Highlanders.

Shell shock: result of psychological strain during prolonged engagement in warfare. The term was first used by Charles Myers, a medical officer, in 1917.

Shrapnel: the red-hot strands of metal produced by a bursting shell. Shrapnel shells were developed by Lt Shrapnel RA in 1784. These shells were superseded during the First World War by high-explosive shells, which had a similar deadly effect.

Star shells: used to illuminate the battlefield with a magnesium flare. The shell contained a parachute to allow slow descent.

Stationary Hospital: despite the name, these could be movable units. There were two to every division holding from 300 to over 1,300 beds. These were often specialist hospitals and frequently situated in the existing hospitals of large towns.

'Strafe': ground attack by low-flying aircraft using machine guns.

Stunt: an action of outstanding skill, daring or effectiveness.

Subcutaneous saline: saline is a solution containing 0.9% sodium chloride administered by injection as a plasma substitute.

Suffolks: Suffolk Regiment.

Taube: First World War German monoplane. It was covered in linen painted with nitrate dope, which made the wings almost transparent and therefore difficult to spot in the sky. Term often also used for all German aircraft.

Thomas splint: a metal frame to hold and protect the wounded leg. Developed by Hugh Owen Thomas, a Welsh surgeon known as the Father of our modern orthopaedic surgery. Introduced in 1916 it reduced deaths from 80% to 8% for femur fractures.

Tin hat: a steel combat helmet invented in Britain by John Brodie in 1915 and designed to protect from shrapnel. Until general issue in 1916 soft hats were worn offering no protection from head wounds. With modifications, it was used through the Second World War. Nicknamed 'salad bowl' by the Germans.

Toc H: Talbot House, Poperinge, Belgium. Opened in 1915 as a refuge for all ranks. Founded by Chaplain Philip (Tubby) Clayton and Neville Talbot.

Tommies: Tommy was a generic name for a British soldier used since the nineteenth century but is now mainly associated with the First World War.

Toxæmia: blood poisoning caused by toxins formed by bacteria in a local site of infection.

Tracer bullets: burn very brightly in their flight from a machine gun to enable accurate aim on the target.

Trench fever: an acute infectious disease characterised by a high fever and muscular aches and pains and transmitted by body lice. Recovery takes a month or more.

Trench foot: caused by exposure of the feet to damp and wet conditions as often experienced in the trenches. A condition that could be eliminated by regular foot inspection and drying of feet. If unattended for long the skin breaks away and can result in gangrene.

Trephine: surgical instrument for removing circular sections of bone, especially from the skull.

Uræmia: the presence of excessive waste compounds in the blood can result in kidney failure, nausea, lethargy and eventually, if untreated, in death.

Verey lights: used as a distress signal or illumination and fired by a single-shot pistol. Invented by Edward Verey (1847–1910), an American Naval Officer.

Warwicks: Warwickshire Regiment.

Wykehamist: former pupil of Winchester College, founded by William of Wykeham in the fourteenth century.

Yorks: Yorkshire Regiment (The Green Howards).

Zeppelin: a type of rigid airship, 150–160 metres long, pioneered by the Germans in 1895. The many separate gas bags were made from cows' intestines. It was invented by Count von Zeppelin and they were used as bombers during the First World War. In 1916 two were brought down in Essex, one of them near Kate's home town of Colchester.

PERSONNEL MENTIONED
IN THE TEXT

Allenby, Field-Marshal Viscount Edmund (1861–1936), Commander of Cavalry Corps, V Corps and 3rd Army. In 1917 and 1918 he led forces in the Middle East against Turkey, and also in the conquest of Palestine and Syria.

Babtie, Lieutenant General Sir William (1859–1920), Director of Medical Services at the War Office from March 1916. He won the VC in the Second Boer War for treating the wounded whilst under heavy fire.

Bairnsfather, Captain Bruce (1887–1959) served in the Royal Warwickshire Regt on the Front until 1915 when he was wounded. He developed his famous cartoon character 'Old Bill' and was then commissioned to draw cartoons for the Allied forces.

Bowlby, Major General Sir Anthony (1855–1929), Consulting Surgeon to 2nd Army and Advisor on Surgery to the British Army. He instituted advanced surgery at Casualty Clearing Stations.

Brooke, Rupert (1887–1915), war poet who died at 28 from a septic mosquito bite on his way to the Dardanelles while serving as a lieutenant in the RNVR. He is buried on the Greek island of Skyros.

Capper, Major General Sir Thompson (1863–1915), GOC 7th Division, who had served with distinction in the Second Boer War. He was killed in action by a sniper at the Battle of Loos in September, 1915.

Chavasse, Captain Noel Godfrey VC and Bar, DSO, MC, RAMC (1864–1917), son of the Bishop of Liverpool, was the only person to be awarded the VC twice during the First World War. He died at the 3rd Battle of Ypres where he was nursed at No. 32 CCS by K.E. Luard, who also attended his funeral. He is buried at Brandhoek New Military Cemetery and his decorations are on display at the Imperial War Museum.

Cottar (Cotter), Corporal William (1882–1916), 6 Battalion The Buffs (East Kent Regiment), was awarded the VC for bravery in action in March 1916, when he died of his wounds after leading an attack at the Hohenzollern Redoubt. He was nursed by K.E. Luard and is buried at Lillers Communal Cemetery.

Dundonald, Lord Thomas Hesketh Blair Cochrane (1886–1958), 13th Earl Dundonald. Captain in the Scots Guards and ADC to General Sir Henry Wilson in the First World War.

Foch, Maréchal Ferdinand (1851–1929), Marshal of France and C-in-C of Allied Armies in 1918. He halted the German advance on Paris at the 2nd Battle of the Marne and later accepted the German Surrender. He was made an honorary Field Marshal of the British Empire.

French, Field Marshal Sir John (1852–1925) commanded the British Expeditionary Force for the first two years of the war, before becoming C-in-C, Home Forces. He had distinguished himself commanding the Cavalry Division during the Second Boer War.

Gough, General Sir Hubert (1870–1963) commanded 7th Division and 1 Corps in 1915 and 5th Army from 1916 to 1918.

Gray, Colonel Sir Henry, Consulting Surgeon to the 3rd Army who introduced the débridement of wounds with Major Mulligan, an Australian MO. Colonel Gray's paper 'Treatment of gunshot wounds by excision of damaged tissues' was published in the journal of the RAMC in June 1915.

Haig, Field Marshal Sir Douglas (1861–1928) commanded the BEF from 1915 to 1918. He founded the Haig fund for the welfare of ex-servicemen.

Henderson, Lieutenant Malcom RFC (1891–1978), 'the Flying Boy'. Whilst on photographic reconnaissance, his plane was hit by an anti-aircraft shell at 7,000 feet and his left leg severed. Once safely landed, he and his observer continued firing at the enemy from a nearby trench whilst under enemy shell-fire. His leg was amputated at scene and he was nursed for several days by KEL until evacuated to England. He was awarded the DSO and later became an Air Vice-Marshal and was Air Officer Commanding No.14 Fighter Group during the Battle of Britain.

Herringham, Major-Gen Sir Wilmot (1855–1936), distinguished doctor, author and academic who investigated treatment for poison gas. He was consultant physician to the British forces in France with the RAMC from 1914 to 1919.

Irwin, Major General Sir James Murray (1858–1938), an army doctor who had served in Sudan and the Boer War and was the RAMC's Director of Medical Services for the 3rd Army in 1916.

Kaiser Wilhelm II (1859–1941), Emperor of Germany and King of Prussia. He was a cousin of King George V and of Tsar Nicholas II of Russia.

King George V (1865–1936), known as the Sailor King because of his time serving in the Royal Navy. George (and Queen Mary) visited the Western Front on many occasions. In 1916 on a visit to the front and Casualty Clearing Stations, he expressed a wish for more names of nurses and sisters to be submitted for decorations. In 1917 he changed his German titles to The House of Windsor.

Kitchener, Field Marshal, 1st Earl Kitchener of Khartoum (1850–1916), Minister of War 1914-15. He succeeded Lord Roberts as C-in-C in the Second Boer War in South Africa and was also famous as victor of the Battle of Omdurman in 1898 and securing control of Sudan. He played a central role in raising Britain's 'New Armies' at the outset of the First World War. He died at sea on June 5, 1916.

Ludendorff, General Erich (1865–1937), chief manager of the German war effort with Paul Von Hindenburg. He became a dedicated member of the Nazi party in the 1930s but warned that Hitler would 'cast the Reich into the Abyss'.

Macpherson, Major General Sir William Grant 'Tiger Mac' (1858–1927), Director of Medical Services 1st Army 1914-15. He became Colonel Commandant RAMC and wrote a medical history of the Great War.

McCarthy, Dame Emma Maude QAIMNS, RRC (1859–1949), Matron-in-Chief with the British troops in France and Flanders, 1914-19. She also served in the Boer War and helped to form the QAIMNS.

Monro, General Sir Charles (1860–1929), Commander of Britain's 3rd Army in 1915 and the 1st Army in 1916.

Paris, Major General Sir Archibald (1861–1937) Royal Marines. During the First War War he commanded the Royal Naval Division until he was severely wounded in October 1916.

Pétain, Maréchal Phillippe (1856–1951), hero of the Battle of Verdun, was considered the outstanding commander of the First World War. He became Marshal of France and was an inspiration to General Charles de Gaulle. In the Second World War he was head of the Vichy Government of France from June 1940 to August 1944.

Prince Arthur, Duke of Connaught (1850–1942), third son of Queen Victoria, had a distinguished career as an officer in the Rifle Brigade. During the First World War he was Governor General of Canada and took a close interest in the role of Canadian troops. He rose to the rank of Field Marshal.

Prince of Wales, later Edward VIII (1894–1972), joined the Grenadier Guards at the outbreak of war. Although keen to serve on the front, he was not allowed to do this by order of Lord Kitchener. He visited the front line and trenches on many occasions, including dug-outs when they were being heavily shelled, and caused great concern to those attending him. He was popular with the troops and was awarded the Military Cross.

Rawlinson, General Sir Henry, 1st Baron Rawlinson, (1864–1925), GOC 4th Division and IV Corps in 1914, Commander 4th Army 1916 and 2nd Army 1917-18. He was held mainly responsible for the heavy British casualties on the Somme but was also credited for the Allied success in the Battle of Amiens. Later he was made C-in-C in India.

Robinson, William Leefe (1895–1918) was awarded the VC after becoming the first British airman to shoot down a German airship over the UK. He was injured at Lille in 1915. He died soon after the war, having suffered ill health in captivity after being shot down in 1917.

Rothenstein, Sir William (1872–1945), distinguished painter and Principal of the Royal College of Art. He was an Official War Artist in both world wars. In 1918 he and K.E. Luard met when both were drawing the ruins of Péronne Cathedral. She describes him helping on the wards 'like an orderly'.

Sloggett, Lieutenant-Gen Sir Arthur FRCS, (1857–1919), Director General of Army Medical Services. He was Mentioned in Despatches seven times.

Williamson H S (1892–1978) was famous for his posters for the General Post Office and London Transport during the 1920s and 30s. He served in France as a rifleman, was wounded, and returned to France in 1917 as an Official War Artist. He was Principal of Chelsea School of Art from 1930 to 1950. A collection of his work is in the Imperial War Museum. One of his paintings from 1918 forms the frontispiece of this book.

Wilson, Lieutenant General Sir Henry (1864–1922), a protégé of Lord Roberts who played an important role in Anglo-French military relations. His only experience of field command was as Commander of IV Corps in 1916 when he met KEL. In 1918 he became Field Marshal and Chief of the Imperial General Staff. He was responsible for trebling the size of the Tank Corps. He was assassinated by the IRA in 1922.

Wright, Sir Almroth (1861–1947), eminent bacteriologist and immunologist who developed an anti-typhoid vaccine in 1892 and insisted that the vaccine was given to the Forces in the First World War. During the First World War he served in France, investigating wound infections, particularly gas gangrene. He was a strong advocate of preventative medicine and warned that antibiotics would create resistant bacteria. He was one of the great medical/scientific intellects of his time. Sir Alexander Fleming worked under him at St Mary's Hospital, London.

BIBLIOGRAPHY

Anonymous, *Diary of a Nursing Sister on the Western Front 1914–1915* (Edinburgh and London, William Blackwood and Sons, 1915)

Anonymous, 'Miss K.E. Luard, RRC: Obituary' *Bradfield College Alumni Magazine,* 1962

Clayton, Philip, MS Letter written 17 August 1915; Archives of Talbot House, Poperinge, Belgium

Hallett, Christine, *Containing Trauma: Nursing Work in the First World War* (Manchester, Manchester University Press, 2009)

Louagie-Nouf, Jan en Katrien, *Talbot House, Poperinge De Eerst Halte na de Hel* (Lannoo, Tielt, 1998)

Luard Family Papers; Essex Record Office, Chelmsford, UK; Files D/ DLu 55/13/1-6; 4/2; 9/6; 10/5; 11/3; 14/4; 15/4; 16/5; 58

Luard, Jock, *Charging The Memory* (Acorn Press, Stanway, Colchester, 1991)

Luard, Kate, War Office File: WO 399/5023; Register No 4862/ Reserve/3387; National Archives, Kew, UK

Register for Nurses for 1923, General Part; The Archive of the Nursing and Midwifery Council, 23, Portland Place, London, UK

Summers, Anne, *Angels and Citizens: British Women as Military Nurses, 1854–1914* (London, Routledge and Kegan Paul, 1988)

Yamaguchi, Midori, '"Unselfish Desires": Daughters of the Anglican Clergy: 1830–1914', unpublished PhD thesis, The University of Essex

Extracts from books by K.E. Luard appear in the following titles:

Hallett, Christine, *Containing Trauma: Nursing Work in the First World War* (Manchester University Press, 2009)

McEwen, Yvonne, *It's a Long Way to Tipperary: British and Irish Nurses in the Great War* (Cualann Press, 2006)

Powell, Anne, *Women in the War Zone: Hospital Service in the First World War* (The History Press, 2009)

Forthcoming Publications

Hallett, Christine, *Veiled Warriors: Allied Nurses of the First World War* (Oxford University Press, 2014)

Hallett, Christine, *Nurse Writers of the Great War* (under review with John's Hopkins University Press; anticipated publication date 2015)

McEwen, Yvonne, *In the Company of Nurses: The History of the British Army Nursing Service in the Great War* (Edinburgh University Press, July 2014)

Yamaguchi, Dr Midori, *Daughters of the Anglican Clergy, Gender and Identity in Victorian England* (Palgrave Macmillan, 2014)

Further Reference

McEwen, Yvonne and Fisken, Fiona, *Journalism and History: War Correspondents in the Two World Wars* (Peter Lang AG, Switzerland, September 2012)

www.scarletfinders.co.uk A source of information about military nurses and hospitals before and during the Great War; including transcriptions of many original documents relating to both nursing and women's work during the conflict.

www.greatwarnurses.blogspot.com

www.kateluard.co.uk

INDEX

Not included, but with frequent references throughout: ambulance cars, motors and trains; amputations, Australians; Boche; CCSs; DMS; French; gas gangrene; Germans; Gerry; Hun; Jerry.

As well as the wards, mentioned in the text, are numerous huts and tents for acute surgical, church, dressing, preparation, Red Cross, resuscitation, and surgical shock.

INDEX OF PLACE NAMES

All places are in France unless otherwise indicated